*Bloomsbury 35*

# Bloomsbury 35

## An Anthology

Edited by

*Liz Calder and Alexandra Pringle*

BLOOMSBURY PUBLISHING
LONDON · OXFORD · NEW YORK · NEW DELHI · SYDNEY

BLOOMSBURY PUBLISHING
Bloomsbury Publishing Plc
50 Bedford Square, London, WC1B 3DP, UK
29 Earlsfort Terrace, Dublin 2, Ireland

BLOOMSBURY, BLOOMSBURY PUBLISHING and the Diana logo are
trademarks of Bloomsbury Publishing Plc

First published in Great Britain 2022

A catalogue record for this book is available from the British Library

ISBN: TPB: 978-1-5266-3504-4; EBOOK: 978-1-5266-3503-7; SPECIAL EDITION: 978-1-5266-5802-9

2 4 6 8 10 9 7 5 3 1

Typeset by Integra Software Services Pvt. Ltd.
Printed and bound in Great Britain by CPI Group (UK) Ltd, Croydon CR0 4YY

To find out more about our authors and books visit www.bloomsbury.com
and sign up for our newsletters

# Contents

# CONTENTS

# Nigel Newton

## Preface

It is a happy moment as I write this introduction to thirty-five years of fiction on the Bloomsbury Adult Trade list as Abdulrazak Gurnah has just been awarded the Nobel Prize in Literature.

Bloomsbury's previous winner of the Nobel was Nadine Gordimer in 1991. It is interesting that the continent of Africa provided inspiration for both novelists.

I conceived the idea of Bloomsbury in February 1984 whilst on leave from Sidgwick & Jackson Publishers following the birth of Joanna's and my first daughter, Catherine. I decided to start a new, independent, medium-sized publisher of books of editorial excellence and originality with high standards of design and production.

During the London Book Fair in March 1985, David Reynolds, a publisher with Shuckburgh Reynolds, joined me and we began meeting early each morning to plan the detail of the company that was to be, before going off to our day jobs elsewhere in publishing. By May 1986 and with plentiful advice from Mike Mayer, a venture capitalist, we wrote a business plan which served initially as a fundraising document and, to this day, as an operating manual for the company. It incorporated several unique ideas, including the creation of the Bloomsbury Authors' Trust, which was to own 5 per cent of the company on behalf of the future authors of Bloomsbury whose books were to be published between the founding of the company in 1986 and its flotation on the London stock market in 1994.

I chose the name Bloomsbury not only as Bloomsbury Way was the street where my previous employers Sidgwick & Jackson Publishers were based and because I liked the name, but also as it was the neighbourhood of London associated with traditional publishing at a time when the industry was being taken over by foreign-owned multinational conglomerates, who were moving out to more distant parts of London. An intimation of the Bloomsbury Group was not the idea, but did no harm.

We approached the first investors in May 1986 and one of them, ECI, was to come through with £500,000 of the £1.75 million which we were seeking to raise. At this time, I approached Alan Wherry of Penguin, who was to become the first Marketing Director of Bloomsbury, also responsible for sales and publicity, and Liz Calder of Jonathan Cape, who was to become Editorial Director and then Editor-in-Chief in charge of all fiction publishing and some non-fiction. David Reynolds would commission the main non-fiction list.

After some hiccups along the way, three investors, being Caledonia Investments, who were the lead investor, ECI, and Legal & General Ventures came on board. We then set about conceiving a logo for the new company and Liz Calder suggested Diana, Goddess of Hunting. During August 1986, the four of us resigned from our existing jobs en masse on the same day. By late September, a day was chosen when briefings about the new publishing house would be given in secret to Louis Baum, Editor of *The Bookseller*, and Rodney Burbeck of *Publishing News*, and also to journalists from *The Times* and the *Guardian*. All four stories appeared on the same day and the existence of Bloomsbury was thus announced to a surprised publishing industry. The same day, Baring Brothers Hambrecht & Quist, the fourth and final investor, was secure, impressed that the company they were expected to help start had already been launched earlier that day.

I had booked a stand in secret for that October's Frankfurt Book Fair in the name of Bloomsbury three months previously and the company simply had to exist by the following week when the Book Fair was to begin. Five days after the press announcement, the four of us were standing on our beautifully designed stand in Frankfurt with not a single book on it. At the same time, Liz Calder signed up Bloomsbury's first novel, and David Reynolds signed up the first titles in the company's non-fiction list. The industry came to visit the Frankfurt stand in fascination that the five-day-old publisher had only quarter bottles of Bollinger to offer, but no books yet.

Premises were found above a Chinese restaurant in Putney near where David and I lived and the new company was based there for three months as we began to recruit future colleagues, ranging from Kathy Rooney, who was to found the company's reference list, to Nigel Batt, who was to become the first Finance Director and Caroline Michel, our first Publicity Director.

The company entered a mode of vertical take-off as it commissioned its first year's list and at the same time prepared to publish it only six months later, on 2 April 1987, when Mary Flanagan's *Trust* came out together with *The Land That Lost Its Heroes* by Jimmy Burns, a book about Argentina and the Falklands War which went on to win the Somerset Maugham Award. There was a tremendous launch party that night at the Braganza restaurant in Frith Street in Soho. *Trust* went straight into the *Sunday Times* bestseller list in the number 5 position.

A number of design innovations made the look of each Bloomsbury book quite distinctive, ranging from a reading ribbon in each novel, which was Reynolds' idea, to wide flaps on the jackets, and the high standard of paper, typography, and book production. I chose the ISBN prefix 747 as £747,000 was the company's profit target in its five-year business plan.

Highlights of the company's first Christmas season in 1987 were the launch of *Presumed Innocent* by the new author Scott Turow and *Marilyn Among Friends* by Sam Shaw and Norman Rosten. At this time, Liz Calder also signed up Jeanette Winterson, as well as Margaret Atwood and, in short order, John Irving, Joanna Trollope, Brian Moore, Jay McInerney, Nadine Gordimer, and Michael Ondaatje. These authors – old and new – were to win literary prizes from the Booker Prize to the Pulitzer and the Nobel in the years ahead. Calder's list of brilliant literary authors was to become the soul of the new Bloomsbury. By December 1987, the company finished its first full year with a staff of twenty-six, a turnover of £2,231,198 (which rose to circa £200,000,000 and 900 people by 2022) and was a vibrant new presence in world publishing.

In 1999, I was lucky that Alexandra Pringle joined us as Editor-in-Chief of the Adult list and since that time has built one of the finest lists of authors in world publishing with her authors including Abdulrazak Gurnah, Susanna Clarke, Kamila Shamsie, Elizabeth Gilbert, Esther Freud, Hannah Rothschild, Anne Patchett, Madeline Miller, Colum McCann and Jhumpa Lahiri. In 2021, authors published by Alexandra won both the Nobel Prize and the Women's Prize.

These have been an extraordinary thirty-five years culminating in the company being voted both Trade Publisher of the Year by the IPA and Academic Publisher of the Year by the British Book Awards in 2021.

I am grateful to my friend Sigrid Rausing for the anthology of Granta 40 which inspired me to suggest to Liz and Alexandra that we do this one.

All choices are invidious and this selection is in particular because it just concerns Bloomsbury's UK Adult list and mainly fiction. We are, after all, very famous as a children's publisher, not least because of J. K. Rowling, Neil Gaiman and Sarah J. Maas and not to mention the great academic, special interest and professional authors as well as other children's authors we publish – about 70,000 books from which these thirty-five have been selected.

So please everyone forgive us for doing this to mark our thirty-fifth anniversary. It seemed more fun than doing nothing. I am deeply indebted to Liz and Alexandra and all of my Bloomsbury colleagues and our authors who have made the last thirty-five years so enjoyable.

The company is not backward-looking – we have a new Editor-in-Chief of Adult, Paul Baggaley – and we have just had the most successful year in our history thanks to our authors, colleagues, customers and to the surge in reading which has accompanied the horrible pandemic we are still living through.

I hope this volume provides welcome distraction, inspiration and joy to you.

# *Liz Calder*

## *The Early Years*

### Editor-in-Chief, 1987–2000*

In early June 1986, I received a mysterious invitation to lunch at Les Halles Restaurant in Theobalds Road, where it emerged, in conspiratorial tones, that Nigel Newton and David Reynolds had been planning and plotting over countless late nights and early mornings the establishment of a major independent publishing company, fuelled by ambitious, groundbreaking ideas, to be known as Bloomsbury. Would I like to join them as a founding editorial director?

Since the early seventies I had worked as an editor for two long-established, highly respected independent publishing houses: Victor Gollancz and Jonathan Cape. Why would I want to jump ship and join a risky venture like that?

Well, first of all, the business plan was impressive. It factored in every putative title Bloomsbury would publish for the next five years, with innovative ideas for how to publish these books

---

*Liz Calder continued to work part-time for Bloomsbury for several years after handing over to AP in 2000. During this time she edited *Middlesex* by Jeffrey Eugenides (2002) and *Come Dance With Me* (2005) by Russell Hoban.

successfully, and profitably. Next, the team were attractive: Nigel, engaging, international, and a brilliant publisher at Sidgwick & Jackson; David Reynolds, experienced editor of non-fiction, gifted writer, and a complex, unflappable human being; and Alan Wherry, super-salesman at Penguin with an irresistible talent for pitching a book to booksellers.

Also, I had for some time nursed an urge to be part of a start-up, where the response to a new idea would not invariably be: 'But we've always done it this way.' I had been inspired by my friend Carmen Callil and her exciting start-up at Virago, which I had observed at close hand a few years earlier.

Besides, change was in the air, and it seemed that publishing could be done in new ways. We wanted to capitalise on that; most importantly by engaging authors more fully in the whole publishing process, making books that were individually and beautifully designed and produced, and making the publicity and marketing more author-involving, more inventive and original. In short, to make what might be called The Bloomsbury Effect come into being.

To achieve some of our ambitions, we captured the up-and-coming queen of PR, Caroline Michel, as publicity director, to ensure the widest possible coverage of our launch. This paid off handsomely when, after the launch, the Bloomsbury Gang of Four hit the front pages and caused a bit of a stir at the Frankfurt Book Fair a few weeks later. At the same time our books in their handsome trappings, complete with reading ribbons, wide flaps, a glamorous new logo featuring Diana the Huntress and notes on typefaces, encouraged booksellers, especially the newborn Waterstones and BOOKS Etc. shops, to put larger than usual quantities of our books in heaving displays on their tables.

My task was to build a fiction list from scratch, and to have fiction for the first catalogue ready in four months.

This first spring catalogue was beautifully designed by the young team at Newell & Sorrell, where Sarah Massini also designed that Diana the Huntress logo, still found on the spine of Bloomsbury books thirty-five years later. The fiction list was headed by a beguiling first novel, appropriately called *Trust*. The author was Mary Flanagan, whose collection of delicious short stories, *Bad Girls*, I had published at Cape. There were two more first novels, both from the US, Mona Simpson's *Anywhere But Here* and Joseph Olshan's *A Warmer Season*.

These first novels were the springboard not only for the careers of the writers but also for Bloomsbury's continuing fiction list. This included Rupert Thompson's *Dreams of Leaving*, Candia McWilliam's *A Case of Knives*, Jay McInerney's *Story of My Life* and Scott Turow's *Presumed Innocent*. Publishing a writer's early books, then gradually building a reputation and a close relationship, were guiding principles of our publishing in the early years. The much-loved novels of Joanna Trollope were perfect examples of this.

Reaching out further and extending the range of the fiction we took on meant scouring publishers' lists from around the world: both English-speaking and in other languages. Book fairs like Frankfurt and visits to the US, Canada, Australia and New Zealand provided excellent shopping opportunities. Bloomsbury's first Booker winner was the result of a visit to the Adelaide Festival in 1988, where on a sunny lawn I sat talking with Michael Ondaatje, an encounter which meant that Bloomsbury was included in, and went on to win, the auction for *The English Patient*.

Our first office was situated above a Chinese restaurant in Putney, where, as it happened, all three of my new colleagues lived. I made the long trek over there from my North London home each day, but became much happier when we moved into central London, first to Bloomsbury and finally to No. 2 Soho Square, our first proper home, next door to Paul McCartney's office.

Our first employees began to be signed up. The first editorial assistant was a young American, Isobel Fonseca, who gamely tackled the mountains of submissions which were piling up around us waiting to be read. She went on to be a fine writer herself. Maggie Traugott, discerning reader and *blurbiste extraordinaire*, joined us from Cape, and we also took on copyeditors Sarah Jane Forder and Mary Tomlinson. Lucy Juckes became our highly effective sales manager.

Every time we secured a new deal with an author or agent, we all climbed on to our chairs and cheered. Don't ask me why. Euphoria perhaps? There were no mobile phones in those heady days, and even new landlines were subject to weeks of waiting. We had one phone for fifteen of us: so we queued up to do business. But magically, business got done, and by early 1987 we had our first list. Incidentally, someone told me that there is nothing quite like the adrenaline-fuelled energy that is pumped into a start-up company. I can confirm that. It is like nothing else: days run into nights into days to get the show on the road.

For me, selecting which extracts from which books published to be included in this anthology has been both very pleasurable and agonisingly difficult. To leave out, simply for reasons of space, works by Patricia Highsmith, David Grossman, Scott Turow, Pauline Melville; not to include a taste of Ian Hamilton's exquisite selections of poetry in the Bloomsbury Classics series of small hardbacks, and to leave out his brilliant life of Matthew Arnold; or to neglect the incomparable Alasdair Gray: these glorious works not included are victims of cruel space controllers and are heartbreaking. But I do feel that in the case of Alasdair Gray, his manic laughter will continue to haunt the stairs of No. 2 Soho Square for years to come. Perhaps forever.

# Jeanette Winterson

## 1987

## *The Passion*

It was Napoleon who had such a passion for chicken that he kept his chefs working around the clock. What a kitchen that was, with birds in every state of undress; some still cold and slung over hooks, some turning slowly on the spit, but most in wasted piles because the Emperor was busy.

Odd to be so governed by an appetite.

It was my first commission. I started as a neck wringer and before long I was the one who carried the platter through inches of mud to his tent. He liked me because I am short. I flatter myself. He did not dislike me. He liked no one except Joséphine and he liked her the way he liked chicken.

No one over five foot two ever waited on the Emperor. He kept small servants and large horses. The horse he loved was seventeen hands high with a tail that could wrap round a man three times and still make a wig for his mistress. That horse had the evil eye and there's been almost as many dead grooms in the stable as chickens on the table. The ones the beast didn't kill itself with an easy kick, its master had disposed of because its coat didn't shine or the bit was green.

'A new government must dazzle and amaze,' he said. Bread and circuses I think he said. Not surprising then that when we did find a groom, he came from a circus himself and stood as high as the horse's flank. When he brushed the beast he used a ladder with a stout bottom and a triangle top, but when he rode him for exercise he took a great leap and landed square on the glossy back while the horse reared and snorted and couldn't throw him, not even with its nose in the dirt and its back legs towards God. Then they'd vanish in a curtain of dust and travel for miles, the midget clinging to the mane and whooping in his funny language that none of us could understand.

But he understood everything.

He made the Emperor laugh and the horse couldn't better him, so he stayed. And I stayed. And we became friends.

We were in the kitchen tent one night when the bell starts ringing like the Devil himself is on the other end. We all jumped up and one rushed to the spit while another spat on the silver and I had to get my boots back on ready for that tramp across the frozen ruts. The midget laughed and said he'd rather take a chance with the horse than the master, but we don't laugh.

Here it comes surrounded by parsley the cook cherishes in a dead man's helmet. Outside the flakes are so dense that I feel like the little figure in a child's snowstorm. I have to screw up my eyes to follow the yellow stain that lights up Napoleon's tent. No one else can have a light at this time of night.

Fuel's scarce. Not all of this army have tents.

When I go in, he's sitting alone with a globe in front of him. He doesn't notice me, he goes on turning the globe round and round, holding it tenderly with both hands as if it were a breast. I give a short cough and he looks up suddenly with fear in his face.

'Put it here and go.'

'Don't you want me to carve it, Sir?'

'I can manage. Goodnight.'

I know what he means. He hardly ever asks me to carve now. As soon as I'm gone he'll lift the lid and pick it up and push it into his mouth. He wishes his whole face were mouth to cram a whole bird.

In the morning I'll be lucky to find the wishbone.

There is no heat, only degrees of cold. I don't remember the feeling of a fire against my knees. Even in the kitchen, the warmest place in any camp, the heat is too thin to spread and the copper pans cloud over. I take off my socks once a week to cut my toe-nails and the others call me a dandy. We're white with red noses and blue fingers.

The tricolour.

He does it to keep his chickens fresh.

He uses winter like a larder.

But that was a long time ago. In Russia.

Nowadays people talk about the things he did as though they made sense. As though even his most disastrous mistakes were only the result of bad luck or hubris.

It was a mess.

Words like devastation, rape, slaughter, carnage, starvation are lock and key words to keep the pain at bay. Words about war that are easy on the eye.

I'm telling you stories. Trust me.

I wanted to be a drummer.

The recruiting officer gave me a walnut and asked if I could crack it between finger and thumb. I could not and he laughed and said a drummer must have strong hands. I stretched out my palm, the walnut resting there, and offered him the same challenge. He coloured up and had a Lieutenant take me to the kitchen tents. The cook sized up my skinny frame and reckoned I was not a cleaver man. Not for me the mess of unnamed meat that had to be chopped for the daily stew. He said I was lucky, that I would be working for Bonaparte himself, and for one brief, bright moment I imagined a training as a pastry cook building delicate towers of sugar and cream. We walked towards a small tent with two impassive guards by the flaps.

'Bonaparte's own storeroom,' said the cook.

The space from the ground to the dome of the canvas was racked with rough wooden cages about a foot square with tiny corridors running in between, hardly the width of a man. In each cage there were two or three birds, beaks and claws cut off, staring through the slats with dumb identical eyes. I am no coward and I've seen plenty of convenient mutilation on our farms but I was not prepared for the silence. Not even a rustle. They could have been dead, should have been dead, but for the eyes. The cook turned to go. 'Your job is to clear them out and wring their necks.'

I slipped away to the docks, and because the stone was warm in that early April and because I had been travelling for days I fell asleep dreaming of drums and a red uniform. It was a boot that woke me, hard and shiny with a familiar saddle smell. I raised my head and saw it resting on my belly the way I had rested the walnut in my palm. The officer didn't look at me, but said, 'You're a soldier now and you'll get plenty of opportunity to sleep in the open air. On your feet.'

He lifted his foot and, as I scrambled up, kicked me hard and still looking straight ahead said, 'Firm buttocks, that's something.'

I heard of his reputation soon enough but he never bothered me. I think the chicken smell kept him away.

I was homesick from the start. I missed my mother. I missed the hill where the sun slants across the valley. I missed all the everyday things I had hated. In spring at home the dandelions streak the fields and the river runs idle again after months of rain. When the army recruitment came it was a brave band of us who laughed and said it was time we saw more than the red barn and the cows we had birthed. We signed up straight away and those of us who couldn't write made an optimistic smear on the page.

Our village holds a bonfire every year at the end of winter. We had been building it for weeks, tall as a cathedral with a blasphemous spire of broken snares and infested pallets. There would be plenty of wine and dancing and a sweetheart in the dark and because we were leaving we were allowed to light it. As the sun went down we plunged our five burning brands into the heart of the pyre. My mouth went dry as I heard the wood take and splinter until the first flame pushed its way out. I wished I were a holy man then with an angel to protect me so I could jump inside the fire and see my sins burned away. I go to confession but there's no fervour there. Do it from the heart or not at all.

4

We're a lukewarm people for all our feast days and hard work. Not much touches us, but we long to be touched. We lie awake at night willing the darkness to part and show us a vision. Our children frighten us in their intimacy, but we make sure they grow up like us. Lukewarm like us. On a night like this, hands and faces hot, we can believe that tomorrow will show us angels in jars and that the well-known woods will suddenly reveal another path.

Last time we had this bonfire, a neighbour tried to pull down the boards of his house. He said it was nothing but a stinking pile of dung, dried meat and lice. He said he was going to burn the lot. His wife was tugging at his arms. She was a big woman, used to the churn and the field, but she couldn't stop him. He smashed his fist into the seasoned wood until his hand looked like a skinned lamb's head. Then he lay by the fire all night until the early wind covered him in cooling ash. He never spoke of it. We never spoke of it. He doesn't come to the bonfire any more.

I sometimes wonder why none of us tried to stop him. I think we wanted him to do it, to do it for us. To tear down our long-houred lives and let us start again. Clean and simple with open hands. It wouldn't be like that, no more than it could have been like that when Bonaparte set fire to half of Europe.

But what other chance had we?

Morning came and we marched away with our parcels of bread and ripe cheese. There were tears from the women and the men slapped us on the back and said soldiering is a fine life for a boy. One little girl who always followed me around pulled at my hand, her eyebrows close together with worry.

'Will you kill people, Henri?'

I dropped down beside her. 'Not people, Louise, just the enemy.'

'What is enemy?'

'Someone who's not on your side.'

We were on our way to join the Army of England at Boulogne. Boulogne, a sleepy nothing port with a handful of whorehouses, suddenly became the springboard of Empire. Only twenty miles away, easy to see on a clear day, was England and her arrogance. We knew about the English; how they ate their children and ignored the Blessed Virgin. How they committed suicide with unseemly cheerfulness. The English have the highest suicide rate in Europe. I got that straight from a priest. The English with their John Bull beef and frothing beer. The English who are even now waist-high in the waters off Kent practising to drown the best army in the world.

We are to invade England.

All France will be recruited if necessary. Bonaparte will snatch up his country like a sponge and wring out every last drop.

We are in love with him.

At Boulogne, though my hopes of drumming head high at the front of a proud column are dashed, I'm still head high enough because I know I'll see Bonaparte himself. He comes regularly rattling from the Tuileries and scanning the seas like an ordinary man checks his rain barrel. Domino the midget says that being near him is like having a great wind rush about your ears. He says that's how Madame de Staël put it and she's famous enough to be right. She doesn't live in France now. Bonaparte had her exiled because she complained about him censoring the theatre and suppressing the newspapers. I once bought a book of hers from a travelling pedlar who'd had it from a ragged nobleman. I didn't understand much but I learned the word 'intellectual' which I would like to apply to myself.

Domino laughs at me.

At night I dream of dandelions.


The cook grabbed a chicken from the hook above his head and scooped a handful of stuffing from the copper bowl.

He was smiling.

'Out on the town tonight, lads, and a night to remember, I swear it.' He rammed the stuffing inside the bird, twisting his hand to get an even coating.

'You've all had a woman before I suppose?'

Most of us blushed and some of us giggled.

'If you haven't then there's nothing sweeter and if you have, well, Bonaparte himself doesn't tire of the same taste day after day.'

He held up the chicken for our inspection.

I had hoped to stay in with the pocket Bible given to me by my mother as I left. My mother loved God, she said that God and the Virgin were all she needed though she was thankful for her family. I've seen her kneeling before dawn, before the milking, before the thick porridge, and singing out loud to God, whom she has never seen. We're more or less religious in our village and we honour the priest who tramps seven miles to bring us the wafer, but it doesn't pierce our hearts.

St Paul said it is better to marry than to burn, but my mother taught me it is better to burn than to marry. She wanted to be a nun. She hoped I would be a priest and saved to give me an education while my friends plaited rope and trailed after the plough.

I can't be a priest because although my heart is as loud as hers I can pretend no answering riot. I have shouted to God and the Virgin, but they have not shouted back and I'm not interested in the still small voice. Surely a god can meet passion with passion?

She says he can.

Then he should.

My mother's family were not wealthy but they were respectable. She was brought up quietly on music and suitable literature, and politics were never discussed at table, even when the rebels were breaking down the doors. Her family were monarchists. When she was twelve she told them that she wanted to be a nun, but they disliked excess and assured her that marriage would be more fulfilling. She grew in secret, away from their eyes. Outwardly she was obedient and loving, but inside she was feeding a hunger that would have disgusted them if disgust itself were not an excess. She read the lives of saints and knew most of the Bible off by heart. She believed that the Blessed Virgin herself would aid her when the time came.

The time came when she was fifteen, at a cattle fair. Most of the town was out to see the lumbering bullocks and high-pitched sheep. Her mother and father were in holiday mood and in a rash moment her papa pointed to a stout, well-dressed man carrying a child on his shoulders. He said she couldn't do better for a husband. He would be dining with them later and very much hoped that Georgette (my mother) would sing after supper. When the crowd thickened my mother made her escape, taking nothing with her but the clothes she stood in and her Bible that she always carried. She hid in a haycart and set off that sunburnt evening out of the town and slowly through the quiet country until the cart reached the village of my birth. Quite without fear, because she believed in the power of the Virgin, my mother presented herself to Claude (my father) and asked to be taken to the nearest convent. He was a slow-witted but kindly man, ten years older than her, and he offered her a bed for the night, thinking to take her home the next day and maybe collect a reward.

She never went home and she never found the convent either. The days turned into weeks and she was afraid of her father, who she heard was scouring the area and leaving bribes at any religious houses he passed. Three months went by and she discovered that she had a way with plants and that she could quiet frightened animals. Claude hardly ever spoke to her and never bothered her, but sometimes she would catch him watching her, standing still with his hand shading his eyes.

One night, late, as she slept, she heard a tapping at the door and turning up her lamp saw Claude in the doorway. He had shaved, he was wearing his nightshirt and he smelled of carbolic soap.

'Will you marry me, Georgette?'

She shook her head and he went away, returning now and again as time continued, always standing by the door, clean shaven and smelling of soap.

She said yes. She couldn't go home. She couldn't go to a convent so long as her father was bribing every Mother Superior with a mind to a new altar piece, but she couldn't go on living with this quiet man and his talkative neighbours unless he married her. He got into bed beside her and stroked her face and taking her hand put it to his face. She was not afraid. She believed in the power of the Virgin.

After that, whenever he wanted her, he tapped at the door in just the same way and waited until she said yes.

Then I was born.

She told me about my grandparents and their house and their piano, and a shadow crossed her eyes when she thought I would never see them, but I liked my anonymity. Everyone else in the village had strings of relations to pick fights with and know about. I made up stories about mine. They were whatever I wanted them to be depending on my mood.

Thanks to my mother's efforts and the rusty scholarliness of our priest I learned to read in my own language, Latin and English and I learned arithmetic, the rudiments of first aid and because the priest also supplemented his meagre income by betting and gambling I learned every card game and a few tricks. I never told my mother that the priest had a hollow Bible with a pack of cards inside. Sometimes he took it to our service by mistake and then the reading was always from the first chapter of Genesis. The villagers thought he loved the creation story. He was a good man but lukewarm. I would have preferred a burning Jesuit, perhaps then I might have found the ecstasy I need to believe.

I asked him why he was a priest, and he said if you have to work for anybody an absentee boss is best.

We fished together and he pointed out the girls he wanted and asked me to do it for him. I never did. I came to women late like my father.

When I left, Mother didn't cry. It was Claude who cried. She gave me her little Bible, the one that she had kept for so many years, and I promised her I would read it.

The cook saw my hesitation and poked me with a skewer. 'New to it, lad? Don't be afraid. These girls I know are clean as a whistle and wide as the fields of France.' I got ready, washing myself all over with carbolic soap.

Bonaparte, the Corsican. Born in 1769, a Leo.

Short, pale, moody, with an eye to the future and a singular ability to concentrate. In 1789 revolution opened a closed world and for a time the meanest street boy had more on his side than any aristocrat. For a young Lieutenant skilled in artillery, the chances were kind and in a few years General Bonaparte was turning Italy into the fields of France.

'What is luck,' he said, 'but the ability to exploit accidents?' He believed he was the centre of the world and for a long time there was nothing to change him from this belief. Not even John Bull. He was in love with himself and France joined in. It was a romance. Perhaps all romance is like that; not a contract between equal parties but an explosion of dreams and desires that can find no outlet in everyday life. Only a drama will do and while the fireworks last the sky is a different colour. He became an Emperor. He called the Pope from the Holy City to crown him but at the last second he took the crown in his own hands and placed it on his own head. He divorced the only person who understood him, the only person he ever really loved, because she couldn't give him a child. That was the only part of the romance he couldn't manage by himself.

He is repulsive and fascinating by turns.

What would you do if you were an Emperor? Would soldiers become numbers? Would battles become diagrams? Would intellectuals become a threat? Would you end your days on an island where the food is salty and the company bland?

He was the most powerful man in the world and he couldn't beat Josephine at billiards.

I'm telling you stories. Trust me.

# Candia McWilliam

## 1988

## *A Case of Knives*

I needed a woman. Or, better, a girl. A woman would be too set in her mould. I required for my purposes something unrefined and eventually ductile. I would perform the smelting and hall-marking myself. I wanted the pure substance I obtained to be worth my effort. I was thinking in terms of ingots, not of pigs.

I have found out recently of women, that, although they are less than pigs to me, since I do not have to eschew the devouring of them, as I do of pigs, to some these fleshy creatures are precious and worthy of the assay.

Occasionally I see in the street a man whose bearing tells me he has endured many of the same privileges and ostracisms as I, and read many of the same books; we have what is called a lot in common, yet we care to remain separate, poised, attentive and distant above our secret parishes, like birds of prey. Our quarry is shared, and our romantic hunger common. We require, like policemen or vicars, a beat. What we hunt is monsters who will turn on us, victims who will show themselves panthers and Calibans; they may be meter-readers, good husbands, fine fathers, but briefly, in the dark or the excoriating snowy brightness of underground, they are to me, and to these other well read, civilised, gentlemen, everything we have wanted. I have never woken up in the bed of someone I have made love to; nor has someone who has made love to me woken up in my bed. The people I have seen in that touching, crumpled state of waking up have all been my patients. One cannot feel violence towards a person one has seen asleep.

But then there was Hal, and he changed the regular, discrete, unadmitted quarterly satisfaction of this essential service in my life. It was clear at once that I could not forbid this boy my home, nor deal him banknotes just out of the lamp-posts' sight.

★★★

When I first saw him, I was thirty-nine and he twenty. He was entering a chemist's shop in St James's Street. The Palace looked on, a toy fort full of courtiers. I saw at once that he was not to be picked up. Even in St James's, there is provision for that sort of thing. I fell in love with him as I looked; the sensation was of sinking, without end. As I sank into the sight of him, I caught on nothing. I saw he had no archaeology. He was simply what he appeared to be. My past is full of bones and ghostly shapes traced in salt and acid. I saw he was an untroubled English boy, his past a simple matter of roots and earth.

My appearance is elegant. I wear conventional clothes. I have been told I look like a man who has had at least one child. Whether this is on account of my profession, I do not know. At any rate, it has been useful to me.

In the chemist's, this young man and I each purchased a wooden bowl of shaving soap. I said, to the assistant, but of course to the young man, 'I find the floral soaps leave you with the blue cheeks of a baboon.' He smiled – did he even shave? The respectable shop fronts were dark but festive as we walked up the street, as though khaki cigars and chestnut hats and dusty-shouldered green bottles were emblems of love.

But that had been six years ago and now I needed a girl.

Here, I thought, she was, smiling, her back to a tall looking-glass, her arms athwart the marble mantelpiece. A woman with her back to a mirror is a rare enough thing, one who will keep her hands still almost unique.

I even felt something of the twinge of recognition which is a presentiment of intimacy. Housemaid's memory, Tertius calls this, meaning the realignment of recollection so its nap lies smooth with the velvet of sentiment and comfortable untruth. His snobbish name for this emotional editing has its source in the frequent employment of the device in detective novels. When his Lordship is found dead on the library bearskin, the housemaid remembers that his Lordship always was funny about bears, never could abide them really. When you come to like someone, you recall the first meeting dignified by time's paragraphing; they were not drunk, they were recently bereaved, their orange sombrero was a welcome note of colour at the funeral. It is far easier to reorder memories than to admit to repeated errors.

I was struck by this girl. She appeared to meet all my superficial requirements. Classical beauties draw to themselves light, their faces pearly in any room. This girl drew to her face and arms not light but colour. A painter will tell you these are the same thing, but at first glance they are different. Light is all take and colour is all give, at least until you look again. She flashed colour like a witchball, bright not pale. There were some pearly girls in the room, and they would surely wear better, if kept in padded cases and held close always to scrupulously soaped flesh, but they were not to my purpose.

Had she held, balanced on her lifted face, a disproportionate sphere, glowing like ectoplasm, she would have resembled one of those Art Deco lamps which have twice been fashionable this century. She had the uselessly sportive length of limb, and the base-metallic glow. She appeared covetable without being unattainable; had auction houses dealt in young women, she might have been picked up quite reasonably at a fairly popular specialist sale in Geneva, with invited bids. She was listening far too attentively to an old Greek three-quarters her height. She looked down her face to his, and moved her features in response to his. The thick brows of the Greek beetled; her thinner eyebrows flinched. His eyes, the red-brown of prune flesh, gave a warm leer; her blue eyes hid behind mauve lids. His grey jaw jutted; she tucked in her chin like a dove. Unless she really was horribly shy, this submission was unconvincing, and gauche in one so big.

Her clothes were not those of a shy girl. She appeared not to realise her size. Unless she learnt soon that her little ways would sour and leave her, like a pale old cheese, on the shelf, she would be wasted. But if she grew into herself, well, then, she would be the perfect picture for the frame I had in mind. In her appearance there was something unEnglish which appealed to me. I was pleased to see this combination of confidence and unease; it is a suggestible compound.

The girl seemed also to have big breasts. I wanted that, too. It was, perforce, to be a full-length picture.

I sought our hostess. Anne was upstairs in her fur cupboard, shivering. There was no sign that anyone had been with her.

If it is possible to admire a person intellectually for their storage system, I did Anne. Her clothes cupboards were tall lozenges of space, obscure and cool. So all cupboards might be described, but hers were a cathedral of sartorial labour, its craftsmen Siamese mulberry tenders, French button piercers, Amazonian crocodile skinners, small men pulling shards off beetles in jungles below warring helicopters, men in palazzi weaving fields of cloth from dreams of past power. The guildsmen of bonded beauty all contributed to her cupboards' satisfaction, and, unlike Nana, the end of all this endeavour was not the pleasure Anne might give men, or the money and power she might gain from this pleasure. She was like the bibliophile of pornographic books. She had all these lovely things created solely for adornment, yet her pleasure was in their contemplation more than in their employment. She told her clothes like a miser, but dressed almost invariably in immaculate constructs of no definite colour.

From the east of her cupboards came the glow of sequined dresses beneath stoles of chiffon; there was a lady chapel of underwear sewn by nuns. Anne's own faith, as far as I could tell, was the limiting of chaos by external control, the absolute control of passion by ritual. Anne kept her clothes in an order logical and convenient, ready, like a soldier, for any contingency. Her cupboards were a thesaurus of social possibilities. I would tease her by inventing absurd putative events and making her select clothes to wear to attend them. She could always do it. We played in her cupboards like children.

Both Anne's houses contained their air-conditioned armoury of skins, muslins, wools, and the braced infantries of shoes. Each item bore a card which was inscribed with the date and place of its last wearing. I once asked her whether she notched the satin heels of her evening shoes for each conquest. She replied that she had her conquests made into coats. I was not sure whether she had lovers.

This evening, I sat with her in the gloom among the furs, the coldest part of the clothes-cathedral, giving a faint winter smell of naphtha and gauze-bagged dry flowers, downy buttons of immortelles, with their petals like small fallen pointed fingernails.

The furs were shouldered with shawls of chiffon to prevent chafing. These capes looked, on the congregation of sleek or brindled shoulders, pitifully domestic.

Anne was not vain. She had short light hair which lay where it was placed, a creased face with prominent cheekbones, very pale blue eyes, and an expression without guile. She was thin, not slim, and never wrinkled her nose, swivelled her hips or licked her mouth before or after telling a lie. So far as I knew, she had never told me one. Her posture was that of a sailor; she was always braced against some greater force, hooked to a chair, set against a wall. Her skin and hair were of a similar light brown, which grew more differentiated in sunlight. After prolonged exposure, her skin would darken to the colour of soft brown sugar, and her hair lighten to the colour of cara-mel. She was always neat, but she pushed her sleeves up from her wrists. She had thin feet and hands and the eyebrows and gaze of a boy. She had no greed but I sometimes worried that she was easily bored. I despised this, but she never seemed to be bored by me, so I was mollified. She was never bored, she said, at Stone. Stone was home, the house of her dead husband.

'Lucas, come in at once, take a pew.' Anne would adopt phrases, use them for a time in a voice different from her own to show she was joking, then forget to highlight them in this way, so that they became assimilated into her speech.

She had no blood which was not Scots, but often her speech was like that of those anglophile continentals who have tellingly twisted our tongue, somewhere between E. F. Benson and the War. I enjoyed seeing askance looks as she spoke.

I hear this, although I am not English. I hear also the diction of expatriates, speaking as though they are reading aloud the fourth leader of a four weeks' late airmail *Times*.

I put on my camp, shopwalker's voice, to disarm her.

We sat in the aisle, between the gowns and crusted capes, she on the floor, I on a set of library steps Anne used to reach her hat-boxes, white drums above us. Her gloves prayed in flat pairs above the silent drums. Above them, the air conditioners rarefied the air, charged it with ions and emitted it once more.

'What's new, Lucas, I haven't seen you in an age.' We had seen each other only the day before.

I had no intention of allowing her to know, although she was probably my best friend, that today had been a hinge in my life. She looked at me. Her eyes were as blue as eggs in a nest. She had a very nice face. Momentarily, I was tempted to tell her of my plan. To control myself, I concentrated very hard on the fabric of one of the hanging dresses.

'One too many, dearie?' asked Anne.

'Annie' (I did not like doing this; she was shrewd enough to hear the wrong note), 'Annie, could you introduce me to someone?'

'I hadn't realised there were any who were quite your toolbag here, dear, but, why, yes of course, though you must realise that it could be no better than a pig, whoops sorry, in a poke.'

I do not like the type of woman who habitually fraternises with homosexuals, though of course this sounds as though I do not like my own female friends. What I mean is women who seek to join in, to nudge, to use argot, to be all but men. They invariably claim also the privileges due to them as women, the softer flesh.

I become cold when this line is crossed. My lawyerly recti-
tude of manner stiffens.

'It's a girl, actually, Anne, the tall one being talked at by
Leonidas. Have you any idea who she is? And please don't tell
me the only reason I am interested is that she is really a boy. I've
seen enough, I mean she is showing enough, to make it quite
clear what she is.'

'I know,' said Anne, serious now the subject warranted it.
'Aren't those clothes terrifying? But there is something there.
With care, I think she could learn to dress.' She spoke of this
capacity as though it were as necessary as walking yet as magical
as transforming matter into gold.

'Why is she here? Who is she?'

'Why do you want to know?' The jealousy was not sexual. It
was the jealousy of sculptors over an untouched block in which
each sees different things. I gave the most evasive reply I could.

'It's to do with work.'

'Lucas, darling, you're not getting spare parts from the living
now, are you? Did your X-ray eyes tell you a particularly fine
pair of ventricles pumps beneath those breasts?'

I am a surgeon; I do not perform transplants very often, but
it is surprising how even the most intelligent prefer to believe
nonsense about something they do not understand. I specialise
in the repair of the small hearts of babies and children. A new
heart is about the size of a matchbox. Of course, I attend to
adults too, but I must admit that the bulk of the fame and the
money has come from the little ones.

'I can't say, Anne, I will when I can.' Could she really not penetrate this false mystique, indispensable to the professional man?

'Oh, Lucas, that's fine, I'll tell you, but she's newish on me too.
I met her a fortnight ago at home.'

'Met her? In your own house? Annie, do tell.' Ask a person
to tell and they are back with their childhood and its plain little
codes of decency swapped, a peek for a peek, an eye for an eye, a
feel for a feel. Traded secrets are part of the old code. She looked
down.

'Tertius brought her, without asking. George and George were angry till they saw her and then they fell about to make her little messes on dishes and diddle in her vanity case.' George and George were the butler and the footman. One was married to the cook, the other to the chambermaid. Or were they all brothers and sisters?

'Where did Tertius find her?' Old Tertius, older than me, living in Albany, cataloguing his frames, pinchbeck, ormolu, palisander, gesso, what could he want with a young woman?

'Apparently she's broke, she went to a vernissage, mostly for something to eat, got picked up by one of those wide-boys with a line in new masters of frigates in the spume, and, to cut a long story, woke up in the chambers opposite Tertius's. She rang his doorbell to ask where she was, and when at last he heard he gave her an egg flip and took her on as the lady who does. And she does very well.'

'Does she need to?' I was interested. Particularly in Anne's world, one was unlikely to find young women willing to take the job of charwoman to a total stranger. 'Is she foreign, without a work permit?'

'No, she's English, as English as you or I.'

I am the son of Polish Jews and Anne makes much of being a Scot. I left it alone, because I wanted more information and even the most fair-minded women are distracted by anything they can possibly take personally, which includes objectively truthful correction.

'But no money.'

'No money.'

'And family, what about that?'

'Not much of it.' As though it were a dry good, measured out like haricots or gems.

'Name?'

'Not a name name. Rather the sort it would be better to drop like a hot cake than simply drop, if you get me.'

I hate the idiom, to get, loathe it, but I did not say a word. I dream sometimes of faces close to mine screaming, 'D'you get me, d'you get me?' and I wake up afraid. The expression seems to push the breath of another hard into your own lungs.

'Still, tell it me,' I appealed to Anne.

'Cora Godfrey.'

'Cora. Miss Godfrey. Or does Tertius call her Mrs Godfrey as an honorific?'

'Tertius seems very fond of her, Lucas, though it can hardly be anything remotely under the blanket.'

Tertius had damp unrequited feeling for boys in shops and long dry passions with very old multiple duchesses. Once a week, a man of upright bearing came to help with the dusting of the stock, and I imagined that, even were Cora Godfrey to dust all day, the upright man would have his place in Tertius's timetable.

'So, she's gerontophile, clean, what else? How did she get on at Stone?'

'Not a foot wrong, even the boot on the other foot in a way, a bit too good, trying too hard. Very careful with everyone, fetching and carrying for Tertius without being proprietary, asking me about the garden, knowing not to ask about Mordred, not jumping every time drowning was mentioned, and eating too much, attractively, as the young should. She did not roll her eyes about when Tertius got tertiary, nor did she fail to mend the cistern in the bachelor's bathroom which I break as a trap for newcomers once in a while.'

Mordred Cowdenbeath had been Anne's husband; it was said that he had been found by Anne, his gun at his side. She had told me one evening that this was not so. By definition a crime, but a crime of passion, she had said, and slipped the oyster into her mouth as the tears slipped out of her eyes, trebly fluent salt.

# John Irving

## 1989

## *A Prayer for Owen Meany*

### The Foul Ball

I am doomed to remember a boy with a wrecked voice – not because of his voice, or because he was the smallest person I ever knew, or even because he was the instrument of my mother's death, but because he is the reason I believe in God; I am a Christian because of Owen Meany. I make no claims to have a life in Christ, or with Christ – and certainly not *for* Christ, which I've heard some zealots claim. I'm not very sophisticated in my knowledge of the Old Testament, and I've not read the New Testament since my Sunday school days, except for those passages that I hear read aloud to me when I go to church. I'm somewhat more familiar with the passages from the Bible that appear in The Book of Common Prayer; I read my prayer book often, and my Bible only on holy days – the prayer book is so much more orderly.

I've always been a pretty regular churchgoer. I used to be a Congregationalist – I was baptized in the Congregational Church, and after some years of fraternity with Episcopalians (I was confirmed in the Episcopal Church, too), I became rather vague in my religion: in my teens I attended a 'nondenominational' church. Then I became an Anglican; the Anglican Church of Canada has been my church – ever since I left the United States, about twenty years ago. Being an Anglican is a lot like being an Episcopalian – so much so that being an Anglican occasionally impresses upon me the suspicion that I have simply become an

Episcopalian again. Anyway, I left the Congregationalists and the Episcopalians – and my country once and for all.

When I die, I shall attempt to be buried in New Hampshire – alongside my mother – but the Anglican Church will perform the necessary service *before* my body suffers the indignity of trying to be sneaked through U.S. Customs. My selections from the Order for the Burial of the Dead are entirely conventional and can be found, in the order that I shall have them read – *not* sung – in The Book of Common Prayer. Almost everyone I know will be familiar with the passage from John, beginning with '... whosoever liveth and believeth in me shall never die.' And then there's '... in my Father's house are many mansions: If it were not so, I would have told you.' And I have always appreciated the frankness expressed in that passage from Timothy, the one that goes '... we brought nothing into this world, and it is certain we can carry nothing out.' It will be a by-the-book Anglican service, the kind that would make my former fellow Congregationalists fidget in their pews. I am an Anglican now, and I shall die an Anglican. But I skip a Sunday service now and then; I make no claims to be especially pious; I have a church-rummage faith – the kind that needs patching up every weekend. What faith I have I owe to Owen Meany, a boy I grew up with. It is Owen who made me a believer.

In Sunday school, we developed a form of entertainment based on abusing Owen Meany, who was *so* small that not only did his feet not touch the floor when he sat in his chair – his knees did not extend to the edge of his seat; therefore, his legs stuck out straight, like the legs of a doll. It was as if Owen Meany had been born without realistic joints.

Owen was so tiny, we loved to pick him up; in truth, we couldn't resist picking him up. We thought it was a miracle: how little he weighed. This was also incongruous because Owen came from a family in the granite business. The Meany Granite Quarry was a big place, the equipment for blasting and cutting the granite slabs was heavy and dangerous-looking; granite itself is such a rough, substantial rock. But the only aura of the granite quarry that clung to Owen was the granular dust, the gray powder that sprang off his clothes whenever we lifted him up. He was the color of a gravestone; light was both absorbed and reflected by his skin, as with a pearl, so that he appeared translucent at times – especially at his temples, where his blue veins showed through his skin (as though, in addition to his extraordinary size, there were other evidence that he was born too soon).

His vocal cords had not developed fully, or else his voice had been injured by the rock dust of his family's business. Maybe he had larynx damage, or a destroyed trachea; maybe he'd been hit in the throat by a chunk of granite. To be heard at all, Owen had to shout through his nose.

Yet he was dear to us – 'a little doll,' the girls called him, while he squirmed to get away from them; and from all of us.

I don't remember how our game of lifting Owen began.

This was Christ Church, the Episcopal Church of Gravesend, New Hampshire. Our Sunday school teacher was a strained, unhappy-looking woman named Mrs Walker. We thought this name suited her because her method of teaching involved a lot of walking out of class. Mrs Walker would read us an instructive passage from the Bible. She would then ask us to think seriously about what we had heard – 'Silently and seriously, that's how I want you to think!' she would say. 'I'm going to leave you alone with your thoughts, now,' she would tell us ominously – as if our thoughts were capable of driving us over the edge. 'I want you to think *very* hard,' Mrs Walker would say. Then she'd walk out on us. I think she was a smoker, and she couldn't allow herself to smoke in front of us. 'When I come back,' she'd say, 'we'll talk about it.'

By the time she came back, of course, we'd forgotten everything about whatever *it* was – because as soon as she left the room, we would fool around with a frenzy. Because being alone with our thoughts was no fun, we would pick up Owen Meany and pass him back and forth, overhead. We managed this while remaining seated in our chairs – that was the challenge of the game. Someone – I forget who started it – would get up, seize

Owen, sit back down with him, pass him to the next person, who would pass him on, and so forth. The girls were included in this game; some of the girls were the most enthusiastic about it. Everyone could lift up Owen. We were very careful; we never dropped him. His shirt might become a little rumpled. His necktie was so long, Owen tucked it into his trousers – or else it would have hung to his knees – and his necktie often came untucked; sometimes his change would fall out (in our faces). We always gave him his money back.

If he had his baseball cards with him, they, too, would fall out of his pockets. This made him cross because the cards were alphabetized, or ordered under another system – all the infielders together, maybe. We didn't know what the system was, but obviously Owen had a system, because when Mrs Walker came back to the room – when Owen returned to his chair and we passed his nickels and dimes and his baseball cards back to him – he would sit shuffling through the cards with a grim, silent fury.

He was not a good baseball player, but he did have a very small strike zone and as a consequence he was often used as a pinch hitter – not because he ever hit the ball with any authority (in fact, he was instructed never to swing at the ball), but because he could be relied upon to earn a walk, a base on balls. In Little League games he resented this exploitation and once refused to come to bat unless he was allowed to swing at the pitches. But there was no bat small enough for him to swing that didn't hurl his tiny body after it – that didn't thump him on the back and knock him out of the batter's box and flat upon the ground. So, after the humiliation of swinging at a few pitches, and missing them, and whacking himself off his feet, Owen Meany selected that *other* humiliation of standing motionless and crouched at home plate while the pitcher *aimed* the ball at Owen's strike zone – and missed it, almost every time.

Yet Owen loved his baseball cards – and, for some reason, he clearly loved the game of baseball itself, although the game was cruel to him. Opposing pitchers would threaten him. They'd tell him that if he didn't swing at their pitches, they'd hit him with the ball. 'Your head's bigger than your strike zone, pal,' one pitcher told him. So Owen Meany made his way to first base after being struck by pitches, too.

Once on base, he was a star. No one could run the bases like Owen. If our team could stay at bat long enough, Owen Meany could steal home. He was used as a pinch runner in the late innings, too; pinch runner and pinch hitter Meany − pinch *walker* Meany, we called him. In the field, he was hopeless. He was afraid of the ball; he shut his eyes when it came anywhere near him. And if by some miracle he managed to catch it, he couldn't throw it; his hand was too small to get a good grip. But he was no ordinary complainer; if he was self-pitying, his voice was so original in its expression of complaint that he managed to make whining lovable.

In Sunday school, when we held Owen up in the air − especially, in the air! − he protested so uniquely. We tortured him, I think, in order to hear his voice; I used to think his voice came from another planet. Now I'm convinced it was a voice not entirely of this world.

'PUT ME DOWN!' he would say in a strangled, emphatic falsetto. 'CUT IT OUT! I DON'T WANT TO DO THIS ANYMORE. ENOUGH IS ENOUGH. PUT ME DOWN! YOU ASSHOLES!'

But we just passed him around and around. He grew more fatalistic about it, each time. His body was rigid; he wouldn't struggle. Once we had him in the air, he folded his arms defiantly on his chest; he scowled at the ceiling. Sometimes Owen grabbed hold of his chair the instant Mrs Walker left the room; he'd cling like a bird to a swing in its cage, but he was easy to dislodge because he was ticklish. A girl named Sukey Swift was especially deft at tickling Owen; instantly, his arms and legs would stick straight out and we'd have him up in the air again.

'NO TICKLING!' he'd say, but the rules to this game were our rules. We never listened to Owen.

Inevitably, Mrs Walker would return to the room when Owen was in the air. Given the biblical nature of her instructions to us:

'to think *very* hard ...' she might have imagined that by a supreme act of our combined and hardest thoughts we had succeeded in levitating Owen Meany. She might have had the wit to suspect that Owen was reaching toward heaven as a direct result of leaving us alone with our thoughts.

But Mrs Walker's response was always the same – brutish and unimaginative and incredibly dense. 'Owen!' she would snap. 'Owen Meany, you get back to your seat! You get *down* from up there!'

What could Mrs Walker teach us about the Bible if she was stupid enough to think that Owen Meany had put himself up in the air?

Owen was always dignified about it. He never said, '*THEY DID IT! THEY ALWAYS DO IT! THEY PICK ME UP AND LOSE MY MONEY AND MESS UP MY BASEBALL CARDS – AND THEY NEVER PUT ME DOWN WHEN I ASK THEM TO! WHAT DO YOU THINK, THAT I FLEW UP HERE?*'

But although Owen would complain to us, he would never complain about us. If he was occasionally capable of being a stoic in the air, he was always a stoic when Mrs Walker accused him of childish behavior. He would never accuse us. Owen was no rat. As vividly as any number of the stories in the Bible, Owen Meany showed us what a martyr was.

It appeared there were no hard feelings. Although we saved our most ritualized attacks on him for Sunday school, we also lifted him up at other times – more spontaneously. Once someone hooked him by his collar to a coat tree in the elementary-school auditorium; even then, even there, Owen didn't struggle. He dangled silently, and waited for someone to unhook him and put him down. And after gym class, someone hung him in his locker and shut the door. 'NOT FUNNY! NOT FUNNY!' he called, and called, until someone must have agreed with him and freed him from the company of his jockstrap – the size of a slingshot.

How could I have known that Owen was a hero?

# Joanna Trollope

## 1989

## *A Village Affair*

On the day that contracts were exchanged on the house, Alice Jordan put all three children into the car and went to visit it. Natasha made her usual seven-year-old fuss about her seat-belt, and James was crying because he had lost the toy man who rode his toy stunt motorbike, but the baby lay peaceably in his carrycot and was pleased to be joggling gently along while a fascinating pattern of bare branches flickered through the slanting back window of the car on to his round upturned face. Natasha sang 'Ten Green Bottles' to drown James and James amplified his crying to yelling. Alice switched on the car radio and a steady female voice from *Woman's Hour* explained calmly to her how to examine herself for any sinister lumps. Mud flew up from the winter lanes and made a gritty veil across the windscreen. James stopped yelling abruptly and put his thumb in his mouth.

'You are an utter baby,' his sister said to him disdainfully. He began to cry again, messily, round his thumb.

Alice could see his smeary wet red face reflected in the driving mirror. The voice on the wireless said that if you disliked touching yourself, you should get someone else to feel for you. The interviewer said – perfectly reasonably, Alice thought – how would anyone else be able to feel what you could feel, not being, as it were, on the inside of yourself?

'Crying like that,' Natasha said to James, 'makes people think you are a girly.'

James let out a wild squeal and flung his motorbike-clutching fist out sideways at his sister, just able to reach her cheek.

Eyes wide with outrage and turned at once upon her mother, Natasha began to cry. In the very back, conscious of an atmosphere he didn't like, Charlie's soft round face gathered itself up in distress. He opened his mouth and screwed his eyes up tight. Alice stopped the car.

'The lymph nodes—' said the *Woman's Hour* woman into the racket.

Alice turned her off. She undid her seat-belt and twisted herself around.

'Be quiet!' she shouted. 'You beastly, beastly children. I won't have this. You are not to quarrel in the car. How can I drive? Do you want me to drive you into a wall? Because that's what will happen.'

Natasha stopped crying and looked out of the window for walls. There were none, only a hedge and a hilly field and some black and white cows.

She said, 'There aren't any walls.'

Alice ignored her.

'Where did I say we were going?'

'In the car,' James said unsteadily.

His sister looked at him witheringly.

'To our new house.'

'Yes. Don't you *want* to see it?'

'Yes,' Natasha said.

James said nothing. At that moment he didn't want anything except to put his thumb back in, which he dared not do.

'Then,' Alice said, 'nobody will say one single word until we get there. Otherwise you will have to stay in the car while I get out and look at everything. Is that clear?'

She buckled herself in again and started the car. Natasha watched her. She was the only mother Natasha knew who had a pigtail. It was very long. It started high up, almost on top of her head, and ended up half-way down her back. It was fat, too. Usually, she pulled it over one shoulder. Natasha wanted one like it, so did her friend Sophie. Sophie's mother had sort of ordinary hair you couldn't really remember, like mothers usually had. Looking at her mother's pigtail made Natasha suddenly feel affectionate, out of pride.

'I'm sorry,' she said, in a minute voice, because of the ban.

Alice beamed at her quickly, flashing the smile over her shoulder.

'Nearly there.'

# *Paul Bailey*

## 1990

## *An Immaculate Mistake*

I was born in February, 1937, in Battersea, south London, the third and last child of Arthur Oswald Bailey and his wife, Helen Maud. He was fifty-four years old, and she was forty-one. He was employed as a roadsweeper, she as a domestic help. They had me christened Peter Harry. Such are the plain facts.

'He who is not very strong in memory should not meddle with lying': these scenes from childhood and beyond were written with Montaigne's caution in mind.

### In Error

'You were our mistake,' said my mother. 'You ought not to be here, by rights.'

She was old now, and letting go of her secrets. This one, she knew, would be of particular interest to me.

'We didn't plan to have you, is what I'm saying. People like us had to be very careful when it came to having children. You took me by surprise, and your poor father, too. That was typical of you – determined to be different even before you were born.'

On the night of my conception, in May 1936, my parents thoroughly enjoyed their love-making. 'We had no fear of the consequences, because we didn't think there'd be any. A few weeks later, we found out we were wrong.'

I asked her to tell me why they had had no fear.

Well, it was her body, and what had been happening to it lately – that was the reason why they had been able to enjoy themselves. At forty, soon to be forty-one, she was certain that the change had come upon her a little bit earlier than expected. It did with some women. All the signs were there – the hot flushes, the horrible black moods that had no cause she could see, plus the fact that her monthlies – if I understood her meaning – had stopped. With evidence like this, there seemed no need – as there always had in the past – for caution.

'Which we threw to the winds, I have to say.'

This revelation, made when she was eighty-four, did not upset me. She had guessed that it wouldn't, and that I might even be amused by it. I was 'old enough and ugly enough' to face the truth.

Walking home that afternoon, I hesitated for a moment on Albert Bridge and looked down at the water that hadn't claimed me, as I had once assured her it would. Two phrases from childhood came back to me while I stood there: my own 'I wish I'd never been born', which I must have said on the Sunday of the gas oven, and my mother's 'Giving birth to you was the worst day's work I ever did'. I could smile at them now, those expressions of unhappiness and exasperation, in the light of the awareness of my accidental entrance into life.

I was pleased, warmed, by this new knowledge. I could say, as Gloucester says of his bastard son Edmund, that I had come 'something saucily to the world' and that 'there was good sport at (my) making'. Why should it matter to me that I had not been planned? 'You were *our* mistake,' she had said – not *a* mistake. She had chosen the word with care, with affection, I realised.

Then I walked on, thanking my father and mother for the error of their loving ways on a late spring night of thorough enjoyment.

## Confetti

There had been a wedding at the church that morning. I wanted to pick up and scatter the confetti that lay outside, but my mother pulled me on, eager to get to the shops before the few miserable things worth buying vanished into other women's bags. It was a Saturday in June, and the sunlit street was crowded.

Then the crowd dispersed, in the familiar manner of wartime. The siren had sounded, alerting everyone to the prospect of an air raid. It was necessary to take cover, quickly. Some friends of friends lived near by, and it was to their house my mother decided to go, in the hope of finding them in. I remember how she knocked and knocked at their door, how she shouted our names through the letter-box, how afraid she was that the couple was somewhere else. 'Oh, thank God,' she said when she at last heard footsteps, and a voice advising her to keep her hair on.

My mother apologised to the man who let us in. She was sorry for the inconvenience. 'It's the Germans who should be sorry, not you,' he responded, leading us through the kitchen to the back yard, where the concrete shelter had been built. His wife was already inside. She had tried to make it as homely as she could, she explained. With their favourite ornaments and family photographs for decoration, and a strip of carpet on the floor, it looked less dark and dreary, less like what it really was. We were invited to sit down – a chair for my mother, a cushion for me – and to wait until the All Clear went.

('You had your nose in a book all the while that raid was going on,' my mother told me, years later. 'I swear you didn't hear a single bang. If Hitler himself had come goosestepping into that shelter, you wouldn't have noticed him.')

When the raid was over, my mother thanked the friends of friends for protecting us, and declined their offer of tea – she had to rush back to her husband, who would be as worried about her as she was worried about him.

We returned to the sunshine, and to a street that had changed. I saw, beyond the smoke and dust, that the church had gone, and that the confetti I'd wanted to play with was buried under broken stone and shattered glass, entirely out of sight.

★

The second bomb – we called it the 'doodlebug' – that destroyed the Railway Tavern damaged the house where I was born as well: it was declared unsafe and we were ordered to leave. In another of the neighbouring houses affected by the blast, a small boy died strangely. When the explosion occurred in the middle of the night, the pillow on which his head was resting burst open and he was suffocated by the feathers flying out of it.

My mother took me off to the tiny house in a Hampshire village where my grandmother had given birth to five daughters and four sons. (These were the living, but it was hinted that there had been others who had come into the world for a mere matter of hours or days. And there might have been more children if my grandfather had not been killed in an accident at the tanning factory, at the age of forty-six.) 'You should count yourself lucky you're staying with the family. Most London kiddies are sent off to complete strangers, and God only knows what happens to them after that. You hear some terrible stories.'

'What stories, Mum?'

'Never you mind what stories.'

'Tell me,' I implored her. 'Tell me.'

'There's stories,' she pronounced, 'and then there's stories. And that's my last word on the subject.'

('There's doctors, and then there's doctors'; 'There's books, and then there's books'; 'There's women, and then there's women' – she used this adaptable phrase to differentiate between the respectable and the dissolute, the worthy and the unworthy, the good and the bad. Once, praising the Cox's Orange Pippin, she observed, 'There's apples, and then there's apples.' As a child, I was irritated by these pronouncements, for they left too much unsaid: 'There's war, and then there's war' seeming peculiarly inadequate.)

Travelling to the country was not a simple business for my mother. If the train departed at eleven in the morning, she insisted on our being at the station by nine. 'You'd think you were going to Timbuctoo, to judge by the fret you're in,' my father would complain. 'Calm yourself, woman.'

'It's the way I am. I can't help it.'

During the inevitable two hours of waiting, she wondered aloud if she had remembered to write to her mother to say we were coming – 'She'll have our guts for garters, otherwise' – and mentioned the items she imagined she had forgotten to pack.

I suggested, once, that she open the suitcase and look inside. Then she would know exactly what was missing.

'And have people peering at our belongings? I should think not.'

After my father's death, she became even more fretful on journeys. She had the gas to worry about now. 'If your dad was still alive, he'd soon smell it escaping and turn it off.' Her Gas Moment, as I named it, came when the train, or coach, in which we had been among the first to seat ourselves, started moving. 'I've left the gas on,' she whispered. 'No, you haven't,' I assured her. 'How would you know? You never see what's in front of you.' It was pointless to argue. There would be a telegram waiting for her at the other end, with the news that our house and everything we owned, not to mention the family who lived downstairs, had been blown to bits. I advised her to pull the communication cord and stop the train. 'Don't be so wicked,' she scolded. Wicked? 'Think of the people who'd be missing their connections and having their Christmas holidays ruined. It's a wicked idea.'

'The country' in my childhood meant either Hampshire or Sussex, and it was the latter I preferred. I had more freedom there, with no stern grandmother to reprimand me. My Uncle Bill was the head gardener on the large estate at Herstmonceux Castle and I and my cousins played on the lawns while he worked.

One post-war summer afternoon, when my uncle had gone home, they dared me to climb an oak tree. I climbed up and up and up, amazed at my daring and prowess. Then I stopped and looked down, and in an instant felt the keenest terror of my life. I was too frightened to scream. I clung to the branch on which I was perched, and prayed that I wouldn't fall. Descent was impossible now that I had been robbed of the courage I had possessed only minutes earlier. 'Ladder,' I managed to say. 'Get a ladder.'

My cousins responded with taunts of 'Cowardy cowardy custard' and ran off, laughing. I remained high in the oak tree until it was almost dark. I cried when my uncle rescued me, from shame as much as relief. Boys, I was told, do not cry. Crying was what little girls did, because it was in their nature.

That was my cousins' single act of cruelty, as inexplicable today as it was then. Both girls abetted me when I pretended to be my twin brother, who did not exist. Of all the games I played as a boy, this was the one I enjoyed most. It was fun being someone else, escaping from the Peter that I was into the Paul of my imagination, giving him different characteristics, different interests. Paul was a livelier creature than his dull impersonator, it seemed to me. He had to be created afresh, newly imagined, each time I decided to become him.

Another Paul, *Sir* Paul, was talked about in Castle Cottage, the big and beautiful house where my uncle and aunt and their daughters lived. 'Poor Sir Paul' was the phrase I often heard. I did not understand. How could he be poor when he was rich? The castle was his, and the gardens. How was he poor? 'He's poor because he's been unlucky,' was the answer I received. Back in London, I asked my mother why Sir Paul was poor and unlucky. 'That would be telling,' she said. 'It's not a story for young ears.'

(In 1941, Sir Paul Latham, a Conservative Member of Parliament and an officer in the Royal Artillery, was accused of committing an 'improper act' with two gunners. Fearing scandal, he attempted suicide by crashing his motorbike. He survived the crash, but had to have a leg amputated. He was sentenced to two years' imprisonment for misbehaving with the soldiers and for the suicide attempt. The scandal persisted. Yet my uncle never said a derogatory word about his employer, and neither did my mother, who considered Sir Paul a 'true gentleman'. Years later, when she and other members of my family informed me that pansies were the sons of the idle rich, they must have been thinking of 'poor Sir Paul'. The two gunners – from back-street homes, like the Peter who was being educated – were forgotten.)

The three names I associate with those summers in Sussex are not English. My cousins collected signed photographs of film stars, which they obtained by writing to an address in Culver City, California. The smiling likenesses of the famous adorned their bedroom walls. I copied out their regular letter and posted it to America, to Turhan Bey. I wrote to him simply because I loved the sound of 'Turhan Bey'. There was no one called Turhan Bey in Battersea or Herstmonceux or Titchfield, where my grandmother had her domain. Turhan Bey, in desert robes, sent his best to Peter, wishing him everything he wished himself.

My aunt and uncle gave an annual children's party in the garden behind their home. She prepared the food and drink – jellies, jam tarts, trifle, orange and lemon squash – and he supplied the entertainment. Uncle Bill's party piece was to dress up as a woman and sing a slightly risqué song. He was hairy and simian in appearance, the black stubble showing through the make-up he had applied to his weather-beaten face. He sported balloons for breasts, which he always burst at the end of his act: 'Bang goes the left titty, bang goes the right.' One year, he disguised himself, with limited resources, as Carmen Miranda, the film star noted rather for the exotic fruits she carried on her person than for any ability as a singer and dancer. Carmen Miranda bore a pineapple on her head, and used bananas as earrings. In wartime England, my uncle was restricted to apples, pears and cherries.

*I, I, I, I, I, I like you very much*
*I, I, I, I, I, I think you're grand*

he sang, swishing his wife's polka-dot frock from side to side. That was all he knew of the song, so he then made a joke about maracas, which only the adults appreciated. He repeated the two lines again and again, and tried to dance the rumba – which wasn't easy for him, in high-heeled shoes – and brought his performance to a close with a protracted fruit striptease: 'You want my cherry? You fancy my pear? How much you pay for my apples?'

The third foreign name is that of a German prisoner-of-war, Matthias Hess, who was dear to my mother's memory. His calm and gentle nature is celebrated in a separate story.

# *Will Self*

## 1991
## *The Quantity Theory of Insanity*

### The North London Book of the Dead

I suppose that the form my bereavement took after my mother died was fairly conventional. Initially I was shocked. Her final illness was mercifully quick, but harrowing. Cancer tore through her body as if it were late for an important meeting with a lot of other successful diseases.

I had always expected my mother to outlive me. I saw myself becoming a neutered bachelor, who would be wearing a cardigan and still living at home at the age of forty, but it wasn't to be. Mother's death was a kind of a relief, but it was also bizarre and hallucinatory. The week she lay dying in the hospital I was plagued by strange sensations; gusts of air would seem personalised and, driving in my car, I had the sensation not that I was moving forward but that the road was being reeled back beneath the wheels, as if I were mounted on some giant piece of scenery.

The night she died my brother and I were at the hospital. We took it in turns to snatch sleep in a vestibule at the end of the ward and then to sit with her. She breathed stertorously. Her flesh yellowed and yellowed. I was quite conscious that she had no mind any more. The cancer – or so the consultant told me – had made its way up through the meningitic fluid in the spine and into her brain. I sensed the cancer in her skull like a cloud of inky pus. Her self-consciousness, sentience, identity, what you will, was cornered, forced back by the cloud into a confined space, where it pulsed on and then off, with all the apparent humanity of a digital watch.

One minute she was alive, the next she was dead. A dumpy nurse rushed to find my brother and me. We had both fallen asleep in the vestibule, cocooned within its plastic walls. 'I think she's gone,' said the nurse. And I pictured Mother striding down Gower Street, naked, wattled.

By the time we reached the room they were laying her out. I had never understood what this meant before; now I could see that the truth was that the body, the corpse, really laid itself out. It was smoothed as if a great wind had rolled over the tired flesh. And it, Mother, was changing colour, as I watched, from an old ivory to a luminous yellow. The nurse, for some strange reason, had brushed Mother's hair back off her forehead. It lay around her head in a fan on the pillow and two lightning streaks of grey ran up into it from either temple. The nurses had long since removed her dentures, and the whole ensemble – Mother with drawn-in cheeks and sculpted visage, lying in the small room, around her the loops and skeins of a life-supporting technology – made me think of the queen of an alien planet, resplendent on a high-tech palanquin, in some Buck Rogers style sci-fi serial of the Thirties.

There was a great whooshing sensation in the room. This persisted as a doctor of Chinese extraction – long, yellow, and divided at the root – felt around inside her cotton nightie for a non-existent heartbeat. The black, spindly hairs on his chin wavered. He pronounced her dead. The whooshing stopped. I felt her spirit fly out into the orange light of central London. It was about 3.00 a.m.

★ ★ ★

When I began to accept the fact that Mother really was gone, I went into a period of intense depression. I felt that I had lost an adversary. Someone to test myself against. My greatest fan and my severest critic and above all a good talker, who I was only just getting to know as a person – shorn of the emotional prejudices that conspire to strait-jacket the relationships between parents and children.

When my depression cleared the dreams started. I found myself night after night encountering my mother in strange situations. In my dreams she would appear at dinner parties (uninvited), crouched behind a filing cabinet in the office where I worked, or on public transport balefully swinging from a strap. She was quite honest about the fact that she was dead in these dreams, she made no attempt to masquerade as one of the living, rather she absorbed the effect that death had had on her personality much the way she had taken the rest of the crap that life had flung at her: a couple of failed marriages and a collection of children who, on the whole, were a bit of a disappointment to her.

When I tried to remonstrate with her, point out to her that by her own lights (she was a fervent atheist and materialist), she ought to be gently decomposing somewhere, she would fix me with a weary eye and say in a characteristically deadpan way, 'So I'm dead but won't lie down, huh? Big deal.'

It was a big deal. Mother had banged on about her revulsion at the idea of an afterlife for as long as I could remember. The chief form that this took was an extended rant aimed at all the trappings of death that society had designed. She despised the undertaking business especially. To Mother it was simply a way of cheating money out of grieving people who could ill afford it.

She had told me a year or two before she died that if it was at all possible I was to try and give her a kind of do-it-yourself funeral. Apparently the Co-op retailed one that allowed you to get the cost of the whole thing down to about £250. You had to build your own casket though and I was never any good at anything remotely practical. At school it took me two years to construct an acrylic string-holder. And even then it wouldn't work.

So, after Mother died we arranged things conventionally, but austerely. Her corpse was burnt at Golders Green Crematorium. My eldest brother and I went alone – knowing that she would have disapproved of a crowd. We sat there in the chapel contemplating the bottom-of-the-range casket. One of the undertakers came waddling down the aisle, he gestured to us to stand and then moved off to one side, conspicuously scratching his grey bottom, either inadvertently or because he considered us of no account. Electric motors whirred, Mother lurched towards what, to all intents and purposes, was her final resting place.

A week or so later when I was going through more of Mother's papers I found a newspaper clipping about the DIY funeral. I threw it away guiltily. I also found a deposit book that showed that mother had invested £370 in something called the Ecological Building Society. I phoned the society and was told by a Mr Hunt that it was true. Mother had been the owner of a seventh of a traditional Mongolian *yurt*, which was sited for some reason in a field outside Wincanton. I told Mr Hunt to keep the seventh; it seemed a suitable memorial.

Meanwhile, the dreams continued. And Mother managed to be as embarrassing in them as she had been alive, but for entirely different reasons. With death she had taken on a mantle of candour and social sharpness that I tended to attribute to myself rather than her. At the dream dinner parties she would make asides to me the whole time about how pretentious people were and what bad taste they displayed, talking all the while in a loud and affected voice which, needless to say, remained inaudible to her subjects. After a while I ceased trying to defeat her with the logic of her own extinction; it was pointless. Mother had long since ceased to be susceptible to reasoning. I think it was something to do with my father, a man who uses dialectics the way the Japanese used bamboo slivers during the war.

About six months after Mother's death the dreams began to decline in frequency and eventually they petered out altogether. They were replaced for a short while by an intense period during which I kept seeing people in the street who I thought were Mother. I'd be walking in the West End or the City and there, usually on the other side of the road, would be Mother, ambling along staring in shop windows. I would know it was

Mother because of the clothes. Mother tended to wear slacks on loan from hippopotami, or else African-style dresses that could comfortably house a scout troop. She also always carried a miscellaneous collection of bags, plastic and linen, dangling from her arm. These were crammed with modern literature, groceries and wadded paper tissues.

And then, invariably, as I drew closer the likeness would evaporate. Not only wasn't it Mother, but it seemed absurd that I ever could have made the mistake. This late-middle-aged woman looked nothing like Mother, she was dowdy and conventional. Not the sort of woman at all who would say of effete young men that they 'had no balls', or of precious young women that they 'shat chocolate ice cream'. Yet each time the fact that Mother was dead hit me again, it was as if it hadn't really occurred to me before and that her failure to get in touch with me over the past six months had been solely because she was 'hellishly busy'.

When I stopped seeing fake Mothers in the street I reckoned that I had just about accepted her death. Every so often I thought about her, sometimes with sadness, sometimes with joy, but her absence no longer gnawed at me like a rat at a length of flex. I was over it. Although, like Marcel after Albertine has gone, from time to time I felt that the reason I no longer missed Mother with such poignancy was that I had become another person. I had changed. I was no longer the sort of person who had had a mother like Mother. Mother belonged to someone else. If I had run into her at a dinner party fully conscious, she probably wouldn't have recognised me. My mother was dead.

All of this made the events that transpired in the winter of the year she died even more shocking. I was walking down Crouch Hill towards Crouch End on a drizzly, bleak Tuesday afternoon. It was about three o'clock. I'd taken the afternoon off work and decided to go and see a friend. When, coming up the other side of the road I saw Mother. She was wearing a sort of bluish, tweedish long jacket and black slacks and carrying a Barnes & Noble book bag, as well as a large handbag and a carrier bag from Waitrose. She had a CND badge in her lapel and was observing the world with a familiar 'there will be tears before bedtime' sort of expression.

The impression I had of Mother in that very first glance was so sharp and so clear, her presence so tangible, that I did not for a moment doubt the testimony of my senses. I looked at Mother and felt a trinity of emotions: affection and embarrassment mingled with a sort of acute embarrassment. It was this peculiarly familiar wash of feeling that must have altogether swamped the terror and bewilderment that anyone would expect to experience at the sight of their dead mother walking up Crouch Hill.

I crossed the road and walked towards her. She spotted me when I was about twenty feet off. Just before a grin of welcome lit up her features I spotted a little *moue* of girlish amusement – that was familiar too, it meant 'You've been had'. We kissed on both cheeks; Mother looked me up and down to see how I was weighing in for the fight with life. Then she gestured at the shop window she'd been looking into. 'Can you believe the prices they're charging for this crap, someone must be buying it.' Her accent was the same, resolutely mid-Atlantic, she had the same artfully yellowed and unevened dentures. It was Mother.

'Mother,' I said, 'what are you doing in Crouch End? You never come to Crouch End except to take the cat to the vet, you don't even like Crouch End.'

'Well, I live here now.' Mother was unperturbed. 'It's OK, it's a drag not being able to get the tube, but the buses are fairly regular. There's quite a few good shops in the parade and someone's just opened up a real deli. Want some halva?' Mother opened her fist under my face. Crushed into it was some sticky halva, half-eaten but still in its gold foil wrapping. She grinned again.

'But Mother, what are you doing in Crouch End? You're dead.'

Mother was indignant, 'Of course I'm dead, dummy, whaddya think I've been doing for the last ten months? Cruising the Caribbean?'

'How the hell should I know? I thought we saw the last of you at Golders Green Crematorium, I never expected to see you in Crouch End on a Tuesday afternoon.' Mother had me rattled, she seemed to be genuinely astonished by my failure to comprehend her resurrection.

'More to the point, what are you doing in Crouch End? Why aren't you at work?'

'I thought I'd take the afternoon off. There's not a lot on at the office. If I stayed there I'd just be shuffling paper back and forth trying to create some work.'

'That's an attitude problem talking, young man. You've got a good job there. What's the matter with you? You always want to start at the top, you've got to learn to work your way up in life.'

'Life, Mother? I hardly think "Life" is the issue here! Tell me about what it's like to be dead! Why didn't you tell any of us you were having life after death in Crouch End? You could have called ...'

Mother wasn't fazed, she looked at her watch, another crappy Timex, indistinguishable from the last one I'd seen her wearing. 'It's late, I've got to go to my class. If you want to know about life after death come and see me tomorrow. I'm living at 24 Rosemount Avenue, in the basement flat, we'll have tea, I'll make you some cookies.' And with that she gave me the sort of perfunctory peck on the cheek she always used to give me when she was in a hurry and toddled off up Crouch Hill, leaving me standing, bemused.

What I couldn't take was that Mother was so offhand about life after death, rather than the fact of it. That and this business of living in Crouch End. Mother had always been such a crushing snob about where people lived in London; certain suburbs – such as Crouch End – were so incredibly non-U in Mother's book of form. The revelation that there was life after death seemed to me relatively unimportant set beside Mother's startling new attitudes.

I probably should have gone and told someone about my encounter. But who? All a shrink could have offered would have been full board and medication. And anyway, the more I told people how real the experience had been, the more certain they would become that I was the victim of an outlandishly complex delusionary state.

I had no desire to be psychiatric cannon fodder, so I went off to see my friend and had a fulfilling afternoon playing Trivial Pursuit. Just suppose it was all for real? I had to find out more about Mother's resurrection, she'd always been so emphatic about what happened to people after they die: 'They rot, that's it. You put 'em in a box and they rot. All that religious stuff, it's a load of crap.' Setting aside the whole issue of the miraculous I really wanted to see Mother eat humble pie over this after-life issue, so much so that I went through the next thirty-odd hours as if nothing had happened. It was an exercise in magical thinking. I figured that if I behaved as if nothing had happened, Mother would be waiting for me, with cookies, in Rosemount Avenue, but if I said anything to anyone, the gods might take offence and whisk her away.

# Michael Ondaatje

## 1992

## *The English Patient*

The first time she dreamed of him she woke up beside her husband screaming.

In their bedroom she stared down onto the sheet, mouth open. Her husband put his hand on her back.

'Nightmare. Don't worry.'

'Yes.'

'Shall I get you some water?'

'Yes.'

She wouldn't move. Wouldn't lie back into that zone they had been in.

The dream had taken place in this room – his hand on her neck (she touched it now), his anger towards her that she had sensed the first few times she had met him. No, not anger, a lack of interest, irritation at a married woman being among them. They had been bent over like animals, and he had yoked her neck back so she had been unable to breathe within her arousal.

Her husband brought her the glass on a saucer but she could not lift her arms, they were shaking, loose. He put the glass awkwardly against her mouth so she could gulp the chlorinated water, some coming down her chin, falling to her stomach. When she lay back she hardly had time to think of what she had witnessed, she fell into a quick deep sleep.

That had been the first recognition. She remembered it sometime during the next day, but she was busy then and she refused to nestle with its significance for long, dismissed it; it was an accidental collision on a crowded night, nothing more.

A year later the other, more dangerous, peaceful dreams came. And even within the first one of these she recalled the hands at her neck and waited for the mood of calmness between them to swerve to violence.

Who lays the crumbs of food that tempt you? Towards a person you never considered. A dream. Then later another series of dreams.

He said later it was propinquity. Propinquity in the desert. It does that here, he said. He loved the word – the propinquity of water, the propinquity of two or three bodies in a car driving the Sand Sea for six hours. Her sweating knee beside the gear-box of the truck, the knee swerving, rising with the bumps. In the desert you have time to look everywhere, to theorize on the choreography of all things around you.

When he talked like that she hated him, her eyes remaining polite, her mind wanting to slap him. She always had the desire to slap him, and she realized even that was sexual. For him all relationships fell into patterns. You fell into propinquity or distance. Just as, for him, the histories in Herodotus clarified all societies. He assumed he was experienced in the ways of the world he had essentially left years earlier, struggling ever since to explore a half-invented world of the desert.

At Cairo aerodrome they loaded the equipment into the vehicles, her husband staying on to check the petrol lines of the Moth before the three men left the next morning. Madox went off to one of the embassies to send a wire. And was going into town to get drunk, the usual final evening in Cairo, first at Madame Badin's Opera Casino, and later to disappear into the streets behind the Pasha Hotel. He would pack before the evening began, which would allow him to just climb into the truck the next morning, hung over.

So he drove her into town, the air humid, the traffic bad and slow because of the hour.

'It's so hot. I need a beer. Do you want one?'

'No, I have to arrange for a lot of things in the next couple of hours. You'll have to excuse me.'

'That's all right,' she said. 'I don't want to interfere.'

'I'll have one with you when I come back.'

'In three weeks, right?'

'About that.'

'I wish I were going too.'

He said nothing in answer to that. They crossed the Bulaq Bridge and the traffic got worse. Too many carts, too many pedestrians who owned the streets. He cut south along the Nile towards the Semiramis Hotel, where she was staying, just beyond the barracks.

'You're going to find Zerzura this time, aren't you.'

'I'm going to find it this time.'

He was like his old self. He hardly looked at her on the drive, even when they were stalled for more than five minutes in one spot.

At the hotel he was excessively polite. When he behaved this way she liked him even less; they all had to pretend this pose was courtesy, graciousness. It reminded her of a dog in clothes. To hell with him. If her husband didn't have to work with him she would prefer not to see him again.

He pulled her pack out of the rear and was about to carry it into the lobby.

'Here, I can take that.' Her shirt was damp at the back when she got out of the passenger seat.

The doorman offered to take the pack, but he said, 'No, she wants to carry it,' and she was angry again at his assumption. The doorman left them. She turned to him and he passed her the bag so she was facing him, both hands awkwardly carrying the heavy case in front of her.

'So. Good-bye. Good luck.'

'Yes. I'll look after them all. They'll be safe.'

She nodded. She was in shadow, and he, as if unaware of the harsh sunlight, stood in it.

Then he came up to her, closer, and she thought for a moment he was going to embrace her. Instead he put his right arm forward and drew it in a gesture across her bare neck so her skin was touched by the whole length of his damp forearm.

'Good-bye.'

He walked back to the truck. She could feel his sweat now, like blood left by a blade which the gesture of his arm seemed to have imitated.

She picks up a cushion and places it onto her lap as a shield against him. 'If you make love to me I won't lie about it. If I make love to you I won't lie about it.'

She moves the cushion against her heart, as if she would suffocate that part of herself which has broken free.

'What do you hate most?' he asks.

'A lie. And you?'

'Ownership,' he says. 'When you leave me, forget me.'

Her fist swings towards him and hits hard into the bone just below his eye. She dresses and leaves.

Each day he would return home and look at the black bruise in the mirror. He became curious, not so much about the bruise, but about the shape of his face. The long eyebrows he had never really noticed before, the beginning of grey in his sandy hair. He had not looked at himself like this in a mirror for years. That was a long eyebrow.

Nothing can keep him from her.

When he is not in the desert with Madox or with Bermann in the Arab libraries, he meets her in Groppi Park – beside the heavily watered plum gardens. She is happiest here. She is a woman who misses moisture, who has always loved low green hedges and ferns. While for him this much greenery feels like a carnival.

From Groppi Park they arc out into the old city, South Cairo, markets where few Europeans go. In his rooms maps cover the walls. And in spite of his attempts at furnishing there is still a sense of base camp to his quarters.

They lie in each other's arms, the pulse and shadow of the fan on them. All morning he and Bermann have worked in the archaeological museum placing Arabic texts and European histories beside each other in an attempt to recognize echo, coincidence, name changes – back past Herodotus to the *Kraab al Kaiuz*, where Zerzura is named after the bathing woman in a desert caravan. And there too the slow blink of a fan's shadow. And here too the intimate exchange and echo of childhood history, of scar, of manner of kiss.

'I don't know what to do. I don't know what to do! How can I be your lover? He will go mad.'

A list of wounds.

The various colours of the bruise – bright russet leading to brown. The plate she walked across the room with, flinging its contents aside, and broke across his head, the blood rising up into the straw hair. The fork that entered the back of his shoulder, leaving its bite marks the doctor suspected were caused by a fox.

He would step into an embrace with her, glancing first to see what movable objects were around. He would meet her with others in public with bruises or a bandaged head and explain about the taxi jerking to a halt so that he had hit the open side window. Or with iodine on his forearm that covered a welt. Madox worried about his becoming suddenly accident-prone. She sneered quietly at the weakness of his explanation. Maybe it's his age, maybe he needs glasses, said her husband, nudging Madox. Maybe it's a woman he met, she said. Look, isn't that a woman's scratch or bite?

It was a scorpion, he said. *Androctonus australis.*

A postcard. Neat handwriting fills the rectangle.

*Half my days I cannot bear not to touch you.*
*the rest of the time I feel it doesn't matter*

*if I ever see you again. It isn't the*
*morality, it is how much you can bear.*

No date, no name attached.

Sometimes when she is able to spend the night with him they are wakened by the three minarets of the city beginning their prayers before dawn. He walks with her through the indigo markets that lie between South Cairo and her home. The beautiful songs of faith enter the air like arrows, one minaret answering another, as if passing on a rumour of the two of them as they walk through the cold morning air, the smell of charcoal and hemp already making the air profound. Sinners in a holy city.

He sweeps his arm across plates and glasses on a restaurant table so she might look up somewhere else in the city hearing this cause of noise. When he is without her. He, who has never felt alone in the miles of longitude between desert towns. A man in a desert can hold absence in his cupped hands knowing it is something that feeds him more than water. There is a plant he knows of near El Taj, whose heart, if one cuts it out, is replaced with a fluid containing herbal goodness. Every morning one can drink the liquid the amount of a missing heart. The plant continues to flourish for a year before it dies from some lack or other.

He lies in his room surrounded by the pale maps. He is without Katharine. His hunger wishes to burn down all social rules, all courtesy.

Her life with others no longer interests him. He wants only her stalking beauty, her theatre of expressions. He wants the minute and secret reflection between them, the depth of field minimal, their foreignness intimate like two pages of a closed book.

He has been disassembled by her.

And if she has brought him to this, what has he brought her to?

When she is within the wall of her class and he is beside her in larger groups he tells jokes he doesn't laugh at himself. Uncharacteristically manic, he attacks the history of exploration. When he is unhappy he does this. Only Madox recognizes the habit. But she will not even catch his eye. She smiles to everyone, to the objects in the room, praises a flower arrangement, worthless impersonal things. She misinterprets his behaviour, assuming this is what he wants, and doubles the size of the wall to protect herself.

But now he cannot bear this wall in her. You built your walls too, she tells him, so I have my wall. She says it glittering in a beauty he cannot stand. She with her beautiful clothes, with her pale face that laughs at everyone who smiles at her, with the uncertain grin for his angry jokes. He continues his appalling statements about this and that in some expedition they are all familiar with.

The minute she turns away from him in the lobby of Groppi's bar after he greets her, he is insane. He knows the only way he can accept losing her is if he can continue to hold her or be held by her. If they can somehow nurse each other out of this. Not with a wall.

Sunlight pours into his Cairo room. His hand flabby over the Herodotus journal, all the tension in the rest of his body, so he writes words down wrong, the pen sprawling as if without spine. He can hardly write down the word *sunlight*. The words *in love*.

In the apartment there is light only from the river and the desert beyond it. It falls upon her neck her feet the vaccination scar he loves on her right arm. She sits on the bed hugging nakedness. He slides his open palm along the sweat of her shoulder. This is my shoulder, he thinks, not her husband's, this is my shoulder. As lovers they have offered parts of their bodies to each other, like this. In this room on the periphery of the river.

In the few hours they have, the room has darkened to this pitch of light. Just river and desert light. Only when there is the rare shock of rain do they go towards the window and put their arms out, stretching, to bathe as much as they can of themselves in it. Shouts towards the brief downpour fill the streets.

'We will never love each other again. We can never see each other again.'

'I know,' he says.

The night of her insistence on parting.

She sits, enclosed within herself, in the armour of her terrible conscience. He is unable to reach through it. Only his body is close to her.

'Never again. Whatever happens.'

'Yes.'

'I think he will go mad. Do you understand?'

He says nothing, abandoning the attempt to pull her within him.

An hour later they walk into a dry night. They can hear the gramophone songs in the distance from the Music for All cinema, its windows open for the heat. They will have to part before that closes up and people she might know emerge from there.

They are in the botanical garden, near the Cathedral of All Saints. She sees one tear and leans forward and licks it, taking it into her mouth. As she has taken the blood from his hand when he cut himself cooking for her. Blood. Tear. He feels everything is missing from his body, feels he contains smoke. All that is alive is the knowledge of future desire and want. What he would say he cannot say to this woman whose openness is like a wound, whose youth is not mortal yet. He cannot alter what he loves most in her, her lack of compromise, where the romance of the poems she loves still sits with ease in the real world. Outside these qualities he knows there is no order in the world.

This night of her insistence. Twenty-eighth of September. The rain in the trees already dried by hot moonlight. Not one cool drop to fall down upon him like a tear. This parting at Groppi Park. He has not asked if her husband is home in that high square of light, across the street.

He sees the tall row of traveller's palms above them, their outstretched wrists. The way her head and hair were above him, when she was his lover.

Now there is no kiss. Just one embrace. He untugs himself from her and walks away, then turns. She is still there. He comes back within a few yards of her, one finger raised to make a point.

'I just want you to know. I don't miss you yet.'

His face awful to her, trying to smile. Her head sweeps away from him and hits the side of the gatepost. He sees it hurt her, notices the wince. But they have separated already into themselves now, the walls up at her insistence. Her jerk, her pain, is accidental, is intentional. Her hand is near her temple.

'You will,' she says.

From this point on in our lives, she had whispered to him earlier, we will either find or lose our souls.


How does this happen? To fall in love and be disassembled.

I was in her arms. I had pushed the sleeve of her shirt up to the shoulder so I could see her vaccination scar. I love this, I said. This pale aureole on her arm. I see the instrument scratch and then punch the serum within her and then release itself, free of her skin, years ago, when she was nine years old, in a school gymnasium.

# Brian Moore

## 1993

## *No Other Life*

In the old days they would have given me a gold watch. I never understood why. Was it to remind the one who is being retired that his time is past? Instead of a watch I have been presented with a videotape of the ceremonies. My life here has ended. My day is done.

Next week I will leave Ganae and fly to a retreat house in Cuba. I have never lived in Cuba. Canada, where I was born and bred, is only a memory. You might ask why I was not permitted to end my days here. I am one of the last white priests on this island and the last foreign principal of the Collège St Jean. At the ceremonies on Tuesday night, this was not mentioned. But yesterday, alone in the sitting room of our residence, watching the videotape which they have made for me, I saw myself as they must now see me. The ceremony was held in the college auditorium. Priests, nuns, students and dignitaries, all were mulatto or black. On the wall behind the microphones and the podium there was a large photograph of our new Pope, himself a man of mixed blood. And then, walking towards the podium, a ghost from the past, this stooped white man in a frayed cassock, incongruous as the blackamoor attendant in a sixteenth-century painting of the French court. I am a reminder of a past they feel is best forgotten. They are happy to see me go.

And yet, on the videotape, they weep, they embrace me. Some profess love for me. One of my former students, now the Minister for Foreign Affairs, praised me in his address for my efforts to bring the benefits of higher education to scholarship students from city slums and rural backwaters. There was applause when he said it, but how many in his audience thought of Jeannot at that moment? Jeannot, the most important milestone of my life, is nowhere mentioned in this farewell ceremony. On the video screen, surrounded by smiling faces, I cut slices from a large cake. The videotape, like the gold watch of other days, attests that I lived and worked with these people for most of my adult life. It is a memento.

But what sort of memento? I am a member of the Albanesians, a Catholic teaching Order, founded in France. Unlike lay people who retire, I have no family, no children, or grandchildren, no link with normal life. My brother and my sister are strangers I have not seen for many years. When a religious retires it is as though he is struck down with a fatal illness. His earthly task is over. Now he must prepare himself for death. In another age it was a time of serenity, of waiting to be joined with God and those who have gone before. But, for me, death is a mystery, the answer to that question which has consumed my life.

At the ceremonies last Tuesday, our boys' choir sang the school song. The words were composed by Father Ricard, a French priest who was principal here before my time. It is a sort of hymn in which God is asked to bless our school and, through education, to bring wealth and happiness to Ganae and its people. Father Pinget makes mock of this song saying that, evidently, God does not speak French. French, of course, is out of favour now. When I came here it was the opposite. Creole was the language of the poor. To speak French was to show that one belonged, or aspired to belong, to the mulatto elite. Now, Creole is the official tongue. But does God speak Creole? I think of these things because I am looking at the empty pages of my life. My years here have counted for little. I have failed in most of the things that I set out to do. But I am a man with a secret, with a story never told. Even now, as I write it down, is it the moment to tell the truth?

Where should I begin? Shall I begin with the anxiety that came upon me last night as I removed from the walls of my room the photograph of my parents and a second photograph showing my graduating class, long ago, at the University of Montreal? I put them in the trunk that contains my belongings, the same flat tin trunk which was carried up to this room when I first arrived in Ganae, thirty years ago. Next week, when they carry that trunk downstairs, there will be no sign that I ever lived here. I think it is that – the knowledge that the truth of these events may never be known – that makes me want to leave this record.

But how should I tell it? When we are young we assume that, in age, we will be able to look back and remember our lives. But just as we forget the details of a story a few months after hearing it, so do the years hang like old clothes, forgotten in the wardrobe of our minds. Did I wear that? Who was I then?

That is a question I cannot answer. I can tell you that my name is Paul Michel and that I was born sixty-five years ago in the town of Ville de la Baie in Northern Quebec. My father was a doctor in that town and when he died my younger brother, Henri, took over the practice. Why did *I* not become a doctor? I do not remember that, as a child, I was especially devout. I was educated by the Albanesian Fathers at their college in Montreal and when I showed some glimmerings of literary talent the Order offered me a chance to do graduate work at McGill University and, later, sent me for a year to read French literature at the Sorbonne. Now, looking back, I do not know if I had a true vocation for the priesthood. I was attracted to the Order by its propaganda about devoting one's life to teaching the poor in faraway places. I became an Albanesian Father much as others of my generation were to join the Peace Corps.

The priesthood meant celibacy and that, for me, caused a terrible confusion. I would feel hopeless longings for a girl seen in the street, followed by a depression which my prayers could not cure. In Paris, I fell in love. She was a fellow student at the Sorbonne. On her part, it was innocent. I was just a friend. I thought for a time of giving up the priesthood and asking her ... but I did nothing. It was not until I was posted to Ganae that my longing for her was eased. Here, far from any world I had known, I would live my life as God's servant, doing His work.

I was soon disappointed. I had come to teach the poor. Ganae is in the Caribbean, but is as poor as any African country. Eighty per cent of the population is illiterate. The few state schools are pathetically inefficient. The state university is an inferior training college which turns out substandard doctors and engineers. Our school, the Collège St Jean in Port Riche, is the only private institution of higher education. It was founded to produce students who could gain admission to foreign universities when they completed their high-school studies and went abroad. For this reason it was, from the beginning, a school for the sons of the mulatto elite, an elite who lived in large estates behind high walls and security gates, waited on by black servants, an elite who aped French manners, served champagne and *haute cuisine*, and gossiped about the new couture collections and the latest Parisian *scandale*. When I began to teach at the Collège St Jean, we had fewer than twenty black students in our classrooms.

Why was this so? Our Principal, Father Bourque, explained it this way. 'The mulattos run Ganae, they always have. They control the parliament, they have business ties with the US and France. By educating their children we have a chance to influence events. This is a black republic but the shade of black is all important. Light skins rule. When a *noir* becomes successful he tries to marry into the *mulâtre* class. Besides, our Archbishop is a conservative. He wants to maintain the status quo.'

What would I have done if things had not held out some hope of change? Would I have become disillusioned and pragmatic like Father Bourque? Luckily, I was not put to the test. A few months after my arrival, in one of those political shifts not unknown in Ganae, a black country dentist named Jean-Marie Doumergue ran for election, promising to abolish torture, promote democracy, and curb the powers of the police. The Army saw in Doumergue a puppet they could use to control the black masses. Doumergue was elected. But, at once, he began to attack the privileges of the mulatto elite.

Why do we remember certain mornings, certain meetings? I can still recall my anxiety on that morning when I stood outside our Principal's office with eight black boys clustered around me. The Archbishop had just arrived. Our Principal opened his office door and beckoned me to bring the boys inside. I bowed humbly to Archbishop Le Moyne, a cold Breton whom I did not know. He and the Principal went on talking as though the boys were not in the room.

'We are dealing with a new situation,' Father Bourque said. 'We now have a president who repeats constantly that he has a mandate to improve the education of his fellow *noirs*, a president who complains about schools like ours. There are no other schools like ours. He is talking about our school. And so, Your Grace, if you will bear with me, I would like to propose that we increase the number of our scholarship pupils immediately. I am thinking of a sizeable number of scholarships. Perhaps forty. And they should all be *noirs*.'

But the Archbishop did not agree. 'I'm afraid the elite will not tolerate their children mixing with children of the slums. A few more *noirs*, yes. The elite does not wish to seem bigoted, especially with a *noir* in power. But forty black students – where would you find them?'

Our Principal turned to me. 'Father Michel has been doing some groundwork in that regard. Father?'

I was holding a sheaf of test results. I was, as always in those days, nervous and overanxious. 'Your Grace,' I said, 'I have been travelling around the rural districts, and, believe me, I have had no trouble finding *noir* children of higher than average intelligence. Here are eight of them. For example, this little fellow seems quite exceptional. And yet he is an orphan, from the poorest of the poor – the village of Toumalie, if that means anything to Your Grace?'

As I was speaking I kept an eye on the boys. The other seven stood humbly, like animals whose sale was in the balance. But the one I had singled out, the boy named Jeannot, stared at us as though he, not we, were deciding his future. And then, suddenly, this boy said, 'I wish to be a priest, Your Grace. No one from Toumalie has ever been a priest.'

Afterwards, at lunch, the Archbishop asked, 'Surely you are not planning to make priests out of these little *noirs*? The college is not a seminary.'

Our Principal laughed. 'The boy from Toumalie? I don't know why he said that. Probably to make us take him in. Do you know, Paul?'

I suppose Father Bourque was merely trying to bring me into the conversation. I had sat tongue-tied throughout the meal. But, because I desperately wanted to have the boys accepted by the school, I answered with an evasion.

'I have no idea,' I said. 'I hardly know the boy.'

It was true, yet not true. By then, I was much involved with Jeannot although I had met him only two weeks before, while combing the few rural schools in the north of the island. A teacher in the village of Toumalie took me to his tin-roofed schoolhouse, excitedly talking of a thirteen-year-old boy, an orphan who, he said, 'is a vessel into which you can put anything and bring it back out again'. I tested the boy. I was astonished. The following day I rode on muleback over a road never travelled by motor vehicles, up to a mud-walled mountain shack on land denuded by three hundred years of ignorant and relentless agriculture. There, a woman with the flayed face and wasted body of those who live on the rim of starvation sat on a ramshackle porch, breast-feeding a child. She was a widow with four children of her own and two boys who were the orphaned children of her brother, a warehouse clerk who had died three years ago. One of these orphans was the boy, Jean-Paul Cantave, known as Jeannot. When I told her my plan she gave him into my care as casually as she would give away a puppy from a litter.

An hour later I rode back down the mountainside, the boy hanging on behind me, his arms around my waist as the mule picked its way over the rutted road. He was small and frail. His clothes were a dirty denim shirt, patched trousers and wooden-soled clogs. Imagine – no papers, no signature, no document of any kind. What would I do with him if the Archbishop refused to accept him? He had been given to me. I wondered if people back in Canada had any idea of what life was like here. No one in the world had any idea. This was Ganae.

The other children I had selected were not orphans and so remained at home until the day, two weeks later, when we brought them before the Archbishop. But Jeannot I took straight back to the college, where I installed him in a dormitory with ten other boarders, all of them mulattos. After the first night he came to me. 'They are laughing at me because they have clothes to go to bed in. I do not.'

He did not speak to me as a teenaged boy might speak to a person in authority. From the beginning, it was as though we were friends. I went out at once and bought pyjamas and underclothes. And, although he had not yet been accepted in the school, I arranged for him to be provided with the school uniform. In the next several days he learned to eat in the same manner as the rich boys, to blow his nose in a handkerchief, to take a daily shower and, above all, to use French as his first language. Until then it was the tongue he had learned in school, but now, surrounded by boys who spoke it in preference to Creole, he became fluent with astonishing speed. In fact, when two weeks later the other black scholarship students showed up, Jeannot was no longer of their world. The village teacher in Toumalie was right. He was a vessel into which you could put anything and bring it back out again.

He had been given to me. Almost every day when his classes ended he would leave the college and walk six streets to the staff residence where I lived. Hyppolite would admit him and he would sit on a stool in the corridor, reading and studying, but waiting to see if I would go with him for a walk. Yes, like a dog. I often thought of that. But I cannot say that he was devoted to me. He watched me, he studied me, he tried to find out how my mind worked. From the time he came into my care he completely cut himself off from his former life. When I asked if he had written to his brother and cousins, he said, 'What use would it be to write? They will forget me. All that is over, isn't it, Father? Now, I live in the city. I would never have seen the city if you had not taken me from Toumalie. You will not be sorry. I will do well for you. I am your boy.'

# Caryl Phillips

## 1993

## *Crossing the River*

A desperate foolishness. The crops failed. I sold my children. I remember. I led them (two boys and a girl) along weary paths, until we reached the place where the mud flats are populated with crabs and gulls. *Returned across the bar with the yawl, and prayed a while in the factory chapel.* I watched as they huddled together and stared up at the fort, above which flew a foreign flag. *Stood beneath the white-washed walls of the factory, waiting for the yawl to return and carry me back over the bar.* In the distance stood the ship into whose keep I would soon condemn them. The man and his company were waiting to once again cross the bar. We watched a while. And then approached. *Approached by a quiet fellow.* Three children only. I jettisoned them at this point, where the tributary stumbles and swims out in all directions to meet the sea. *Bought 2 strong man-boys, and a proud girl.* I soiled my hands with cold goods in exchange for their warm flesh. A shameful intercourse. I could feel their eyes upon me. Wondering, *why?* I turned and journeyed back along the same weary paths. *I believe my trade for this voyage has reached its conclusion.* And soon after, the chorus of a common memory began to haunt me.

For two hundred and fifty years I have listened to the many-tongued chorus. And occasionally, among the sundry restless voices, I have discovered those of my own children. My Nash. My Martha. My Travis. Their lives fractured. Sinking hopeful roots into difficult soil. For two hundred and fifty years I have longed to tell them: Children, I am your father. I love you. But understand. There are no paths in water. No signposts. There is no return. To a land trampled by the muddy boots of others. To a people encouraged to war among themselves. To a father consumed with guilt. You are beyond. Broken-off, like limbs from a tree. But not lost, for you carry within your bodies the seeds of new trees. Sinking your hopeful roots into difficult soil. And I, who spurned you, can blame only myself for my present misery. For two hundred and fifty years I have waited patiently for the wind to rise on the far bank of the river. For the drum to pound across the water. For the chorus to swell. Only then, if I listen closely, can I rediscover my lost children. A brief, painful communion. A desperate foolishness. The crops failed. I sold my children.

# Nadine Gordimer

## 1994

## *None to Accompany Me*

And who was that?

There's always someone nobody remembers. In the group photograph only those who have become prominent or infamous or whose faces may be traced back through experiences lived in common occupy that space and time, flattened glossily.

Who could it have been? The dangling hands and the pair of feet neatly aligned for the camera, the half-smile of profile turned to the personage who was to become the centre of the preserved moment, the single image developed to a higher intensity; on the edge of this focus there's an appendage, might as well trim it off because, in the recognition and specific memory the photograph arouses, the peripheral figure was never present.

But if someone were to come along—wait!—and recognize the one whom nobody remembers, immediately another reading of the photograph would be developed. Something else, some other meaning would be there, the presence of what was taken on, along the way, then. Something secret, perhaps. Caught so insignificantly.

Vera Stark, lawyer-trained and with the impulse to order that brings tidiness with ageing, came upon a photograph she had long thought thrown out with all she had discarded in fresh starts over the years. But it wasn't any print she had overlooked. It was the photograph she had sent to her first husband in his officers' quarters in Egypt during the war—their war, the definitive war, not those following it which spawn without the resolution of victory parades. He must have kept the photograph. Must have brought it back in his kit. It was a postcard—the postcard—she had sent when on a trip to the mountains; a photograph of the little group of friends who made up the holiday party. What she had written on the back (turning it over now, the lifting of a stone) was the usual telegraphic few lines scribbled while buying stamps—the weather perfect, she was climbing, walking miles a day, swimming in clear pools, the hotel was as he would remember it but rather run-down. Best wishes from this one and that—for those linking arms were their mutual friends, there was only one new face: a man on her left, a circle round his head. He was identified by name in a line squeezed vertically alongside her account of the weather.

What was written on the back of the photograph was not her message. Her message was the inked ring round the face of the stranger: this is the image of the man who is my lover. I am in love with him, I'm sleeping with this man standing beside me; there, I've been open with you.

Her husband had read only the text on the back. When he came home he did not understand it was not to be to her. She defended herself, amazed, again and again:—I showed you, I ringed his photograph next to me. I thought at least we knew each other well enough ... How could you not understand! You just refused to understand.—

But yes, he must have brought it back in all innocence with his other souvenir knick-knacks, the evidence of his war, brought it back and here it was, somehow hadn't been torn up or thrown away when they divided their possessions in the practical processes of parting in divorce. After forty-five years she was looking at the photograph again and seeing there in its existence, come back to her and lying on a shelf under some old record sleeves, that it was true: the existence of his innocence, for ever.

# David Guterson

## 1995

### Snow Falling on Cedars

The accused man, Kabuo Miyamoto, sat proudly upright with a rigid grace, his palms placed softly on the defendant's table – the posture of a man who has detached himself insofar as this is possible at his own trial. Some in the gallery would later say that his stillness suggested a disdain for the proceedings; others felt certain it veiled a fear of the verdict that was to come. Whichever it was, Kabuo showed nothing – not even a flicker of the eyes. He was dressed in a white shirt worn buttoned to the throat and grey, neatly pressed trousers. His figure, especially the neck and shoulders, communicated the impression of irrefutable physical strength and of precise, even imperial bearing. Kabuo's features were smooth and angular; his hair had been cropped close to his skull in a manner that made its musculature prominent. In the face of the charge that had been leveled against him he sat with his dark eyes trained straight ahead and did not appear moved at all.

In the public gallery every seat had been taken, yet the court-room suggested nothing of the carnival atmosphere sometimes found at country murder trials. In fact, the eighty-five citizens gathered there seemed strangely subdued and contemplative. Most of them had known Carl Heine, a salmon gill-netter with a wife and three children, who was buried now in the Lutheran cemetery up on Indian Knob Hill. Most had dressed with the same communal propriety they felt on Sundays before attending church services, and since the courtroom, however stark, mirrored in their hearts the dignity of their prayer houses, they conducted themselves with churchgoing solemnity.

This courtroom, Judge Llewellyn Fielding's, down at the end of a damp, drafty hallway on the third floor of the Island County Courthouse, was run-down and small as courtrooms go. It was a place of grey-hued and bleak simplicity – a cramped gallery, a bench for the judge, a witness stand, a plywood platform for the jurors, and scuffed tables for the defendant and his prosecutor. The jurors sat with studiously impassive faces as they strained to make sense of matters. The men – two truck farmers, a retired crabber, a bookkeeper, a carpenter, a boat builder, a grocer, and a halibut schooner deckhand – were all dressed in coats and neckties. The women all wore Sunday dresses – a retired waitress, a sawmill secretary, two nervous fisher wives. A hairdresser accompanied them as alternate.

The bailiff, Ed Soames, at the request of Judge Fielding, had given a good head of steam to the sluggish radiators, which now and again sighed in the four corners of the room. In the heat they produced – a humid, overbearing swelter – the smell of sour mildew seemed to rise from everything.

Snow fell that morning outside the courthouse windows, four tall, narrow arches of leaded glass that yielded a great quantity of weak December light. A wind from the sea lofted snowflakes against the windowpanes, where they melted and ran toward the casements. Beyond the courthouse the town of Amity Harbor spread along the island shoreline. A few wind-whipped and decrepit Victorian mansions, remnants of a lost era of seagoing optimism, loomed out of the snowfall on the town's sporadic hills. Beyond them, cedars wove a steep mat of still green. The snow blurred from vision the clean contours of these cedar hills. The sea wind drove snowflakes steadily inland, hurling them against the fragrant trees, and the snow began to settle on the highest branches with a gentle implacability.

The accused man, with one segment of his consciousness, watched the falling snow outside the windows. He had been exiled in the county jail for seventy-seven days – the last part of September, all of October and all of November, the first week of December in jail. There was no window anywhere in his basement cell, no portal through which the autumn light could come to him. He had missed autumn, he realized now – it had passed already, evaporated. The snowfall, which he witnessed out of the corners of his eyes – furious, wind-whipped flakes against the windows – struck him as infinitely beautiful.

San Piedro was an island of five thousand damp souls, named by lost Spaniards who moored offshore in the year 1603. They'd sailed in search of the Northwest Passage, as many Spaniards did in those days, and their pilot and captain, Martín de Aquilar of the Vizcaíno expedition, sent a work detail ashore to cull a fresh spar pole from among the hemlocks at water's edge. Its members were murdered almost immediately upon setting foot on the beach by a party of Nootka slave raiders.

Settlers arrived – mostly wayward souls and eccentrics who had meandered off the Oregon Trail. A few rooting pigs were slaughtered in 1845 – by Canadian Englishmen up in arms about the border – but San Piedro Island generally lay clear of violence after that. The most distressing news story of the preceding ten years had been the wounding of an island resident by a drunken Seattle yachtsman with a shotgun on the Fourth of July, 1951.

Amity Harbor, the island's only town, provided deep moorage for a fleet of purse seiners and one-man gill-netting boats. It was an eccentric, rainy, wind-beaten sea village, downtrodden and mildewed, the boards of its buildings bleached and weathered, their drainpipes rusted a dull orange. Its long, steep inclines lay broad and desolate; its high-curbed gutters swarmed, most winter nights, with traveling rain. Often the sea wind made its single traffic light flail from side to side or caused the town's electrical power to flicker out and stay out for days. Main Street presented to the populace Petersen's Grocery, a post office, Fisk's Hardware Center, Larsen's Pharmacy, a dime-store-with-fountain owned by a woman in Seattle, a Puget Power office, a chandlery, Lottie Opsvig's apparel shop, Klaus Hartmann's real estate agency, the San Piedro Cafe, the Amity Harbor Restaurant, and a battered, run-down filling station owned and operated by the Torgerson brothers. At the wharf a fish packing plant exuded the odor of salmon bones, and the creosoted pilings of the state ferry terminal lay in among a fleet of mildewed boats. Rain, the spirit of the place, patiently beat down everything man-made. On winter evenings it roared in sheets against the pavements and made Amity Harbor invisible.

San Piedro had too a brand of verdant beauty that inclined its residents toward the poetical. Enormous hills, soft green with cedars, rose and fell in every direction. The island homes were damp and moss covered and lay in solitary fields and vales of alfalfa, feed corn, and strawberries. Haphazard cedar fences lined the careless roads, which slid beneath the shadows of the trees and past the bracken meadows. Cows grazed, stinking of sweet dung and addled by summer blackflies. Here and there an islander tried his hand at milling sawlogs on his own, leaving fragrant heaps of sawdust and mounds of cedar bark at roadside. The beaches glistened with smooth stones and sea foam. Two dozen coves and inlets, each with its pleasant muddle of sailboats and summer homes, ran the circumference of San Piedro, an endless series of pristine anchorages.

Inside Amity Harbor's courthouse, opposite the courtroom's four tall windows, a table had been set up to accommodate the influx of newspapermen to the island. The out-of-town reporters – one each from Bellingham, Anacortes, and Victoria and three from the Seattle papers – exhibited no trace of the solemnity evident among the respectful citizens in the gallery. They slumped in their chairs, rested their chins in their hands, and whispered together conspiratorially. With their backs only a foot from a steam radiator, the out-of-town reporters were sweating.

Ishmael Chambers, the local reporter, found that he was sweating, too. He was a man of thirty-one with a hardened face, a tall man with the eyes of a war veteran. He had only one arm, the left having been amputated ten inches below the shoulder joint, so that he wore the sleeve of his coat pinned up with the cuff fastened to the elbow. Ishmael understood that an air of disdain, of contempt for the island and its inhabitants, blew from the knot of out-of-town reporters toward the citizens in the gallery. Their discourse went forward in a miasma of sweat and heat that suggested a kind of indolence. Three of them had loosened their ties just slightly; two others had removed their jackets. They were reporters, professionally jaded and professionally immune, a little too well traveled in the last analysis to exert themselves toward the formalities San Piedro demanded silently of mainlanders. Ishmael, a native, did not want to be like them. The accused man, Kabuo, was somebody he knew, somebody he'd gone to high school with, and he couldn't bring himself, like the other reporters, to remove his coat at Kabuo's murder trial. At ten minutes before nine that morning, Ishmael had spoken with the accused man's wife on the second floor of the Island County Courthouse. She was seated on a hall bench with her back to an arched window, just outside the assessor's office, which was closed, gathering herself, apparently. 'Are you all right?' he'd said to her, but she'd responded by turning away from him. 'Please,' he'd said. 'Please, Hatsue.'

She'd turned her eyes on his then. Ishmael would find later, long after the trial, that their darkness would beleaguer his memory of these days. He would remember how rigorously her hair had been woven into a black knot against the nape of her neck. She had not been exactly cold to him, not exactly hateful, but he'd felt her distance anyway. 'Go away,' she'd said in a whisper, and then for a moment she'd glared. He remained uncertain afterward what her eyes had meant – punishment, sorrow, pain. 'Go away,' repeated Hatsue Miyamoto. Then she'd turned her eyes, once again, from his.

'Don't be like this,' said Ishmael.

'Go away,' she'd answered.

'Hatsue,' said Ishmael. 'Don't be like this.'

'Go away,' she'd said again.

Now, in the courtroom, with sweat on his temples, Ishmael felt embarrassed to be sitting among the reporters and decided that after the morning's recess he would find a more anonymous seat in the gallery. In the meantime he sat facing the wind-driven snowfall, which had already begun to mute the streets outside the courthouse windows. He hoped it would snow recklessly and bring to the island the impossible winter purity, so rare and precious, he remembered fondly from his youth.

*

The first witness called by the prosecutor that day was the county sheriff, Art Moran. On the morning Carl Heine died – September 16 – the sheriff was in the midst of an inventory at his office and had engaged the services of the new court stenographer, Mrs. Eleanor Dokes (who now sat primly below the judge's bench recording everything with silent implacability), as an aide in this annual county-mandated endeavor. He and Mrs. Dokes had exchanged surprised glances when Abel Martinson, the sheriff's deputy, reported over the newly purchased radio set that Carl Heine's fishing boat, the *Susan Marie*, had been sighted adrift in White Sand Bay.

'Abel said the net was all run out and drifting along behind,' Art Moran explained. 'I felt, well, concerned immediately.'

'The *Susan Marie* was on the move?' asked Alvin Hooks, the prosecutor, who stood with one foot perched on the witnesses' podium as if he and Art were talking by a park bench.

'That's what Abel said.'

'With its fishing lights on? Is that what Deputy Martinson reported?'

'That's right.'

'In *day*light?'

'Abel called in nine-thirty a.m., I believe.'

'Correct me if I'm wrong,' Alvin Hooks asked. 'Gill nets, by law, must be on board by nine o'clock – is that right, Sheriff Moran?'

'That's correct,' said the sheriff. 'Nine a.m.'

The prosecutor swiveled with a faintly military flourish and executed a tight circle over the courtroom's waxed floor, his hands against the small of his back neatly. 'What did you do then?' he inquired.

'I told Abel to stay put. To stay where he was. That I would pick him up in the launch.'

'You didn't call the coast guard?'

'Decided I'd hold off just yet. Decided to have a look myself.'

Alvin Hooks nodded. 'Was it your jurisdiction, sheriff?'

'It's a judgment call, Mr. Hooks,' Art Moran said. 'I felt it was the right thing to do.'

The prosecutor nodded one more time and surveyed the members of the jury. He appreciated the sheriff's answer; it cast a favorable moral light on his witness and gave him the authority of the conscientious man, for which there was ultimately no substitute.

'Just tell the court your whole story,' Alvin Hooks said. 'The morning of September 16.'

The sheriff stared at him doubtfully for a moment. By nature Art Moran was an uneasy person, nervous in the face of even trivial encounters. He'd come to his vocation as if driven ineluctably; he had never formed the intention of being sheriff, yet, to his astonishment, here he was. In his liver-colored uniform, black tie, and polished shoes he looked inevitably miscast in life, a man uncomfortable with the accoutrements of his profession, as if he had dressed for a costume party and now wandered about in the disguise. The sheriff was a lean figure, unimposing, who habitually chewed a stick of Juicy Fruit gum (though he wasn't chewing any at the moment, mostly out of deference to the American legal system, which he believed in wholeheartedly despite its flaws). He'd lost much of his hair since turning fifty, and his belly, always undernourished in appearance, now suggested a shriveled emaciation.

Art Moran had lain awake the night before fretting about his role in this trial and remembering the sequence of events with his eyes shut, as if they were occurring in a dream. He and his deputy, Abel Martinson, had taken the county launch into White Sand Bay on the morning of September 16. The tide, steadily on the rise, had turned about three and a half hours before, at six-thirty; by midmorning sunlight lay like a glare over the water, warming his back pleasantly. The preceding night a fog as palpable as cotton had hung suspended over Island County. Later it gently separated at the seams and became vast billows travelling above the sea instead of a still white miasma. Around the launch as it churned toward the *Susan Marie* the last remnants of this night fog sailed and drifted in shreds of vapor toward the sun's heat.

Abel Martinson, one hand on the launch's throttle, the other on his knee, told Art that a Port Jensen fisherman, Erik Syvertsen – Erik the younger, he pointed out – had come across the *Susan Marie* adrift off the south side of White Sand Point with her net set and, it appeared, no one on board. It was more than an hour and a half past dawn and the running lights had been left on. Abel had driven to White Sand Point and walked out to the end of the community pier with his binoculars dangling from his neck. Sure enough, the *Susan Marie* lay drifting on the tide well into the bay on an angle north by northwest, he'd found, and so he'd radioed the sheriff.

In fifteen minutes they came abreast of the drifting boat and Abel turned back the throttle. In the calm of the bay their approach went smoothly; Art set the fenders out; and the two of them made fast their mooring lines with a few wraps each around the forward deck cleats. 'Lights're all on,' observed Art, one foot on the *Susan Marie*'s gunnel. 'Every last one of 'em, looks like.'

'He ain't here,' replied Abel.

'Doesn't look like it,' said Art.

'Went over,' Abel said. 'I got this bad feeling.'

Art winced at hearing this. 'Let's hope not,' he urged. 'Don't say that.'

He made his way just abaft of the cabin, then stood squinting up at the *Susan Marie*'s guys and stays and at the peaks of her stabilizer bars. The red and white mast lights had been left on all morning; the picking light and the jacklight at the end of the net both shone dully in the early sun. While Art stood there, pondering this, Abel Martinson dragged the hatch cover from the hold and called for him to come over.

'You got something?' Art asked.

'Look here,' answered Abel.

Together they crouched over the square hold opening, out of which the odor of salmon flew up at them. Abel maneuvered his flashlight beam across a heap of inert, silent fish. 'Silvers,' he said. 'Maybe fifty of 'em.'

'So he picked his net least once,' said Art.

'Looks like it,' answered Abel.

Men had been known to fall into empty holds before, crack their heads, and pass out even in calm weather. Art had heard of a few such incidents. He looked in at the fish again.

'What time you figure he put out last night?'

'Hard to say. Four-thirty? Five?'

'Where'd he go, you figure?'

'Probably up North Bank,' said Abel. 'Maybe Ship Channel. Or Elliot Head. That's where the fish been running.'

But Art already knew about these things. San Piedro lived and breathed by the salmon, and the cryptic places where they ran at night were the subject of perpetual conversation. Yet it helped him to hear it aloud just now – it helped him to think more clearly.

The two of them crouched by the hold a moment longer in a shared hiatus from their work. The still heap of salmon troubled Art in a way he could not readily articulate, and so he looked at it wordlessly. Then he rose, his knees creaking, and turned away from the dark hold.

'Let's keep looking,' he suggested.

'Right,' said Abel. 'Could be he's up in his cabin, maybe. Knocked out one way or t'other.'

The *Susan Marie* was a thirty-foot stern-picker – a standard, well-tended San Piedro gill-netter – with her cabin just abaft of midship. Art ducked through its stern-side entry and stood to port for a moment. In the middle of the floor – it was the first thing he noticed – a tin coffee cup lay tipped on its side. A marine battery lay just right of the wheel. There was a short bunk made up with a wool blanket to starboard; Abel ran his flashlight across it. The cabin lamp over the ship's wheel had been left on; a ripple of sunlight, flaring through a window, shimmered on the starboard wall. The scene left Art with the ominous impression of an extreme, too-silent tidiness. A cased sausage hanging from a wire above the binnacle swayed a little as the *Susan Marie* undulated; otherwise, nothing moved. No sound could be heard except now and again a dim, far crackle from the radio set. Art, noting it, began to manipulate the radio dials for no other reason than that he didn't know what else to do. He was at a loss.

'This is bad,' said Abel.

'Take a look,' answered Art. 'I forgot – see if his dinghy's over the reel.'

Abel Martinson stuck his head out the entry. 'It's there, Art,' he said. 'Now what?'

For a moment they stared at one another. Then Art, with a sigh, sat down on the edge of Carl Heine's short bunk.

'Maybe he crawled in under the decking,' suggested Abel. 'Maybe he had some kind of engine trouble, Art.'

'I'm sitting on top of his engine,' Art pointed out. 'There's no room for anyone to crawl around down there.'

'He went over,' said Abel, shaking his head.

'Looks like it,' answered the sheriff.

They glanced at each other, then away again.

'Maybe somebody took him off,' suggested Abel. 'He got hurt, radioed, somebody took him off. That – '

'They wouldn't let the boat drift,' put in Art. 'Besides, we'd a heard about it by now.'

'This is bad,' repeated Abel Martinson.

Art tucked another stick of Juicy Fruit between his teeth and wished this was not his responsibility. He liked Carl Heine, knew Carl's family, went to church with them on Sundays. Carl came from old-time island stock; his grandfather, Bavarian born,

had established thirty acres of strawberry fields on prime growing land in Center Valley. His father, too, had been a strawberry
farmer before dying of a stroke in '44. Then Carl's mother, Etta
Heine, had sold all thirty acres to the Jurgensen clan while her
son was away at the war. They were hard-toiling, quiet people, the
Heines. Most people on San Piedro liked them. Carl, Art recalled,
had served as a gunner on the U. S. S. *Canton*, which went down
during the invasion of Okinawa. He'd survived the war – other
island boys hadn't – and come home to a gill-netter's life.

On the sea Carl's blond hair had gone russet colored. He
weighed two hundred and thirty-five pounds, much of it carried
in his chest and shoulders. On winter days, picking fish from his
net, he wore a wool cap knitted by his wife and an infantryman's
battered field jacket. He spent no time at the San Piedro Tavern
or drinking coffee at the San Piedro Cafe. On Sunday mornings
he sat with his wife and children in a back pew of the First Hill
Lutheran Church, blinking slowly in the pale sanctuary light, a
hymnbook open in his large, square hands, a calm expression on
his face. Sunday afternoons he squatted on the aft deck of his
boat, silently and methodically untangling his gill net or knit-
ting its flaws up patiently. He worked alone. He was courteous
but not friendly. He wore rubber boots almost everywhere, like
all San Piedro fishermen. His wife, too, came from old island
people – the Varigs, Art remembered, hay farmers and shake
cutters with a few stump acres on Cattle Point – and her father
had passed away not so long ago. Carl had named his boat after
his wife, and, in '48, built a big frame house just west of Amity
Harbor, including an apartment for his mother, Etta. But – out
of pride, word had it – Etta would not move in with him. She
lived in town, a stout, grave woman with a slight Teutonic edge
to her speech, over Lottie Opsvig's apparel shop on Main. Her
son called at her door every Sunday afternoon and escorted her
to his house for supper. Art had watched them trudge up Old
Hill together, Etta with her umbrella turned against the winter
rain, her free hand clutching at the lapels of a coarse winter coat,
Carl with his hands curled up in his jacket pockets, his wool cap

pulled to his eyebrows. All in all, Art decided, Carl Heine was a good man. He was silent, yes, and grave like his mother, but the war had a part in that, Art realized. Carl rarely laughed, but he did not seem, to Art's way of thinking, unhappy or dissatisfied. Now his death would land hard on San Piedro; no one would want to fathom its message in a place where so many made their living fishing. The fear of the sea that was always there, simmering beneath the surface of their island lives, would boil up in their hearts again.

'Well, look,' said Abel Martinson, leaning in the cabin door while the boat shifted about. 'Let's get his net in, Art.'

'Suppose we better,' sighed Art. 'All right. We'd better do it, then. But we'll do it one step at a time.'

'He's got a power takeoff back there,' Abel Martinson pointed out. 'You figure he hasn't run for maybe six hours. And all these lights been drawing off the battery. Better choke it up good, Art.'

Art nodded and then turned the key beside the ship's wheel. The solenoid kicked in immediately; the engine stuttered once and then began to idle roughly, rattling frantically beneath the floorboards. Art slowly backed the choke off.

'Okay,' he said. 'Like that?'

'Guess I was wrong,' said Abel Martinson. 'She sounds real good and strong.'

They went out again, Art leading. The *Susan Marie* had veered off nearly perpendicular to the chop and angled, briefly, to starboard. With the thrust of the engine she'd begun to bobble a little, and Art, treading across the aft deck, stumbled forward and grabbed at a stanchion, scraping his palm at the heel of the thumb, while Abel Martinson looked on. He rose again, steadied himself with a foot on the starboard gunnel, and looked out across the water.

The morning light had broadened, gained greater depth, and lay in a clean sheet across the bay, giving it a silver tincture. Not a boat was in sight except a single canoe traveling parallel to a tree-wreathed shoreline, children in life jackets at the flashing paddles a quarter mile off. They're *innocent*, thought Art.

'It's good she's come about,' he said to his deputy. 'We'll need time to get this net in.'

'Whenever you're ready,' answered Abel.

For a moment it occurred to Art to explain certain matters to his deputy. Abel Martinson was twenty-four, the son of an Anacortes brick mason. He had never seen a man brought up in a net before, as Art had, twice. It happened now and then to fishermen – they caught a hand or a sleeve in their net webbing and went over even in calm weather. It was a part of things, part of the fabric of the place, and as sheriff he knew this well. He knew what bringing up the net really meant, and he knew Abel Martinson didn't.

Now he put his foot on top of the beaver paddle and looked across at Abel. 'Get over there with the lead line,' he said softly. 'I'll bring her up real slow. You may need to pick some, so be ready.'

Abel Martinson nodded.

Art brought the weight of his foot down. The net shuddered for a moment as the slack went out of it, and then the reel wound it in against the weight of the sea. Surging, and then lowering a note, the engine confronted its work. The two men stood at either end of the gunnel roller, Art with one shoe on the beaver paddle and Abel Martinson staring at the net webbing as it traveled slowly toward the drum. Ten yards out, the float line fell away and hobbled in a seam of white water along the surface of the bay. They were still moving up the tide about north by northwest, but the breeze from the south had shifted just enough to bring them gently to port.

They had picked two dozen salmon from the net, three stray sticks, two dogfish, a long convoluted coil of kelp, and a number of ensnarled jellyfish when Carl Heine's face showed. For a brief moment Art understood Carl's face as the sort of illusion men are prone to at sea – or hoped it was this, rather, with a fleeting desperation – but then as the net reeled in Carl's bearded throat appeared too and the face completed itself. There was Carl's face turned up toward the sunlight and the

76

water from Carl's hair dripped in silver strings to the sea; and now clearly it *was* Carl's face, his mouth open – Carl's *face* – and Art pressed harder against the beaver paddle. Up came Carl, hanging by the left buckle of his rubber bib overalls from the gill net he'd made his living picking, his T-shirt, bubbles of seawater coursing under it, pasted to his chest and shoulders. He hung heavily with his legs in the water, a salmon struggling in the net beside him, the skin of his collarbones, just above the highest waves, hued an icy but brilliant pink. He appeared to have been parboiled in the sea.

Abel Martinson vomited. He leaned out over the transom of the boat and retched and cleared his throat and vomited again, this time more violently. 'All right, Abel,' Art said. 'You get ahold of yourself.'

The deputy did not reply. He wiped his mouth with a handkerchief. He breathed heavily and spat into the sea a half-dozen times. Then, after a moment, he dropped his head and pounded his left fist against the transom. 'Jesus Christ,' he said.

'I'll bring him up slow,' answered Art. 'You keep his head back away from the transom, Abel. Get ahold of yourself. Keep his head back and away now.'

But in the end they had to rattle up the lead line and pull Carl fully into the folds of his net. They cupped the net around him like a kind of hammock so that his body was borne by the webbing. In this manner they brought Carl Heine up from the sea – Abel yarding him over the net roller while Art tapped gingerly at the beaver paddle and squinted over the transom, his Juicy Fruit seized between his teeth. They laid him, together, on the afterdeck. In the cold salt water he had stiffened quickly; his right foot had frozen rigidly over his left, and his arms, locked at the shoulders, were fixed in place with the fingers curled. His mouth was open. His eyes were open too, but the pupils had disappeared – Art saw how they'd revolved backward and now looked inward at his skull. The blood vessels in the whites of his eyes had burst; there were two crimson orbs in his head.

Abel Martinson stared.

Art found that he could not bring forward the least vestige of professionalism. He simply stood by, like his twenty-four-year-old deputy, thinking the thoughts a man thinks at such a time about the ugly inevitability of death. There was a silence to be filled, and Art found himself hard-pressed in the face of it to conduct himself in a manner his deputy could learn from. And so they simply stood looking down at Carl's corpse, a thing that had silenced both of them.

'He banged his head,' whispered Abel Martinson, pointing to a wound Art hadn't noticed in Carl Heine's blond hair. 'Must have banged it against the gunnel going over.'

Sure enough, Carl Heine's skull had been crushed just above his left ear. The bone had fractured and left a dent in his head. Art Moran turned away from it.

# John Berger

## 1995

## *To the Wedding*

*Wonderful a fistful of snow in the mouths*
*of men suffering summer heat*
*Wonderful the spring winds*
*for mariners who long to set sail*
*And more wonderful still the single sheet*
*over two lovers on a bed.*

I like quoting ancient verses when the occasion is apt. I remember most of what I hear, and I listen all day but sometimes I do not know how to fit everything together. When this happens I cling to words or phrases which seem to ring true.

In the quartier around Plaka, which a century or so ago was a swamp and is now where the market is held, I'm called Tsobanakos. This means a man who herds sheep. A man from the mountains. I was given this name on account of a song.

Each morning before I go to the market I polish my black shoes and brush the dust off my hat which is a Stetson. There is a lot of dust and pollution in the city and the sun makes them worse. I wear a tie too. My favourite is a flashy blue and white one. A blind man should never neglect his appearance. If he does, there are those who jump to false conclusions. I dress like a jeweller and what I sell in the market are *tamata*.

Tamata are appropriate objects for a blind man to sell for you can recognise one from another by touch. Some are made of tin, others of silver and some of gold. All of them are as thin as linen and each one is the size of a credit card. The word *tama* comes from the verb *tázo,* to make an oath. In exchange for a promise made, people hope for a blessing or a deliverance. Young men buy a tama of a sword before they do their military service, and this is a way of asking: May I come out of it unhurt.

Or something bad happens to somebody. It may be an illness or an accident. Those who love the person who is in danger make an oath before God that they will perform a good act if the loved one recovers. When you are alone in the world, you can even do it for yourself.

Before my customers go to pray, they buy a tama from me and put a ribbon through its hole, then they tie it to the rail by the ikons in the church. Like this they hope God will not forget their prayer.

Into the soft metal of each tama is pressed an emblem of the part of the body in danger. An arm or a leg, a stomach or a heart, hands, or, as in my case, a pair of eyes. Once I had a tama on which a dog was embossed, but the priest protested and maintained that this was a sacrilege. He understands nothing, this priest. He has lived all his life in Athens, so he doesn't know how in the mountains a dog can be more important, more useful than a hand. He can't imagine that the loss of a mule may be worse than a leg which does not heal. I quoted the Evangelist to him: Consider the ravens: they do not sow or reap, they have no storeroom or barn. Yet God feeds them … When I told him this, he pulled at his beard and turned his back as if on the Devil.

Bouzouki players have more to say than priests about what men and women need.

What I did before I went blind, I'm not going to tell you. And if you had three guesses they'd all be wrong.

The story begins last Easter. On the Sunday. It was mid-morning and there was a smell of coffee in the air. The smell of coffee drifts farther when the sun is out. A man asked me whether I had anything for a daughter. He spoke in broken English.

A baby? I enquired.

She's a woman now.

Where is she suffering? I asked. Everywhere, he said.

Perhaps a heart would be suitable? I eventually suggested, feeling with my fingers to find a tama in the tray and holding it out to him.

Is it made of tin? His accent made me think he was French or Italian. I guess he was my age, perhaps a little older.

I have one in gold if you wish, I said in French. She can't recover, he replied.

Most important is the oath you make, sometimes there's nothing else to do.

I'm a railwayman, he said, not a voodoo man. Give me the cheapest, the tin one.

I heard his clothes squeaking as he pulled out a wallet from his pocket. He was wearing leather trousers and a leather jacket.

There's no difference between tin and gold for God, is there?

You came here on a motorbike?

With my daughter for four days. Yesterday we drove to see the temple of Poseidon.

At Sounion?

You've seen it? You have been there? Excuse me.

I touched my black glasses with a finger and said: I saw the temple before this.

How much does the tin heart cost?

Unlike a Greek, he paid without questioning the price. What is her name?

Ninon.

Ninon?

NINON. He spelt out each letter.

I will think of her, I said, arranging the money. And as I said this, I suddenly heard a voice. His daughter must have been elsewhere in the market. Now she was beside him.

My new sandals – look! Handmade. Nobody would guess I've just bought them. I might have been wearing them for years. Maybe I bought them for my wedding, the one that didn't happen.

The strap between the toes doesn't hurt? the railwayman asked.

Gino would have liked them, she said. He has good taste in sandals.

The way they tie at the ankle is very pretty.

They protect you if you walk on broken glass, she said. Come here a moment. Yes, the leather's nice and soft.

Remember, Papa, when I was small and you dried me after my shower and I sat on the towel on your knee, and you used to tell me how each little toe was a magpie who stole this and that and this and flew away...

She spoke with a cool clipped rhythm. No syllable slurred or unnecessarily prolonged.

Voices, sounds, smells bring gifts to my eyes now. I listen or I inhale and then I watch as in a dream. Listening to her voice I saw slices of melon carefully arranged on a plate, and I knew I would immediately recognise Ninon's voice should I hear it again.

★★★

Several weeks went by. Somebody speaking French in the crowd, my selling another tama with a heart on it, the screech of a motorcycle tearing away from the traffic lights – from time to time such things reminded me of the railwayman and his daughter Ninon. The two of them passed by, they never stayed. Then one night, at the beginning of June, something changed.

In the evenings, I walk home from Plaka. One of the effects of blindness is that you can develop an uncanny sense of time. Watches are useless – though sometimes I sell them – yet I know to the minute what time of day it is. On my way home I regularly pass ten people to whom I say a few words. To them I'm a reminder of the hour.

★★★

Since a year one of the ten has been Kostas but he and I are another story, as yet untold.

On the bookshelves in my room I keep the tamata, my many pairs of shoes, a tray of glasses with a carafe, my fragments of marble, some pieces of coral, some conch shells, my *baglama* on the top shelf – I seldom take it down – a jar of pistachio nuts, a number of framed photographs – yes – and my pot plants: hibiscus, begonia, asphodels, roses. I touch them each evening to see how they are doing and how many new flowers have come out.

After a drink and a wash, I like to take the train to Piraeus. I walk along the quayside, asking the occasional question to inform myself which big ships have docked and which ones are going to sail that night, and then I spend the evening with my friend Yanni. Nowadays he runs a small bar.

Sights are ever-present. That's why eyes get tired. But voices – like everything to do with words – they come from far away. I stand at Yanni's bar and I listen to old men talking.

Yanni is the age of my father. He was a *rembetis*, a bouzouki player, with a considerable following after the war and played with the great Markos Vamvakarious. Nowadays he picks up his six-stringed bouzouki only when old friends ask him. They ask him most nights and he has forgotten nothing. He plays sitting on a cane-seated chair with a cigarette stuck between the fourth and little finger of his left hand, touching the frets. It can happen that if he plays, I dance.

When you dance to a *rembetiko* song, you step into the circle of the music and the rhythm is like a round cage with bars, and there you dance before the man or woman who once lived the song. You dance a tribute to their sorrow which the music is throwing out.

> *Drive Death out of the yard*
> *So I don't have to meet him.*
> *And the clock on the wall*
> *Leads the funeral dirge.*

Listening night after night to rembetika is like being tattooed.

Ah my friend, Yanni said to me that June evening after we'd drunk two glasses of raki, why don't you live with him?

He's not blind, I said.

You repeat yourself, he said.

I left the bar to buy some souvlaki to eat at the corner. Afterwards, as I often do, I asked Vasilli, the grandson, to carry a chair for me and I installed myself on the pavement a good way down the narrow street opposite some trees where the troughs of silence are deeper. Behind my back was a blind wall facing west and I could feel the warmth it had stored during the day.

Distantly I heard Yanni playing a rembetiko which he knew was one of my favourites:

> *Your eyes, little sister,*
> *Crack open my heart.*

For some reason I didn't return to the bar. I sat on the cane-seated chair with my back to the wall and my stick between my legs and I waited, as you wait before you slowly get to your feet to dance. That rembetiko ended, I guess, without anyone dancing to it.

I sat there. I could hear the cranes loading, they load all night. Then a completely silent voice spoke, and I recognised it as the railwayman's.

Federico, he is saying, come stai? It's good to hear you, Federico. Yes, I'm leaving early tomorrow morning, in a few hours, and I will be with you on Tuesday. Don't forget, Federico, all the champagne I pay, I pay, so order three, four crates! Whatever you think. Ninon's my only daughter. And she's getting married. Si. Certo.

The railwayman is talking Italian into a telephone and standing in the kitchen of his three-roomed house in the town of Modane on the French side of the Alps. He is a signalman, Grade II, and the name on his letterbox is Jean Ferrero. His parents were emigrants from the rice town of Vercelli in Italy.

The kitchen is not big and seems smaller because of a large motorbike on its stand behind the front door which gives on to the street. The way the saucepans have been left on the stove shows that the cooking is done by a man. In his room, as in mine in Athens, there's no trace of a feminine touch. A room where a man lives without a woman, and man and room are used to it.

The railwayman hangs up the telephone, goes over to the kitchen table where a map is spread out and picks up a list of road numbers and towns: Pinerolo, Lombriasco, Torino, Casale Monferrato, Pavia, Casalmaggiore, Borgoforte, Ferrara. With scotchtape he sticks the list beside the dials of the bike. He checks the brake fluid, the cooling liquid, the oil, the pressure of the tyres. He feels the weight of the chain with his left forefinger to test whether it's tight enough. He turns the ignition on. The dials light up red. He examines the two headlights. His gestures are methodical, careful and – above all – gentle, as if the bike was alive.

Twenty-six years ago Jean lived in this same three-roomed house with his wife, who was called Nicole. One day Nicole left him. She said she had had enough of him working at nights and spending every other minute organising for the CGT and reading pamphlets in bed – she wanted to live. Then she slammed the front door and never came back to Modane. They had no children.

# Rupert Thomson

## 1996

## *The Insult*

'You've been shot.'

I heard someone say it. I wouldn't have known otherwise; I wouldn't have realised. All I could remember was four tomatoes – three of them motionless, one still rolling. And a black shape, too. A shape that had a curve to it.

*I've been shot.*

Sirens circled me like ghosts.

I slipped away, the feeling of having fallen from a plane, of falling through dark air, and the plane flying on without me ...

Each time I woke up, it was night.

Then voices spoke to me, out of nothing. Voices told me the rest. You'd been shopping, they said. You were in a supermarket car-park when it happened. It was a Thursday evening. You were walking towards your vehicle when you were fired upon, a single shot. The bullet took a horizontal path through the occipital cortex. One millimetre lower and you would've died instantaneously. You suffered no damage to adjacent structures; however, you have lost your vision and that loss is permanent. There were no witnesses to the shooting.

I lay in bed, my neck supported by a padded brace. My head had a strange deadness to it, as if it was an arm and I'd slept on it.

My mouth tasted of flowers.

The voices told me I was in a clinic in the northern suburbs. They told me how much time had passed, and how it had been spent: brain-scans, neuro-surgery, post-traumatic amnesia. They told me that my parents had visited. My fiancée, too. None of what they said surprised me. I could smell bandages and, behind the smell of bandages, methylated spirits, linoleum, dried blood. I imagined, for some reason, that the lino was pale-green with streaks of white in it, like certain kinds of soap or marble. It seemed to me that several people were positioned around my bed, though only one of them was speaking. I turned my face in his direction.

'Something I didn't understand. Occipital something.'

The same voice answered. 'Occipital cortex. It's located at the back of the head, the very base of the brain. It's responsible for visual interpretation. In your case, the damage is bilateral: both lobes are affected.'

'You said the loss of vision is permanent ...'

'That's correct.'

'So there's no chance of recovery?'

'None.' The voice paused. 'I'm sorry.'

Somebody placed a hand on my shoulder. I wasn't sure which one of them it was – the man who'd been talking to me or one of the others. I couldn't have said what it communicated. Pity, maybe. Consolation. It reminded me of the feelings I'd had about churches when I was young. How I'd imagined an angel's touch might be.

I found that my eyes had filled with water.


Bits fly off me as I run.

The place is always the same. It's a city street, though not one I recognise. Sunlight everywhere. The buildings blaze with it.

I can see myself running. The bits flying off me. Two ribs, an ear. One of my arms. Some teeth. They come loose, drop silently away. It's like the way things happen in space. I watch a finger leave my hand, spin backwards through the bright gold air behind me. Soon there's just the running left.

You might think it would stop then, but it doesn't. I keep running, even though I don't have any legs. Even though the body's gone, the elbows too, the lungs.

It's hard to describe. It's like one kind of air passing through another. It's not a bad feeling. The flesh has gone. There's only the spirit left.

I wake up sweating ...

The man who had talked to me before was sitting by my bed. This time he was alone.

'My name's Visser. Bruno Visser.'

'What do you look like?' I said.

'An understandable question.' He mentioned light-brown hair, pale-blue eyes. He was fairly tall, he said. Then he told me he was my neuro-surgeon, as if he thought that detail might complete the picture.

'And what about me?' I said. 'What do I look like?'

He paused, his silence awkward – or perhaps just curious, intrigued.

'I mean, am I disfigured?' I asked him. 'Would I recognise myself?'

'There's only one disfigurement, as you put it, and it's not really apparent.' He explained that I'd lost a small section of bone on the left side of my cranium, shattered by the stranger's bullet as it exited. The normal procedure was to wait until the tissues healed, and then to fit a titanium plate. It was a fairly simple operation, he assured me. There would be a scar, of course, but the hair would grow back over it. Nobody would know.

He continued, more earnest now (he had moved his chair closer to the bed, his voice was lower). I shouldn't underestimate the task that lay ahead, he said. When someone loses their vision suddenly, at least three stages can usually be distinguished. First there's shock, a numbness that may last for weeks – the body's own protective anaesthesia. Then depression sets in. This stage could last longer. Months. Years even. Hopelessness, self-pity, suicidal thoughts – I had to be ready, he said, for any or all of these. Finally, when I'd finished mourning my loss of vision, there was the gradual rehabilitation: the development of a new personality, with different capacities, different potential.

'And now for the bad news,' I said.

'At this clinic, Martin,' Visser said, 'we don't believe you should be under any illusions about your condition.'

'I don't think there's much danger of that.'

There was a silence. 'Perhaps you should get some rest.' His chair creaked twice. He was gone.

I wake sweating, wait for my heart to settle. It always takes a while, after the dream, for my hands to join the smooth, glossy stumps of my wrists. For my body to piece itself together.

This is what must have happened after I was shot. I mean, that must have been the first time it happened. Only then it would have taken longer. Hours, probably. Maybe days. And there were parts of me that didn't reappear, of course. One small section of my skull, measuring, according to Visser, 2.75 cm by 1.93 cm. My eyesight, too. That never came back either.

I lie here with my neck supported by the brace. I move my fingers against the coarse wool of the blanket that covers me. I move my feet against the undersheet. There will come a time, I think to myself, when this won't happen. When I don't wake up in a hospital bed – or any other bed, for that matter. When disintegration's pull can no longer be resisted. When the bits of my body continue to fly outwards, like the universe itself.

Visser returned. I knew him by his footsteps – or, to be more accurate, his shoes. They'd been repaired with metal, those steel crescents that prevent heels or toes from wearing out. I turned my head towards him. He wanted to explain something to me – I sensed his need – but he wasn't sure how to begin.

At last he leaned forwards, his clothes releasing a faint odour of carbolic. 'NPL,' he said.

'I'm sorry?'

'No perception of light. I'll give you a demonstration.' He reached into a trouser or a jacket pocket. 'I'm holding a torch. Now, can you tell me, is it on?'

I stared hard, but I had no awareness of a torch. I wasn't aware of anything.

'Is it off,' Visser said, 'or on?'

'I've no idea.'

'And yet your pupils still contract.' The torch clicked. 'What's interesting about cortical blindness is that it's absolute. Your eyes still see, they still respond to light. It's just that what they're seeing is not being recorded in the brain.' He shifted in his chair. 'Imagine a TV. A TV receives electromagnetic waves from a transmitter and it reconverts those waves into visual images. If the TV's faulty, the electromagnetic waves are not converted. Unfortunately, that's where the analogy ends. Unlike a TV, the occipital cortex cannot be replaced, or even repaired. We simply don't have the technology as yet. Do you understand?'

'I think so.'

'It's perhaps for this reason — the fact that the retina, the optic nerves and the anterior visual pathways are all still functioning as normal — that people who suffer from cortical blindness often believe, despite proof to the contrary, that they can see. This is a condition known as Anton's Syndrome. Rare, admittedly, but it exists.'

I didn't know what he meant by proof to the contrary.

'Oh, falling downstairs,' he said, 'bumping into furniture — that kind of thing.' Visser's tone was light, almost playful, and yet I wasn't offended. I saw what he was describing — it was slapstick, it was farce: policemen walking into lampposts, fat women slipping on banana-skins — and I, too, was entertained.

'You might also experience visual hallucinations,' Visser went on, 'flashes of light and so forth. It's quite common in cases like yours, where there has been a severe insult to the brain —'

'I think I know what you're trying to say, Doctor.'

Visser was silent, waiting.

'You're trying to say that I shouldn't fall into the trap of believing I can still see.'

'Well, yes. Precisely.'

He sounded so surprised, so pleased with me, that I couldn't help feeling proud of myself. In fact, I had the feeling that the pride was mutual, that we were, to some as yet unknown extent, dependent on each other.

Once or twice a year, when I was young, my parents would put me on a train to the city. My grandparents met me at the other end. From the station we caught a tram out to their small house in the suburbs (in my memory it's always the same ride, through streets that are sunlit, tree-lined, deadened by the heat, and my grandmother always offers me a pear, picked from a tree on their allotment). I usually stayed for two weeks, and was always sad when it was time to go.

Not far from where they lived was a big house that stood in a private park. I would ride there on my grandfather's bicycle, slow down as I passed the gates. Standing on the pedals, I'd turn in an unsteady circle, unwilling to stop, but wanting a second glimpse. There was a driveway leading up to the house between two rows of trees. On winter evenings their branches, black and gleaming, seemed to hoard the gold windows in their fingers. In spring, white blossoms lay scattered on the gravel, each petal curved and pale, eyelid-shaped. Otherwise there was nothing much to see. The house itself was a kilometre away, at least, a façade of dark bricks in the distance. Green drainpipes. Chimneys.

When I asked my grandparents about it, they told me it was a sanatorium. That means people who are sick, they said. I was never sure if they meant mad or just ill, and they were dead now, my grandparents; the last time I looked for the sanatorium, I was told it had been pulled down. If I'd been called upon to explain my fascination I don't know what I would have said. It wasn't so much what I saw as what I might see. Part of you recognises a potential. Thinking about it now, I found a cruel irony in it. It occurred to me that if the boy on the bicycle had looked hard enough, if he'd looked really hard, he might have seen the man he would eventually become.

More than twenty years had passed since then, but just for a moment, lying in my bed in the clinic, I'm that boy again, turning circles on his grandfather's bicycle. And, looking up, I notice a man moving down the gravel drive towards me. I drop one foot to the ground and stand there, watching. The man's eyes are bandaged and yet he's walking in a straight line, as though he can see. And when he reaches the gates he stops and looks at me, right through the bandages, right between the black wrought-iron bars.

'Martin?' he says. 'Is that you?'

My hands tighten on the handlebars.

'It's you,' he says, 'isn't it.'

I start pedalling. There's a hill luckily, it's steep, the wind roars in my ears. But even when I'm back with my grandparents and everything's normal again, I can't be sure that I won't turn round and see him walk towards me through the house.

Knowing me, despite the bandages.

Knowing my name.

'Mr Blom?'

It was the nurse, Miss Janssen. She had two detectives with her. One of them, Slatnick, was making noises, strange little squeaks and splashes, which I finally identified as the sound of someone chewing gum. The other man's name was Munck. Munck did most of the talking. His voice was easy to listen to, almost soporific. I wanted to tell him he was in the wrong job; with a voice like that, he should have been a hypnotist.

He was shocked, he said – they both were – by what had happened. He could only express the deepest sympathy for me in my predicament. If there was anything that they could do …

'Thank you,' I said.

Munck talked on. The last ten years had seen a proliferation of firearms in the city. Incidents of the type it had been my misfortune to be involved in had increased a hundredfold. Random violence, seemingly senseless crimes. He had his theories, of course, but now was not the time. He paused. Wind rushed in the trees outside. A window further down the ward blew open; I felt cold air search the room. Munck leaned closer in his chair. The reason they'd come, he said, was to hear my version of the event.

'I'm sorry,' I said. 'I don't have a version.'

'You don't remember anything?'

'No, not really.'

'Did you see anything at all?'

I smiled. 'Tomatoes.'

Slatnick stopped chewing for a moment.

'They must've spilled out of my bag,' I said. 'I suppose I was going to make a salad that night.'

'I see.' I heard Munck stand up and start to pace about. 'Where do you work, Mr Blom?'

'A bookshop.' I mentioned the name of it.

'I know the place. I'm often in there myself.' Munck walked to the end of the bed. 'Do you have any enemies?'

I raised my eyebrows.

'It sounds dramatic, I know,' Munck said, 'but we have to ask.'

'None that I can think of.'

'You have no idea who might've shot at you?'

'I'm afraid not.'

Slatnick spoke next. 'Am I correct in assuming therefore that you would not be able to identify your assailant?'

I stared in his direction. What is it about policemen?

'Slatnick,' Munck said, 'I think the answer's yes.'

'Yes?' Slatnick hadn't understood.

'Yes, you'd be correct in that assumption.'

There was a silence.

'I'm sorry to have disturbed you, Mr Blom,' Munck said. 'I have to say that, in this case, it seems unlikely that justice will be done. All that remains is for us to wish you a speedy recovery. Once again, if there's anything we can do—'

'Thank you, Detective.'

I listened to the two men walk away, their footsteps mingling with those of other visitors. One of them sounded like a diver, the soles of his shoes slapping down like flippers on the floor …

★

Absolute blindness is rare. There's usually some suggestion of movement, some sense of light and shade. Not in my case. What I 'saw' was without texture or definition: it was constant, depthless and impenetrable. Sometimes I thought: *Your eyes are closed. Open them.* But they were already open. Wide open, seeing nothing. I could look straight into the sun and my pupils would contract, but I wouldn't know it was the sun that I was looking at. Or I could put my head inside a cardboard box. Same thing. There were no gradations in the blankness, no fluctuations of any kind. It was what depression would look like, I thought, if you had to externalise it.

Miss Janssen spent part of every morning at my bedside. It was her job to motivate me, though I found most of her efforts infantile and embarrassing. Take the rubber balls, for instance. She told me to hold one in each hand. I was supposed to 'squeeze and then relax, squeeze and then relax'.

'What's it for?' I asked.

'You'd be surprised,' she said, 'how quickly muscles atrophy.'

'Is that so?'

'Yes, it is. If you don't exercise, they just wither away.'

'Well, in that case,' I said, 'there's one muscle we definitely shouldn't overlook.'

She brought the session to an abrupt end.

The next morning she was back again, as usual. She made no reference to what I'd said the day before. In what was intended as a gesture of repentance, I asked her for the rubber balls. I lay there, one in each hand, squeezing and relaxing. I behaved. And, since her voice was all there was, I began to listen to it. Not the words in themselves, but the sound of the words. I tried to work out how old she was, what she did in her spare time, whether she was happy. There were moments when I thought I could picture her, the way you picture strangers on the phone, just from their voices: I saw the colour of her eyes, the shape of her mouth. It was like what happened when the dream I had was over: the gradual assembly of a physical presence. Some mornings I found that I could only see her breasts. Her voice seemed to be telling me that they were large. The curve from the rib-cage to the nipple, for example. That fullness, that wonderful convexity. Not unlike a fruit bowl. But I could never sustain it. Sooner or later the picture always broke up, fell apart, dissolved. And, anyway, they weren't her breasts. They were just breasts. They could have been anybody's.

I tried the same thing with the man in the next bed. His name was Smulders. He used to work for the national railways, first as a signalman and, later, as a station announcer. Then he got cataracts in both eyes. They'd operated during the summer, but the results had been disappointing. I asked him the obvious question, just to start him talking: 'Can you see anything at all?'

'Sometimes I see dancing girls. They move across in front of me, legs kicking, like they're on a stage.' Smulders took a breath. His lungs bubbled.

He must be a smoker, I thought. Forty a day, non-filter. The tips of two of his fingers appeared, stained yellow by the nicotine.

'Anything else?' I said.

'Dogs.'

'Dogs? What kind of dogs?'

'Poodles. With ribbons and bows all over them.'

'No trains?'

'Once.' Smulders chuckled. 'It was the 6.23, I think. Packed, it was.'

He talked on, about his work, his colleagues, his passion for all things connected with the railways; he talked for hours. But nothing came. Nothing except a pair of black spectacles, their lenses stained the same colour as the fingertips. Then I realised that they belonged to a friend of my father's, a man who used to work at the post office, in Sorting. I couldn't seem to picture Smulders at all. Somehow his breathing got in the way, like frosted glass.

These were, in any case, minor entertainments, scant moments of distraction. There were days, whole days, when I lay in bed without moving. Almost without thinking. The TV cackled and muttered, the way a caged bird might. Meals came and went on metal trolleys – hot, damp smells that were lurid, rotten, curiously tropical. My head felt as if it had been wrapped in cloth, layer upon layer of it. I often had to fight for breath. Once I tried to tear the covering from my face, but all I found beneath my fingernails was skin.

My skin.

There was no covering, of course.

Nurse Janssen sat with me each morning, her voice in the air beside me. It was still a kind of seed, yet I could grow nothing from it, no comfort, no desire. I'd lost all my wit, my ingenuity.

'How's your face?' she asked me.

'You tell me.'

'It's looking much better. How does it feel?'

'Feels all right.'

'You know, there are three trees outside your window,' she said, 'three beautiful trees. They're pines.'

If this was an attempt at consolation, it was misconceived, hopelessly naive. I stared straight ahead. 'Pines, you say?'

'Yes.'

'I can smell them.'

'It's a beautiful smell, isn't it?'

I scowled. 'If you like toilet cleaner.'

Later that day I picked up one of my rubber balls and threw it into the blankness in front of me. Now that *was* beautiful, the silence of the ball travelling through the air, an unseen arc, and then the splintering of glass. I hadn't realised there might be a window there. I saw the impact as a flower blooming, from tight green bud to petals in less than a second. It was like those programmes on TV where they speed a natural process up.

The next morning Visser put me on a course of medication. I took the drug in liquid form. It was acrid, syrupy in texture, but I didn't make any fuss. I drank it down and then lay back, waiting for the effect.

What happens is this:

The world shrinks. The world's a ball of dust. It rolls silently along the bottom of a wall, meaningless and round. You watch it go. You don't have to think about it any more. It's got nothing to do with you, nothing whatsoever.

You'd wave goodbye to it if you could lift your arm.

# Tobias Wolff

## 1996

## *The Night in Question*

Frances had come to her brother's apartment to hold his hand over a disappointment in love, but Frank ate his way through half the cherry pie she'd brought him and barely mentioned the woman. He was in an exalted state over a sermon he'd heard that afternoon. Dr. Violet had outdone himself, Frank said. This was his best; this was the gold standard. Frank wanted to repeat it to Frances, the way he used to act out movie scenes for her when they were young.

'Gotta run, Franky.'

'It's not that long,' Frank said. 'Five minutes. Ten – at the outside.'

Three years earlier he had driven Frances' car into a highway abutment and almost died, then almost died again, in detox, of a *grand mal* seizure. Now he wanted to preach sermons at her. She supposed she was grateful. She said she'd give him ten minutes.

It was a muggy night, but as always Frank wore a long-sleeved shirt to hide the weird tattoos he woke up with one morning when he was stationed in Manila. The shirt was white, starched and crisply ironed. The tie he'd worn to church was still cinched up hard under his prominent Adam's apple. A big man in a small room, he paced in front of the couch as he gathered himself to speak. He favored his left leg, whose knee had been shattered in the crash; every time his right foot came down, the dishes clinked in the cupboards.

'Okay, here goes,' he said. 'I'll have to fill in here and there, but I've got most of it.' He continued to walk, slowly, deliberately,

98

hands behind his back, head bent at an angle that suggested meditation. 'My dear friends,' he said, 'you may have read in the paper not long ago of a man of our state, a parent like many of yourselves here today... but a parent with a terrible choice to make. His name is Mike Bolling. He's a railroad man, Mike, a switchman, been with the railroad ever since he finished high school, same as his father and grandfather before him. He and Janice've been married ten years now. They were hoping for a whole houseful of kids, but the Lord decided to give them one instead, a very special one. That was nine years ago. Benny, they named him after Janice's father. He died when she was just a youngster, but she remembered his big lopsided grin and the way he threw back his head when he laughed, and she was hoping some of her dad's spirit would rub off on his name. Well, it turned out she got all the spirit she could handle, and then some.

'Benny. He came out in high gear and never shifted down. Mike liked to say you could run a train off him, the energy he had. Good student, natural athlete, but his big thing was mechanics. One of those boys, you put him in the same room with a clock and he's got it in pieces before you can turn around. By the time he was in second grade he could put the clocks back together, not to mention the vacuum cleaner and the TV and the engine of Mike's old lawn mower.'

This didn't sound like Frank. Frank was plain in his speech, neither formal nor folksy, so spare and sometimes harsh that his jokes sounded like challenges, or insults. Frances was about the only one who got them. This tone was putting her on edge. Something terrible was going to happen in the story, something Frances would regret having heard. She knew that. But she didn't stop him. Frank was her little brother, and she would deny him nothing.

When Frank was still a baby, not even walking yet, Frank Senior, their father, had set out to teach his son the meaning of the word no. At dinner he'd dangle his wristwatch before Frank's eyes, then say no! and jerk it back just as Frank grabbed for it. When Frank persisted, Frank Senior would slap his hand until he was howling with fury and desire. This happened night after night. Frank would not take the lesson to heart; as soon as the watch was offered, he snatched at it. Frances followed her mother's example and said nothing. She was eight years old, and while she feared her father's attention she also missed it, and resented Frank's obstinacy and the disturbance it caused. Why couldn't he learn? Then her father slapped Frank's face. This was on New Year's Eve. Frances still remembered the stupid tasseled hats they were all wearing when her father slapped her baby brother. In the void of time after the slap there was no sound but the long rush of air into Frank's lungs as, red-faced, twisting in his chair, he gathered himself to scream. Frank Senior lowered his head. Frances saw that he'd surprised himself and was afraid tried to think of a moment when their lives might have turned by even a degree, turned and gone some other way, and she always came back to this instant when her father knew the wrong he had done, was shaken and open to rebuke. What might have happened if her mother had come flying out of her chair and stood over him and told him to stop, now and forever?

Or if she had only looked at him, confirming his shame? But her eyes were closed, and stayed closed until Frank blasted them with his despair and Frank Senior left the room. As Frances knew even then, her mother could not allow herself to see what she had no strength to oppose. Her heart was bad. Three years later she reached for a bottle of ammonia, said 'Oh,' sat down on the floor and died.

Frances did oppose her father. In defiance of his orders, she brought food to Frank's room when he was banished, stood up for him and told him he was right to stand up for himself. Frank Senior had decided that his son needed to be broken, and Frank would not break. He went after everything his father said no to, with Frances egging him on and mothering him when he got caught. In time their father ceased to give reasons for his displeasure. As his silence grew heavier, so did his hand. One night

Frances grabbed her father's belt as he started after Frank, and when he flung her aside Frank head-rammed him in the stomach. Frances jumped on her father's back and the three of them crashed around the room. When it was over Frances was flat on the floor with a split lip and a ringing sound in her ears, laughing like a madwoman. Frank was crying. That was the first time.

Frank Senior said no to his son in everything, and Frances would say no to him in nothing. Frank was aware of her reluctance and learned to exploit it, most shamelessly in the months before his accident. He'd invaded her home, caused her trouble at work, nearly destroyed her marriage. To this day her husband had not forgiven Frances for what he called her complicity in that nightmare. But her husband had never been thrown across a room, or kicked, or slammed headfirst into a door. No one had ever spoken to him as her father had spoken to Frank. He did not understand what it was to be helpless and alone. No one should be alone in this world. Everyone should have someone who kept faith, no matter what, all the way.

'On the night in question,' Frank said, 'Mike's foreman called up and asked him to take another fellow's shift at the drawbridge station where he'd been working. A Monday night it was, mid-January, bitter cold. Janice was at a PTA meeting when Mike got the call, so he had no choice but to bring Benny along with him. It was against the rules, strictly speaking, but he needed the overtime and he'd done it before, more than once. Nobody ever said anything. Benny always behaved himself, and it was a good chance for him and Mike to buddy up, batch it a little. They'd talk and kid around, heat up some franks, then Mike would set Benny up with a sleeping bag and air mattress. A regular adventure.

'A bitter night, like I said. There was a furnace at the station, but it wasn't working. The guy Mike relieved had on his parka and a pair of mittens. Mike ribbed him about it, but pretty soon he and Benny put their own hats and gloves back on. Mike brewed up some hot chocolate, and they played gin rummy, or tried to – it's not that easy with gloves on. But they weren't thinking about winning or losing. It was good enough just being together, the two of them, with the cold wind blowing up against the windows. Father and son: what could be better than that? Then Mike had to raise the bridge for a couple of boats, and things got pretty tense because one of them steered too close to the bank and almost ran aground. The skipper had to reverse engines and go back downriver and take another turn at it. The whole business went on a lot longer than it should have, and by the time the second boat got clear Mike was running way behind schedule and under pressure to get the bridge down for the express train out of Portland. That was when he noticed Benny was missing.'

Frank stopped by the window and looked out in an unseeing way. He seemed to be contemplating whether to go on. But then he turned away from the window and started in again, and Frances understood that this little moment of reflection was just another part of the sermon.

'Mike calls Benny's name. No answer. He calls him again, and he doesn't spare the volume. You have to understand the position Mike is in. He has to get the bridge down for that train and he's got just about enough time to do it. He doesn't know where Benny is, but he has a pretty good idea. Just where he isn't supposed to be. Down below, in the engine room.

'The engine room. The mill, as Mike and the other operators call it. You can imagine the kind of power that's needed to raise and lower a drawbridge, aside from the engine itself – all the winches and levers, pulleys and axles and wheels and so on. Massive machinery. Gigantic screws turning everywhere, gears with teeth like file cabinets. They've got catwalks and little crawlways through the works for the mechanics, but nobody goes down there unless they know what they're doing. You have to know what you're doing. You have to know exactly where to put your feet, and you've got to keep your hands in close and wear all the right clothes. And even if you know what you're doing, you never go down there when the bridge is being moved. Never. There's just too much going on, too many ways of getting snagged and pulled into the works. Mike has told

Benny a hundred times, stay out of the mill. That's the iron rule when Benny comes out to the station. But Mike made the mistake of taking him down for a quick look one day when the engine was being serviced, and he saw how Benny lit up at the sight of all that steel, all that machinery. Benny was just dying to get his hands on those wheels and gears, see how everything fit together. Mike could feel it pulling at Benny like a big magnet. He always kept a close eye on him after that, until this one night, when he got distracted. And now Benny's down in there. Mike knows it as sure as he knows his own name.'

Frances said, 'I don't want to hear this story.' Frank gave no sign that he'd heard her. She was going to say something else, but made a sour face and let him go on.

'To get to the engine room, Mike would have to go through the passageway to the back of the station and either wait for the elevator or climb down the emergency ladder. He doesn't have time to do the one or the other. He doesn't have time for anything but lowering the bridge, and just barely enough time for that. He's got to get that bridge down now or the train is going into the river with everyone on board. This is the position he's in; this is the choice he has to make. His son, his Benjamin, or the people on that train.

'Now, let's take a minute to think about the people on that train. Mike's never met any of them, but he's lived long enough to know what they're like. They're like the rest of us. There are some who know the Lord, and love their neighbors, and live in the light. And there are the others. On this train are men who whisper over cunning papers and take from the widow even her mean portion. On this train is the man whose factories kill and maim his workers. There are thieves on this train, and liars, and hypocrites. There is the man whose wife is not enough for him, who cannot be happy until he possesses every woman who walks the earth. There is the false witness. There is the bribe-taker. There is the woman who abandons her husband and children for her own pleasure. There is the seller of spoiled goods, the coward, and the usurer, and there is the man who lives for his drug, who will do anything for that false promise – steal from those who give him work, from his friends, his family, yes, even from his own family, scheming for their pity, borrowing in bad faith, breaking into their very homes. All these are on the train, awake and hungry as wolves, and also on the train are the sleepers, the sleepers with open eyes who sleepwalk through their days, neither doing evil nor resisting it, like soldiers who lie down as if dead and will not join the battle, not for their cities and homes, not even for their wives and children. For such people, how can Mike give up his son, his Benjamin, who is guilty of nothing?

'He can't. Of course he can't, not on his own. But Mike isn't on his own. He knows what we all know, even when we try to forget it: we are never alone, ever. We are in our Father's presence in the light of day and in the dark of night, even in that darkness where we run from Him, hiding our faces like fearful children. He will not leave us. No. He will never leave us alone. Though we lock every window and bar every door, still He will enter. Though we empty our hearts and turn them to stone, yet shall He make His home there.

'He will not leave us alone. He is with all of you, as He is with me. He is with Mike, and also with the bribe-taker on the train, and the woman who needs her friend's husband, and the man who needs a drink. He knows their needs better than they do. He knows that what they truly need is Him, and though they flee His voice He never stops telling them that He is there. And at this moment, when Mike has nowhere to hide and nothing left to tell himself, then he can hear, and he knows that he is not alone, and he knows what it is that he must do. It has been done before, even by Him who speaks, the Father of All, who gave His own son, His beloved, that others might be saved.'

'No!' Frances said.

Frank stopped and looked at Frances as if he couldn't remember who she was.

'That's it,' she said. 'That's my quota of holiness for the year.'

'But there's more.'

'I know, I can see it coming. The guy kills his kid, right? I have to tell you, Frank, that's a crummy story. What're we supposed to get from a story like that – we should kill our own kid to save some stranger?'

'There's more to it than that.'

'Okay, then, make it a trainload of strangers, make it ten train-loads of strangers. I should do this because the so-called Father of All did it? Is that the point? How do people think up stuff like this, anyway? It's an awful story.'

'It's true.'

'True? Franky. Please, you're not a moron.'

'Dr. Violet knows a man who was on that train.'

'I'll just bet he does. Let me guess.' Frances screwed her eyes shut, then popped them open. 'The drug addict! Yes, and he reformed afterward and worked with street kids in Brazil and showed everybody that Mike's sacrifice was not in vain. Is that how it goes?'

'You're missing the point, Frances. It isn't about that. Let me finish.'

'No. It's a terrible story, Frank. People don't act like that. I sure as hell wouldn't.'

'You haven't been asked. He doesn't ask us to do what we can't do.'

'I don't care what He asks. Where'd you learn to talk like that, anyway? You don't even sound like yourself.'

'I had to change. I had to change the way I thought about things. Maybe I sound a little different too.'

'Yeah, well you sounded better when you were drunk.'

Frank seemed about to say something, but didn't. He backed up a step and lowered himself into a hideous plaid La-Z-Boy left behind by the previous tenant. It was stuck in the upright position.

'I don't care if the Almighty poked a gun in my ear, I would never do that,' Frances said. 'Not in a million years. Neither would you. Honest, now, little brother, would you grind me up if I was the one down in the mill, would you push the Francesburger button?'

'It isn't a choice I have to make.'

'Yeah, yeah, I know. But say you did.'

'I don't. He doesn't hold guns to our heads.'

'Oh, really? What about hell, huh? What do you call that? But so what. Screw hell, I don't care about hell. Do I get crunched or not?'

'Don't put me to the test, Frances. It's not your place.'

'I'm down in the mill, Frank. I'm stuck in the gears and here comes the train with Mother Teresa and five hundred sinners on board, *whoo whoo, whoo whoo*. Who, Frank, who? Who's it going to be?'

Frances wanted to laugh. Glumly erect in the chair, hands gripping the armrests, Frank looked like he was about to take off into a hurricane. But she kept that little reflection to herself. Frank was thinking, and she had to let him. She knew what his answer would be – in the end there could be no other answer – but he couldn't just say she's my sister and let it go at that. No, he'd have to noodle up some righteous, high-sounding reasons for choosing her. And maybe he wouldn't, at first, maybe he'd chicken out and come up with the Bible-school answer. Frances was ready for that, she was up for a fight; she could bring him around. Frances didn't mind a fight, and she especially didn't mind fighting for her brother. For her brother she'd fought neighborhood punks, snotty teachers and unappreciative coaches, loan sharks, landlords, bouncers. From the time she was a scabby-kneed girl she'd taken on her own father, and if push came to shove she'd take on the Father of All, that incomprehensible bully. She was ready. It would be like old times, the two of them waiting in her room upstairs while Frank Senior worked himself into a rage below, muttering, slamming doors, stinking up the house with the cigars he puffed when he was on a tear. She remembered it all – the tremor in her legs, the hammering pulse in her neck as the smell of smoke grew stronger. She could still taste that smoke and hear her father's steps on the stairs, Frank panting beside her, moving closer, his voice whispering her name and her own voice answering as fear gave way to ferocity and unaccountable joy, *It's okay, Franky. I'm here.*

# Anne Michaels

## 1997

### *Fugitive Pieces*

Time is a blind guide.

Bog-boy, I surfaced into the miry streets of the drowned city. For over a thousand years, only fish wandered Biskupin's wooden sidewalks. Houses, built to face the sun, were flooded by the silty gloom of the Gasawka River. Gardens grew luxurious in subaqueous silence; lilies, rushes, stinkweed.

No one is born just once. If you're lucky, you'll emerge again in someone's arms; or unlucky, wake when the long tail of terror brushes the inside of your skull.

I squirmed from the marshy ground like Tollund Man, Grauballe Man, like the boy they uprooted in the middle of Franz Josef Street while they were repairing the road, six hundred cockleshell beads around his neck, a helmet of mud. Dripping with the prune-coloured juices of the peat-sweating bog. Afterbirth of earth.

I saw a man kneeling in the acid-steeped ground. He was digging. My sudden appearance unnerved him. For a moment he thought I was one of Biskupin's lost souls, or perhaps the boy in the story, who digs a hole so deep he emerges on the other side of the world.

Biskupin had been carefully excavated for almost a decade. Archaeologists gently continued to remove Stone and Iron Age relics from soft brown pockets of peat. The pure oak causeway that once connected Biskupin to the mainland had been reconstructed, as well as the ingenious nail-less wooden houses, ramparts, and the high-towered city gates. Wooden streets, crowded twenty-five centuries before with traders and craftsmen, were being raised from the swampy lake bottom. When the soldiers arrived they examined the perfectly preserved clay bowls; they held the glass beads, the bronze and amber bracelets, before smashing them on the floor. With delighted strides, they roamed the magnificent timber city, once home to a hundred families. Then the soldiers buried Biskupin in sand.

My sister had long outgrown the hiding place. Bella was fifteen and even I admitted she was beautiful, with heavy brows and magnificent hair like black syrup, thick and luxurious, a muscle down her back. "A work of art," our mother said, brushing it for her while Bella sat in a chair. I was still small enough to vanish behind the wallpaper in the cupboard, cramming my head sideways between choking plaster and beams, eyelashes scraping.

Since those minutes inside the wall, I've imagined that the dead lose every sense except hearing.

The burst door. Wood ripped from hinges, cracking like ice under the shouts. Noises never heard before, torn from my father's mouth. Then silence. My mother had been sewing a button on my shirt. She kept her buttons in a chipped saucer. I heard the rim of the saucer in circles on the floor. I heard the spray of buttons, little white teeth.

Blackness filled me, spread from the back of my head into my eyes as if my brain had been punctured. Spread from stomach to legs. I gulped and gulped, swallowing it whole. The wall filled with smoke. I struggled out and stared while the air caught fire.

I wanted to go to my parents, to touch them. But I couldn't, unless I stepped on their blood.

The soul leaves the body instantly, as if it can hardly wait to be free: my mother's face was not her own. My father was twisted with falling. Two shapes in the flesh-heap, his hands.

I ran and fell, ran and fell. Then the river: so cold it felt sharp.

The river was the same blackness that was inside me; only the thin membrane of my skin kept me floating.

From the other bank, I watched darkness turn to purple-orange light above the town; the colour of flesh transforming to spirit. They flew up. The dead passed above me, weird haloes and arcs smothering the stars. The trees bent under their weight. I'd never been alone in the night forest, the wild bare branches were frozen snakes. The ground tilted and I didn't hold on. I strained to join them, to rise with them, to peel from the ground like paper ungluing at its edges. I know why we bury our dead and mark the place with stone, with the heaviest, most perman-ent thing we can think of: because the dead are everywhere but the ground. I stayed where I was. Clammy with cold, stuck to the ground. I begged: If I can't rise, then let me sink, sink into the forest floor like a seal into wax.

Then – as if she'd pushed the hair from my forehead, as if I'd heard her voice – I knew suddenly my mother was inside me. Moving along sinews, under my skin the way she used to move through the house at night, putting things away, putting things in order. She was stopping to say goodbye and was caught, in such pain, wanting to rise, wanting to stay. It was my responsibility to release her, a sin to keep her from ascending. I tore at my clothes, my hair. She was gone. My own fast breath around my head.

I ran from the sound of the river into the woods, dark as the inside of a box. I ran until the first light wrung the last greyness out of the stars, dripping dirty light between the trees. I knew what to do. I took a stick and dug. I planted myself like a turnip and hid my face with leaves.

My head between the branches, bristling points like my father's beard. I was safely buried, my wet clothes cold as armour. Panting like a dog. My arms tight against my chest, my neck stretched back, tears crawling like insects into my ears. I had no choice but to look straight up. The dawn sky was milky with new spirits. Soon I couldn't avoid the absurdity of daylight even by closing my eyes. It poked down, pinned me like the broken branches, like my father's beard.

Then I felt the worst shame of my life: I was pierced with hunger. And suddenly I realised, my throat aching without sound – Bella.

I had my duties. Walk at night. In the morning dig my bed. Eat anything.

My days in the ground were a delirium of sleep and attention. I dreamed someone found my missing button and came looking for me. In a glade of burst pods leaking their white stuffing, I dreamed of bread; when I woke, my jaw was sore from chewing the air. I woke terrified of animals, more terrified of men.

In this day-sleep, I remembered my sister weeping at the end of novels she loved; my father's only indulgence – Romain Rolland or Jack London. She wore the characters in her face as she read, one finger rubbing the edge of the page. Before I learned to read, angry to be left out, I strangled her with my arms, leaning over with my cheek against hers, as if somehow to see in the tiny black letters the world Bella saw. She shrugged me off or, big-hearted, she stopped, turned the book over in her lap, and explained the plot ... the drunken father lurching home ... the betrayed lover waiting vainly under the stairs ... the terror of wolves howling in the Arctic dark, making my own skeleton rattle in my clothes. Sometimes at night, I sat on the edge of Bella's bed and she tested my spelling, writing on my back with her finger and, when I'd learned the word, gently erasing it with a stroke of her smooth hand.

I couldn't keep out the sounds: the door breaking open, the spit of buttons. My mother, my father. But worse than those sounds was that I couldn't remember hearing Bella at all. Filled with her silence, I had no choice but to imagine her face.

The night forest is incomprehensible: repulsive and endless, jutting bones and sticky hair, slime and jellied smells, shallow roots like ropy veins.

Draping slugs splash like tar across the ferns; black icicles of flesh.

During the day I have time to notice lichen like gold dust over the rocks.

A rabbit, sensing me, stops close to my head and tries to hide behind a blade of grass.

The sun is jagged through the trees, so bright the spangles turn dark and float, burnt paper, in my eyes.

The white nibs of grass get caught in my teeth like pliable little fishbones. I chew fronds into a bitter, stringy mash that turns my spit green.

Once, I risk digging my bed close to pasture, for the breeze, for relief from the dense damp of the forest. Buried, I feel the shuddering dark shapes of cattle thudding across the field. In the distance, their thrusting heads make them look as if they're swimming. They gallop to a stop a few feet from the fence then drift towards me, their heads swinging like slow church bells with every glory step of their heavy flanks. The slender calves quiver behind, fear twitching their ears. I'm also afraid – that the herd will bring everyone from miles away to where I'm hiding – as they gather to rest their massive heads on the fence and stare down at me with rolling eyes.

I fill my pockets and my hands with stones and walk into the river until only my mouth and nose, pink lilies, skim the air. Muck dissolves from my skin and hair, and it's satisfying to see floating like foam on the surface the fat scum of lice from my clothes. I stand on the bottom, my boots sucked down by the mud, the current flowing around me, a cloak in a liquid wind. I don't stay under long. Not only because of the cold, but because with my ears under the surface, I can't hear. This is more frightening to me than darkness, and when I can't stand the silence any longer, I slip out of my wet skin, into sound.

Someone is watching from behind a tree. I stare from my hiding place without moving, until my eyeballs harden, until I'm no longer sure he's seen me. What's he waiting for? In the last possible moment before I have to run, light coming fast, I discover I've been held prisoner half the night by a tree, its dead, dense bole carved by moonlight.

Even in daylight, in the cold drizzle, the tree's faint expression is familiar. The face above a uniform.

The forest floor is speckled bronze, sugar caramelised in the leaves. The branches look painted onto the onion-white sky. One morning I watch a finger of light move its way deliberately towards me across the ground.

I know, suddenly, my sister is dead. At this precise moment, Bella becomes flooded ground. A body of water pulling under the moon.

A grey fall day. At the end of strength, at the place where faith is most like despair, I leaped from the streets of Biskupin; from underground into air.

I limped towards him, stiff as a golem, clay tight behind my knees. I stopped a few yards from where he was digging – later he told me it was as if I'd hit a glass door, an inarguable surface of pure air – "and your mud mask cracked with tears and I knew you were human, just a child. Crying with the abandonment of your age."

He said he spoke to me. But I was wild with deafness. My peat-clogged ears.

So hungry. I screamed into the silence the only phrase I knew in more than one language, I screamed it in Polish and German and Yiddish, thumping my fists on my own chest: dirty Jew, dirty Jew, dirty Jew.

The man excavating in the mud at Biskupin, the man I came to know as Athos, wore me under his clothes. My limbs bone-shadows on his strong legs and arms, my head buried in his neck, both of us beneath a heavy coat. I was suffocating but I couldn't get warm. Inside Athos's coat, cold air streaming in from the edge of the car door. The drone of engine and wheels, once in a while the sound of a passing lorry. In our strange coupling, Athos's voice burrowed into my brain. I didn't understand so I made it up myself: It's right, it's necessary to run ...

For miles through darkness in the back seat of the car, I had no idea where we were or where we were going. Another man drove and when we were signalled to stop, Athos pulled a blanket over us. In Greek-stained but competent German, Athos complained that he was ill. He didn't just complain. He whimpered, he moaned. He insisted on describing his symptoms and treatments in detail. Until, disgusted and annoyed, they waved us on. Each time we stopped, I was numb against his solid body, a blister tight with fear.

My head ached with fever, I smelled my hair burning. Through days and nights I sped from my father and my mother. From long afternoons with my best friend, Mones, by the river. They were yanked right through my scalp.

But Bella clung. We were Russian dolls. I inside Athos, Bella inside me.

I don't know how long we travelled this way. Once, I woke and saw signs in a fluid script that from a distance looked like Hebrew. Then Athos said we were home, in Greece. When we got closer I saw the words were strange; I'd never seen Greek letters before. It was night, but the square houses were white even in the darkness and the air was soft. I was dim with hunger and from lying so long in the car.

Athos said: "I will be your koumbaros, your godfather, the marriage sponsor for you and your sons ..."

Athos said: "We must carry each other. If we don't have this, what are we ..."

On the island of Zakynthos, Athos – scientist, scholar, middling master of languages – performed his most astounding feat. From out of his trousers he plucked the seven-year-old refugee Jakob Beer.

# Jay McInerney

## 1998
## *Model Behaviour*

### MODEL COUPLE

When Philomena looks in the mirror she sees a creature fat and unattractive. This despite the fact that she is a woman whose photographic image is expensively employed to arouse desire in conjunction with certain consumer goods. Or rather, *because* of that fact. Toxic body consciousness being the black lung of her profession. Dressing for the party, she screams that she's bloated and has nothing to wear.

I'm clutching a preparty martini when she makes this declaration. 'You look terrific,' I say. She seizes my glass and hurls it at the mirror, shattering both.

It's all right, really. I drink too much anyway.

### THE PARTY

The name of the party is the Party You Have Been to Six Hundred Times Already. Everybody is here. 'All your friends,' Philomena states in what can only be described as a citric tone. It seems to me that they are *her* friends, that *she* is the reason we grace this fabulous gala, which takes place in the Waiting Room of Grand Central, presumably evicting dozens of homeless people for the night. We're supposedly on hand for the benefit of a disease, but we were comped, as was everyone else we know. 'I'm sick of all this pointless glamour,' my glamorous girlfriend says. 'I want the simple life.' This has become a theme. Weariness with metropolitan life in all its colonoscopic intricacy. I wonder if this ennui is somehow related to that other unstated domestic theme: sex, infrequency thereof.

We are accosted by Belinda, the popular transvestite, whom I am nearly certain is a friend of my girlfriend's, as opposed to one of my very own. I can't exactly remember if I know him from the gossip columns or if I know him personally, from events like these. Belinda is with an actual, ageless woman with striking dark eyebrows and buzzcut white hair, a woman who is always here at the party and whom I always sort of recognize. One of those women with three names: Hi Howareyou Goodtoseeyou. All the women lately have either three names or just one. Even the impersonators.

'Oh God, hide me,' says the woman whose name I always forget, 'there's Tommy Kroger, I had a bad date with him about five thousand years ago.'

'Did you sleep with him?' Philomena asks, raising one of her perfectly defined eyebrows, which looks like a crow in flight in the far distance of a painting by Van Gogh.

'God, who can remember?'

'If you can't, then you did,' says Belinda. 'That's the rule.'

Ah, so *that's* the rule.

'Hello darlings.' Who could it be but Delia McFaggen, the famous designer, streaking toward Belinda, blowing kisses all over everyone. I retreat, slaloming through the thick crowd to find beverages, the first of many trips.

## A FRIENDLY FACE

At the bar I encounter Jeremy Green, an unlikely and conspicuous figure at this venue, his golden locks falling superabundantly across the square shoulders of his rented tux – which juxtaposition suggests a flock of begowned angels camped atop the Seagram Building. He is an actual friend, my best friend, in fact, though he ignores my repeated greetings. Not until I pour vodka on his shirt does he deign to acknowledge my existence.

'Fuck off.'

'Excuse me. Aren't you Jeremy Green, the famous short story writer?'

'That's an oxymoron. Same category as *living poet, French rock star, German cuisine.*'

'How about Chekhov?'

'Dead.' Jeremy pronounces this verdict with a poet maudit manner that seems tinged more than faintly with envy. He doesn't quite add, *Lucky bastard,* but you can see that's what he's thinking.

'Carver?'

'Ditto. Plus, you think the guy who read his gas meter knew who Carver was? You think this bartender knows?'

The bartender, an aspiring model, says *'Shortcuts'* in midpour. 'I saw the movie.'

'I think,' Jeremy says, 'that proves my point. And don't even think about saying *Hemingway.*'

'Wouldn't dream of it. Any particular reason you're ignoring me?'

'I just think I'll feel better about myself if I pretend I don't know anybody at this hideous ratfuck.' Finally he turns his wrathful gaze upon me. 'Besides, if memory serves, you're the slimy lowlife who talked me into attending this fetid fete.'

'Your *editor* talked you into it,' I remind him. 'I merely encouraged you by way of saying that I, personally, would be happier and less chagrined if you were among the throng.'

Why, I wonder, are all the boys and girls blaming *me* tonight? Jeremy has a book coming out, and his editor, Blaine Forrestal, thought it would be good for him to be seen. Blaine is part of this world. She wears terrific suits, has a Radcliffe degree and a house in Sag Harbor; Jeremy is the least commercial of the writers she publishes. In fact, one might surmise that she is publishing Jeremy as a kind of penance for the frothy, wildly successful stuff she generally dispenses – memoirs by disgraced politicians, autobiographies by Emmy-winning TV stars. Jeremy's stories tend to appear in *Antaeus* and the *Iowa Review* and frequently are set in mental institutions.

'I feel,' he says, 'like a whore.'

'Now you know how the rest of us feel.'

'I'm sure this will really boost my lit cred, showing all the media elite that I swim in the same sewer they do.'

'Don't worry, I think the media elite's swimming in some other sewer tonight.' Indeed, excepting a few young black-clad Voguettes and self, I don't see much in the way of the Fourth Estate.

'Who's that fucking midget over there who told me he "rather liked" my first book.'

Following Jeremy's aquiline nose, I spot Kevin Shipley, book assassin for *Beau Monde*, in conversation with the *New York Post*.

'Jesus, I hope you didn't insult him. That's Kevin Shipley.'

'He told me he bought it on the remainder table at Barnes and Noble and I said I was deeply honored that he felt he'd gotten his buck ninety-five's worth.'

'Just pray he doesn't review the new one. His keyboard's made out of human teeth.'

Finally *I* have reached the bar, where I request several cosmopolitans, one of which I hand to Jeremy. 'Your problem,' I say, 'is that you don't drink enough. Where's Blaine, anyway?'

'Last I knew she was kissing Hollywood butt. Some fucking troll from Sony Pictures.'

'Let's go find Phil,' I suggest. 'Maybe you can cheer her up.'


## WHAT'S WITH PHILOMENA?

The love of my life has been decidedly edgy and nervous. I would ask her why, except I'm not entirely certain I want to know. What we need is some ecstasy therapy, drop a few tabs, have a long night of truth and touch. There has been too little rapture of late. Not to mention the touching part.

Fortunately, by the time I find her again, she seems to have undergone a mood transplant. Delighted to see Jeremy, she kisses him and then, for good measure, me.

I introduce myself to the attractive young woman of color with whom Phil has been conversing, whose name sounds familiar.

'Do I know you?' I ask.

'We've never met,' she says. 'I'm Chip Ralston's personal assistant.'

'Well,' says Jeremy, 'bully for you.'

'I was just telling Cherie,' Phil tells me, 'that you're doing the profile for *CiaoBella!*'

A photographer suddenly appears: 'Philomena, let's get a shot.'

My statuesque soulmate breaks into autosmile and gamely reaches for my arm, but, shy guy that I am, I say, 'Do a shot with Jeremy, we're trying to get him noticed.' Shoving them together, I chase after the retreating personal assistant.

'Is Chip *here*,' I ask.

'You just missed him,' she says. 'He's flying back to L.A. tonight, but I gave him your message. I'm sure he'll check in with you next week.'

I'd press her harder, I've got to talk to the bastard, but soon, then I suddenly see that she's edging directly into the path of Jillian Crowe, my formidably glamorous boss; and while I admire Jillian's fashion sense and editorial skills, I'd just as soon avoid her at present. Backtracking, I find Philomena teasing Jeremy about the career that awaits him in modeling. She is more vivacious than I've seen her in days, Jeremy being such a Jeremiah that he tends to spur his companions to sparkle and shine.

Fueled by several uncharacteristic cocktails, Philomena's high spirits last well into the morning; she surprises me by agreeing to join an expedition of fashion folk down to the Baby Doll Lounge, a low strip joint in TriBeCa.

Cabbing down with three revelers – satellites of Planet Fashion – she sits on my lap and sips from a drink she managed to smuggle out of the party. 'I have a joke,' she suddenly announces.

## TOPLESS MODEL IN HEADLESS BAR

At the Baby Doll, Philomena orders another cosmopolitan and, not unkindly, critiques the bodies of the dancing girls. With the body God gave Phil, she can afford to be generous. Finally the guy named Ralph, whom Philomena introduced as 'genius with hair,' suggests that Philomena show us her tits. The cry is taken up by Alonzo – who introduced himself as 'a powder fairy,' which Philomena annotated as 'makeup guy' – and then by the adjoining tables. To my astonishment, she jumps on the bar and pulls her dress down to her waist, giving us a liberal flash of lunar breast. And it is a measure of their excellence of form that I *nearly* swoon – if indeed one can nearly swoon – despite having seen them nearly every day for the past three years of my life. Tumid with desire, I try to coax Philomena home the minute she jumps down from the bar. But she's on a roll. Wants to dance. Wants another cosmopolitan.

For the third time I try the men's room and it's still locked.


## SHIPS IN THE NIGHT

We continue to have an uproarious time, but by now I have lost the feeling of being in the moment, and stand as if on the side-lines watching Philomena entertain her friends, though I dance and drink with the best of them. I don't mind, it's good to see her like this. Alonzo, feeling no pain either, slips me his phone number and says we ought to get together sometime. I explain to him that while I appreciate the thought, he is barking up the wrong telephone pole. He raises a skeptical eyebrow, then plants a hand voguishly on his hip. Working as I do for a young women's magazine with a strong emphasis on fashion, I often encounter this suspicion.

Philomena's mood slips away when I'm not looking, possibly around the time that Ralph's giving me his card and telling me that I have to do something about my haircut immediately, for the sake of the nation. 'They actually let you into the offices of *CiaoBella!* with that do?'

'Maybe he really *is* straight,' says Ralph.

By the time we get in the cab my love is silent and pensive. As we undress for bed, she announces preemptively that she's exhausted.

No nooky for you, buckaroo.

# AT LONG LAST, SEX

The narrator, slightly hungover now, the day after the party, helps Philomena choose the outfits for her trip — a versatile taupe suit from Jill Sander, a Versace jacket and ripped jeans for the plane, a fetching little sheath from Nicole Miller for the audition, as well as an extra pair of ripped, faded jeans plus three immaculate white T-shirts. And some nice clunky boots suitable for heavy construction or light shopping in SoHo. If he were more attentive it's possible the narrator would pick up certain clues from the packing, or from her behaviour, indications that this trip might be something more than advertised, but he is not a suspicious person by nature, and his powers of observation are swamped by a surge of hormones. When, after trying on the sheath, she slips out of it and asks him to fetch some panties from her dainties drawer, he is overcome with desire for the taut, tawny flesh beneath her teddy.

'Please,' he pleads. 'Just a little slice.' He reminds her that it has been five days, nine hours, and thirty-six minutes. And they're not even married yet.

'No we're not, are we?' Oh, dear, a tactical mistake on his part, this allusion to matrimony. This is a sore point, something he has been meaning to get around to addressing for the last couple of years. While she has been waiting for the big question, he is waiting to be worthy of such an honor; he does not believe that anyone, let alone Philomena, could really want to hitch her shining carriage to his lame gelding. Yet for some reason she seems to want to do so. As long as he is only a boyfriend, he believes that his fortunes are still fluid, that his lowly station is merely a stage of gestation. Whereas she believes that the actual obstacle is his sense of superiority. Luckily she doesn't pursue the subject, though perhaps with the absence of a marriage proposal in mind she makes him kneel and beg for it.

Craven, genuflective begging ensues, as per standard form. But heartfelt and genuine on his part. PLEASE PLEASE PLEASE. Feeling like the target audience for the recent beer commercial in which she appeared, oiled and glistening in a bikini, he tells her he will do anything. He will bark like any species of canine she can name and, if necessary, roll over. Finally she peels off the teddy and lies back on the bed like Manet's *Olympia*, ripe and haughty, a bored odalisque.

'Fast,' she commands, 'and no sweating.'

The narrator takes what he can get, a grateful consumer.


## AFTERGLOW


Afterward, lying in bed, a single gemlike tear appears on Philomena's cheek. When I ask what's wrong, she concocts a smile and shakes her head. 'Don't worry,' I say, although I have no idea what I mean by this hollow formula. While I am full of doubt as to the future, my job, I feel, is to reassure her, my consort, my lost little girl. Later, a moment of perfect melancholy: watching Philomena gather her cosmetics at her vanity in front of the cracked mirror, the dusky dimness infiltrated with pulsing red light that strobes through the window slats of our half-basement bedroom. This lurid glow likely signifying a more permanent death than the one I have just experienced; across the street is a nursing home where ambulances call with some regularity. 'Don't go,' I say in a sudden swoon of dread. 'It's just for a few days,' she says, brushing her hair. 'I love you,' I say – a too-rare declaration. She smiles at me from a shard of mirror.

# Ahdaf Soueif

## 1999
## *The Map of Love*

— and there, on the table under her bedroom window, lies the voice that has set her dreaming again. Fragments of a life lived a long, long time ago. Across a hundred years the woman's voice speaks to her — so clearly that she cannot believe it is not possible to pick up her pen and answer.

*The child sleeps. Nur al-Hayah: light of my life.*

Anna must have put aside her pen, Amal thinks, and looked down at the child pressed into her side: the face flushed with sleep, the mouth slightly open, a damp tendril of black hair clinging to the brow.

*I have tried, as well as I could, to tell her. But she cannot — or will not — understand, and give up hope. She waits for him constantly.*

Amal reads and reads deep into the night. She reads and lets Anna's words flow into her, probing gently at dreams and hopes and sorrows she had sorted out, labelled and put away.

Papers, polished and frail with age, sheets and sheets of them. Mostly they are covered in English in a small, firm, sloping hand. Amal has sorted them out by type and size of paper, by colour of ink. Other papers are in French. Some are in envelopes, some loosely bundled together in buff folders. There is a large green journal, and another bound in plain brown leather, a tiny brass keyhole embedded in its chased clasp. The key Amal found later in the corner of a purse made of green felt — a purse with an unwilling feel to it, as though it had been made in a schoolroom project – and with it were two wedding rings, one smaller than the other. She looked carefully at the etchings inside them, and at first the only part of the inscription she could make out on either ring was the date: 1896. A large brown envelope held one writing book: sixty-four pages of neat Arabic *ruq'a* script. Amal recognised the hand immediately: the upright letters short but straight, the sharp angles, the tail of the 'ya' tucked under its body. The definite, controlled hand of her grandmother. The paper is white and narrow-lined, bound between marbled grey boards. The stiff pages crackle and resist. When she smooths them open they lie awkwardly, holding a rigid posture till she closes the book again. Some newspaper cuttings: *al-Ahram, al-Liwa, The Times*, the *Daily News* and others. A programme from an Italian theatre. Another purse, this time of dark blue velvet. She had upended it over her palm and poured out a string of thirty-three prayer beads of polished wood with a short tassel of black silk. For the rest of the day her hand smelled faintly of aged sandalwood. Some sketchbooks with various drawings. Several books of Arabic calligraphy practice. She flicked through them, noting the difference in flow and confidence. Several books of Arabic exercises, quotations, notes, etc. A locket, curious in that it is made of a heavy, dull metal and hangs on a fine chain of steel. When she pressed its spring, it opened and a young woman looked out at her. It is an exquisite painting and she studies it repeatedly. She tells herself she has to get a magnifying glass and look at it properly. The young woman's hair is blonde and is worn loose and crimped in the style made famous by the Pre-Raphaelites. She has a smooth, clear brow, an oval face and a delicate chin. Her mouth is about to break into a smile. But her eyes are the strangest shade of blue, violet really, and they look straight at you and they say – they say a lot of things. There's a strength in that look, a wilfulness; one would almost call it defiance except that it is so good-humoured. It is the look a woman would wear – would have worn – if she asked a man, a stranger, say, to dance. The date on the back is 1870 and into the concave lid someone had taped a tiny golden key. A calico bag, and inside it, meticulously laundered and with a sachet of lavender tucked between the folds, was a baby's frock of the finest white cotton, its top a mass of blue and yellow and pink smocking. And folded once, and rolled in muslin, a curious woven tapestry showing a pharaonic image and an Arabic inscription. There was also a shawl, of the type worn by peasant women on special occasions: 'butter velvet', white. You can buy one today in the Ghuriyya for twenty Egyptian pounds. And there is another, finer one, in pale grey wool with faded pink flowers – so often worn that in patches you can almost see through the weave.

And there were other things too. Things wrapped in tissue, or in fabric, or concealed in envelopes: a box full of things, a treasure chest, a trunk, actually. It is a trunk.

A story can start from the oddest things: a magic lamp, a conversation overheard, a shadow moving on a wall. For Amal al-Ghamrawi, this story started with a trunk. An old-fashioned trunk made of brown leather, cracked now and dry, with a vaulted top over which run two straps fastened with brass buckles black with age and neglect.

The American had come to Amal's house. Her name was Isabel Parkman and the trunk was locked in the boot of the car she had hired. Amal could not pretend she was not wary. Wary and weary in advance: an American woman – a journalist, she had said on the phone. But she said Amal's brother had told her to call and so Amal agreed to see her. And braced herself: the fundamentalists, the veil, the cold peace, polygamy, women's status in Islam, female genital mutilation – which would it be?

But Isabel Parkman was not brash or strident; in fact she was rather diffident, almost shy. She had met Amal's brother in New York. She had told him she was coming to Egypt to do a project on the millennium, and he had given her Amal's number. Amal said she doubted whether Isabel would come across anyone with grand millennial views or theories. She said that she thought Isabel would find that on the whole everyone was simply worried – worried sick about what would become of Egypt, the Arab countries, 'le tiers monde', in the twenty-first century. But she gave her coffee and some names and Isabel went away.

On her second visit Isabel had broached the subject of the trunk. She had found it when her mother had gone into hospital – for good. She had looked inside it, and there were some old papers in English, written, she believed, by her great-grandmother. But there were many papers and documents in Arabic. And there were other things: objects. And the English papers were mostly undated, and some were bound together but seemed to start in midsentence. She knew some of her own history must be there, but she also thought there might be a story. She didn't want to impose but Amal's brother had thought she might be interested ...

Amal was touched by her hesitancy. She said she would have a look at the thing and sent the doorman to bring it upstairs. As he carried it in and put it in the middle of her living room, she said, 'Pandora's box?'

'Oh, I hope not,' Isabel cried, sounding genuinely alarmed.

*My name is Anna Winterbourne. I do not hold (much) with those who talk of the Stars governing our Fate.*

# Margaret Atwood

## 2000

## *The Blind Assassin*

### The Bridge

Ten days after the war ended, my sister Laura drove a car off a bridge. The bridge was being repaired: she went right through the Danger sign. The car fell a hundred feet into the ravine, smashing through the treetops feathery with new leaves, then burst into flames and rolled down into the shallow creek at the bottom. Chunks of the bridge fell on top of it. Nothing much was left of her but charred smithereens.

I was informed of the accident by a policeman: the car was mine, and they'd traced the licence. His tone was respectful: no doubt he recognized Richard's name. He said the tires may have caught on a streetcar track or the brakes may have failed, but he also felt bound to inform me that two witnesses – a retired lawyer and a bank teller, dependable people – had claimed to have seen the whole thing. They'd said Laura had turned the car sharply and deliberately, and had plunged off the bridge with no more fuss than stepping off a curb. They'd noticed her hands on the wheel because of the white gloves she'd been wearing.

It wasn't the brakes, I thought. She had her reasons. Not that they were ever the same as anybody else's reasons. She was completely ruthless in that way.

'I suppose you want someone to identify her,' I said. 'I'll come down as soon as I can.' I could hear the calmness of my own voice, as if from a distance. In reality I could barely get the words out; my mouth was numb, my entire face was rigid with pain. I felt as if I'd been to the dentist. I was furious with Laura for what she'd done, but also with the policeman for implying that she'd done it. A hot wind was blowing around my head, the strands of my hair lifting and swirling in it, like ink spilled in water.

'I'm afraid there will be an inquest, Mrs. Griffen,' he said. 'Naturally,' I said. 'But it was an accident. My sister was never a good driver.'

I could picture the smooth oval of Laura's face, her neatly pinned chignon, the dress she would have been wearing: a shirt-waist with a small rounded collar, in a sober colour – navy blue or steel grey or hospital-corridor green. Penitential colours – less like something she'd chosen to put on than like something she'd been locked up in. Her solemn half-smile; the amazed lift of her eyebrows, as if she were admiring the view.

The white gloves: a Pontius Pilate gesture. She was washing her hands of me. Of all of us.

What had she been thinking of as the car sailed off the bridge, then hung suspended in the afternoon sunlight, glinting like a dragonfly for that one instant of held breath before the plummet? Of Alex, of Richard, of bad faith, of our father and his wreckage; of God, perhaps, and her fatal, triangular bargain. Or of the stack of cheap school exercise books that she must have hidden that very morning, in the bureau drawer where I kept my stockings, knowing I would be the one to find them.

When the policeman had gone I went upstairs to change. To visit the morgue I would need gloves, and a hat with a veil. Something to cover the eyes. There might be reporters. I would have to call a taxi. Also I ought to warn Richard, at his office: he would wish to have a statement of grief prepared. I went into my dressing room: I would need black, and a handkerchief.

I opened the drawer, I saw the notebooks. I undid the criss-cross of kitchen string that tied them together. I noticed that my teeth were chattering, and that I was cold all over. I must be in shock, I decided.

What I remembered then was Reenie, from when we were little. It was Reenie who'd done the bandaging, of scrapes and cuts and minor injuries: Mother might be resting, or doing good deeds elsewhere, but Reenie was always there. She'd scoop us up and sit us on the white enamel kitchen table, alongside the pie dough she was rolling out or the chicken she was cutting up or the fish she was gutting, and give us a lump of brown sugar to get us to close our mouths. *Tell me where it hurts*, she'd say. *Stop howling. Just calm down and show me where.*

But some people can't tell where it hurts. They can't calm down. They can't ever stop howling.

*The Toronto Star, May 26, 1945*

# QUESTIONS RAISED IN CITY DEATH
## SPECIAL TO THE STAR

A coroner's inquest has returned a verdict of accidental death in last week's St. Clair Ave. fatality. Miss Laura Chase, 25, was travelling west on the afternoon of May 18 when her car swerved through the barriers protecting a repair site on the bridge and crashed into the ravine below, catching fire. Miss Chase was killed instantly. Her sister, Mrs. Richard E. Griffen, wife of the prominent manufacturer, gave evidence that Miss Chase suffered from severe headaches affecting her vision. In reply to questioning, she denied any possibility of intoxication as Miss Chase did not drink.

It was the police view that a tire caught in an exposed streetcar track was a contributing factor. Questions were raised as to the adequacy of safety precautions taken by the City, but after expert testimony by City engineer Gordon Perkins these were dismissed.

The accident has occasioned renewed protests over the state of the streetcar tracks on this stretch of roadway. Mr. Herb T. Jolliffe, representing local ratepayers, told *Star* reporters that this was not the first mishap caused by neglected tracks. City Council should take note.

The Blind Assassin. *By Laura Chase.*
*Reingold, Jaynes & Moreau, New York, 1947*

*Prologue: Perennials for the Rock Garden*

She has a single photograph of him. She tucked it into a brown envelope on which she'd written *clippings*, and hid the envelope between the pages of *Perennials for the Rock Garden*, where no one else would ever look.

She's preserved this photo carefully, because it's almost all she has left of him. It's black and white, taken by one of those boxy, cumbersome flash cameras from before the war, with their accordion-pleat nozzles and their well-made leather cases that looked like muzzles, with straps and intricate buckles. The photo is of the two of them together, her and this man, on a picnic. *Picnic* is written on the back, in pencil – not his name or hers, just *picnic*. She knows the names, she doesn't need to write them down.

They're sitting under a tree; it might have been an apple tree; she didn't notice the tree much at the time. She's wearing a white blouse with the sleeves rolled to the elbow and a wide skirt tucked around her knees. There must have been a breeze, because of the way the shirt is blowing up against her; or perhaps it wasn't blowing, perhaps it was clinging; perhaps it was hot. It was hot. Holding her hand over the picture, she can still feel the heat coming up from it, like the heat from a sun-warmed stone at midnight.

The man is wearing a light-coloured hat, angled down on his head and partially shading his face. His face appears to be more darkly tanned than hers. She's turned half towards him, and smiling, in a way she can't remember smiling at anyone since. She seems very young in the picture, too young, though she hadn't considered herself too young at the time. He's smiling too – the whiteness of his teeth shows up like a scratched match flaring – but he's holding up his hand, as if to fend her off in play, or else to protect himself from the camera, from the person who must be there, taking the picture; or else to protect himself from those in the future who might be looking at him, who might be looking in at him through this square, lighted window of glazed paper.

As if to protect himself from her. As if to protect her. In his outstretched, protecting hand there's the stub end of a cigarette.

She retrieves the brown envelope when she's alone, and slides the photo out from among the newspaper clippings. She lays it flat on the table and stares down into it, as if she's peering into a well or pool – searching beyond her own reflection for something else, something she must have dropped or lost, out of reach but still visible, shimmering like a jewel on sand. She examines every detail. His fingers bleached by the flash or the sun's glare; the folds of their clothing; the leaves of the tree, and the small round shapes hanging there – were they apples, after all? The coarse grass in the foreground. The grass was yellow then because the weather had been dry.

Over to one side – you wouldn't see it at first – there's a hand, cut by the margin, scissored off at the wrist, resting on the grass as if discarded. Left to its own devices.

The trace of blown cloud in the brilliant sky, like ice cream smudged on chrome. His smoke-stained fingers. The distant glint of water. All drowned now.

Drowned, but shining.

★★★

## The Blind Assassin: The hard-boiled egg

What will it be, then? he says. Dinner jackets and romance, or shipwrecks on a barren coast? You can have your pick: jungles, tropical islands, mountains. Or another dimension of space – that's what I'm best at.

Another dimension of space? Oh really!

Don't scoff, it's a useful address. Anything you like can happen there. Spaceships and skin-tight uniforms, ray guns, Martians with the bodies of giant squids, that sort of thing.

You choose, she says. You're the professional. How about a desert? I've always wanted to visit one. With an oasis, of course.

Some date palms might be nice. She's tearing the crust off her sandwich. She doesn't like the crusts.

Not much scope, with deserts. Not many features, unless you add some tombs. Then you could have a pack of nude women who've been dead for three thousand years, with lithe, curvaceous figures, ruby-red lips, azure hair in a foam of tumbled curls, and eyes like snake-filled pits. But I don't think I could fob those off on you. Lurid isn't your style.

You never know. I might like them.

I doubt it. They're for the huddled masses. Popular on the covers though – they'll writhe all over a fellow, they have to be beaten off with rifle butts.

Could I have another dimension of space, and also the tombs and the dead women, please?

That's a tall order, but I'll see what I can do. I could throw in some sacrificial virgins as well, with metal breastplates and silver ankle chains and diaphanous vestments. And a pack of ravening wolves, extra.

I can see you'll stop at nothing.

You want the dinner jackets instead? Cruise ships, white linen, wrist-kissing and hypocritical slop?

No. All right. Do what you think is best.

Cigarette?

She shakes her head for no. He lights his own, striking the match on his thumbnail.

You'll set fire to yourself, she says.

I never have yet.

She looks at his rolled-up shirt sleeve, white or a pale blue, then his wrist, the browner skin of his hand. He throws out radiance, it must be reflected sun. Why isn't everyone staring? Still, he's too noticeable to be out here – out in the open. There are other people around, sitting on the grass or lying on it, propped on one elbow – other picnickers, in their pale summer clothing. It's all very proper. Nevertheless she feels that the two of them are alone; as if the apple tree they're sitting under is not a tree but a tent; as if there's a line drawn around them with chalk. Inside this line, they're invisible.

Space it is, then, he says. With tombs and virgins and wolves – but on the instalment plan. Agreed?

The instalment plan? You know, like furniture. She laughs.

No, I'm serious. You can't skimp, it might take days. We'll have to meet again.

She hesitates. All right, she says. If I can. If I can arrange it.

Good, he says. Now I have to think. He keeps his voice casual. Too much urgency might put her off.

On the Planet of – let's see. Not Saturn, it's too close. On the Planet Zycron, located in another dimension of space, there's a rubble-strewn plain. To the north is the ocean, which is violet in colour. To the west is a range of mountains, said to be roamed after sunset by the voracious undead female inhabitants of the crumbling tombs located there. You see, I've put the tombs in right off the bat.

That's very conscientious of you, she says.

I stick to my bargains. To the south is a burning waste of sand, and to the east are several steep valleys that might once have been rivers.

I suppose there are canals, like Mars?

Oh, canals, and all sorts of things. Abundant traces of an ancient and once highly developed civilization, though this region is now only sparsely inhabited by roaming bands of primitive nomads. In the middle of the plain is a large mound of stones. The land around is arid, with a few scrubby bushes. Not exactly a desert, but close enough. Is there a cheese sandwich left?

She rummages in the paper bag. No, she says, but there's a hard-boiled egg. She's never been this happy before. Everything is fresh again, still to be enacted.

Just what the doctor ordered, he says. A bottle of lemonade, a hard-boiled egg, and Thou. He rolls the egg between his palms, cracking the shell, then peeling it away. She watches his mouth, the jaw, the teeth.

Beside me singing in the public park, she says. Here's the salt for it.

Thanks. You remembered everything.

This arid plain isn't claimed by anyone, he continues. Or rather it's claimed by five different tribes, none strong enough to annihilate the others. All of them wander past this stone heap from time to time, herding their *thulks* – blue sheep-like creatures with vicious tempers – or transporting merchandise of little value on their pack animals, a sort of three-eyed camel.

The pile of stones is called, in their various languages, The Haunt of Flying Snakes, The Heap of Rubble, The Abode of Howling Mothers, The Door of Oblivion, and The Pit of Gnawed Bones. Each tribe tells a similar story about it. Underneath the rocks, they say, a king is buried – a king without a name. Not only the king, but the remains of the magnificent city this king once ruled. The city was destroyed in a battle, and the king was captured and hanged from a date palm as a sign of triumph. At moonrise he was cut down and buried, and the stones were piled up to mark the spot. As for the other inhabitants of the city, they were all killed. Butchered – men, women, children, babies, even the animals. Put to the sword, hacked to pieces. No living thing was spared.

That's horrible.

Stick a shovel into the ground almost anywhere and some horrible thing or other will come to light. Good for the trade, we thrive on bones; without them there'd be no stories. Any more lemonade?

No, she says. We've drunk it all up. Go on.

The real name of the city was erased from memory by the conquerors, and this is why – say the taletellers – the place is now known only by the name of its own destruction. The pile of stones thus marks both an act of deliberate remembrance, and an act of deliberate forgetting. They're fond of paradox in that region. Each of the five tribes claims to have been the victorious attacker. Each recalls the slaughter with relish. Each believes it was ordained by their own god as righteous vengeance, because of the unholy practices carried on in the city. Evil must be cleansed with blood, they say. On that day the blood ran like water, so afterwards it must have been very clean.

Every herdsman or merchant who passes adds a stone to the heap. It's an old custom – you do it in remembrance of the dead, your own dead – but since no one knows who the dead under the pile of stones really were, they all leave their stones on the off chance. They'll get around it by telling you that what happened there must have been the will of their god, and thus by leaving a stone they are honouring this will.

There's also a story that claims the city wasn't really destroyed at all. Instead, through a charm known only to the King, the city and its inhabitants were whisked away and replaced by phantoms of themselves, and it was only these phantoms that were burnt and slaughtered. The real city was shrunk very small and placed in a cave beneath the great heap of stones. Everything that was once there is there still, including the palaces and the gardens filled with trees and flowers; including the people, no bigger than ants, but going about their lives as before – wearing their tiny clothes, giving their tiny banquets, telling their tiny stories, singing their tiny songs.

The King knows what's happened and it gives him nightmares, but the rest of them don't know. They don't know they've become so small. They don't know they're supposed to be dead. They don't even know they've been saved. To them the ceiling of rock looks like a sky: light comes in through a pinhole between the stones, and they think it's the sun.

The leaves of the apple tree rustle. She looks up at the sky, then at her watch. I'm cold, she says. I'm also late. Could you dispose of the evidence? She gathers eggshells, twists up wax paper.

No hurry, surely? It's not cold here.

There's a breeze coming through from the water, she says. The wind must have changed. She leans forward, moving to stand up.

Don't go yet, he says, too quickly.

I have to. They'll be looking for me. If I'm overdue, they'll want to know where I've been.

She smoothes her skirt down, wraps her arms around herself, turns away, the small green apples watching her like eyes.

# Alexandra Pringle

## A New Century

Editor-in-Chief 2000–2020

On May Day 1999, I walked into a house in Soho Square. I knew it was the beginning of an important new chapter in my life. Earlier in the year I'd had lunch with Liz Calder. We'd scarcely begun when she said she was looking for someone to take over from her as editor-in-chief in due course. I met some of her colleagues including the founder Nigel Newton. Then I thought about it for four months – how could it have taken more than four minutes? Now I walked in to the offices of Bloomsbury, up the stairs painted burnt orange to the first floor, my home for the next few years. The offices were bursting with people and books. I had a desk in a corridor that an editor had sweetly given up for me, and Liz brought me a bunch of parrot tulips.

My first job was to hire an assistant. I'd heard of a young student at Oxford keen to work in publishing and made a date to meet her in the Groucho Club. Walking in I saw her across the empty afternoon bar. She was called Chiki Sarkar and I knew on the spot I was going to hire her. Chiki arrived a week or so after me, and until a desk was found, took up residence on the floor. We worked together eight years before she left to set up Random House in Delhi and eventually founded her own publishing company.

Those were the last days of an era in publishing. We smoked like chimneys, sat at desks piled high with manuscripts, lunched in Soho, partied hard and worked until late. When I arrived Ahdaf Soueif was shortlisted for the Booker Prize, Harry Potter was beginning to fly, Bloomsbury was made Publisher of the Year and our paperback list had its fifth birthday celebration in a dark basement club.

In America Bloomsbury US had just been set up in the Flatiron Building in New York. Their publisher called to beg that I read a manuscript by a friend of hers, a chef called Anthony Bourdain who had written a memoir, *Kitchen Confidential*. I took it home and was enthralled. In those days I couldn't be bothered much to eat, and certainly didn't dream of cooking; I thought that if I loved this white-knuckle ride of a memoir, then other people in the UK would too. I was right. It was my first Bloomsbury book and it sold one and a half million copies.

On January 1 2000, the first day of a new century, Liz stepped down as editor-in-chief and I stepped up. I have now, after twenty years, executed the same dance with Paul Baggaley, who we lured from Picador in March 2020. In that time we have moved from a house in louche Soho to a row of three Georgian houses in posher literary Bloomsbury, where at night the mice come out to dance. Bloomsbury has grown in every direction, and in our own bit, under the guidance of the energetic, irrepressible Richard Charkin and with the acumen and comradeship of Kathleen Farrar, we started a cookery division, and a crime list. Next we set up a company in India. I flew to Delhi to find a publisher and we launched Bloomsbury India in a garden strung with paper lanterns and garlands of jasmine.

Because of who we are, both mine and Liz's books reach across the world. Liz comes from New Zealand and lived for many years in Brazil; in her hands Bloomsbury was never going to be an exercise in Englishness. As for me, I had a Berber Jewish mother from Morocco, whose family from pre-Babylonian times brought gum arabic and ostrich feathers in caravans from Timbuktu to what was then Mogador. When I was a young teenager my Scottish father taught every summer in West Africa, and one year came back from Nigeria with a book called *Things Fall Apart*. As I read it my world shifted on its axis. Bloomsbury has a list of some of Britain, Ireland and America's finest living writers, but importantly there are books from Brazil, Chile, Egypt, India, Iran, Morocco, Nigeria, Pakistan, Palestine, Sierra Leone, South Africa, Sri Lanka, Sudan, Zanzibar, and many other countries. In 2015 our editor Bill Swainson was made an OBE for services to literary translation.

At the heart of every publishing company are its editors and that mysterious, mercurial thing, their taste. There are, too, their secret weapons, their readers. Mine, Antonia Till, has worked with me from my earliest publishing days. She has been the first reader of so many of our successes. I cannot imagine how life would have been without her. During my time at Bloomsbury I have published mainly fiction with publishing director Michael Fishwick beside me, presiding over his distinguished and distinctive non-fiction list. And there have, too, been generations of bright young women who began as editorial assistants and went on to become distinguished in the world of books.

This anthology represents our fiction years, with a couple of exceptions. Fiction is of course wonderful entertainment. But it is much more than that. Through it we learn history, we learn about ourselves, but more importantly we learn about others, about the world we live in and worlds we can only dream of. At the heart of much I do is politics. My parents were life-long socialists and my father twice stood for Parliament as a Labour candidate. My publishing childhood was spent at the feminist publisher Virago Press, where I arrived as the fourth member of staff, a 24-year-old office skivvy, where I learned to be a publisher, from where I left, twelve years later, as editorial director. I've had a skirmish in the corporate world, but

soon realised it wasn't for me. It was Bloomsbury's independence of ownership – and heart – that made it irresistible to
me. It was Bloomsbury that became my country. As Liz used to
say, at Bloomsbury we publish writers, not books – and she is
right. Patience and sheer bloody-minded belief in an author can
reap the best rewards, impossible without backing from the top.
Liz and I have been blessed with constant support from Nigel
Newton, whose vision for Bloomsbury has informed everything
we do. As Alison MacLeod has written, he has created 'an impec-
cable publishing home for writers'.

Bloomsbury had published George Saunders for many years,
collections of short stories that were highly rated and which sold
pretty dismally. Then came *Lincoln in the Bardo* and the Booker
Prize. Our two most recent Women's Prize winners, Kamila
Shamsie and Susanna Clarke, I have worked with for decades,
in Kamila's case since she was a student. Then the greatest and
most astonishing joy of my publishing life happened one day
in October 2021. In the middle of a meeting, the news broke
that Abdulrazak Gurnah had been awarded the Nobel Prize
in Literature. I burst into tears. I had been publishing him for
twenty years, longing for him to receive the international recognition he deserved, but hope was running a little thin. And so I
would add to Liz's words the words of Tammy Wynette, 'stand
by your man' (or woman).

I hope that in this anthology not only will you be reminded
of some of the triumphs of Bloomsbury's publishing through
the past thirty-five years, but also you will discover some writers
you may not know. In these pages I have chosen work by best-
selling and prize-winning writers and also by authors I value as
highly, but who have not (as yet) received their due recognition.

There have been, of course, many heartbreaks in making this
selection. The authors and their books have been my greatest
joy and choosing one over another has been a painful and sometimes impossible task.

So here we are. You have read some of Bloomsbury's work in
the first half of its life. Now welcome to the second half.

# Anthony Bourdain

## 2000

## *Kitchen Confidential*

My first indication that food was something other than a substance one stuffed in one's face when hungry—like filling up at a gas station—came after fourth-grade elementary school. It was on a family vacation to Europe, on the *Queen Mary*, in the cabin-class dining room. There's a picture somewhere: my mother in her Jackie O sunglasses, my younger brother and I in our painfully cute cruise wear, boarding the big Cunard ocean liner, all of us excited about our first transatlantic voyage, our first trip to my father's ancestral homeland, France.

It was the soup.

It was *cold*.

This was something of a discovery for a curious fourth-grader whose entire experience of soup to this point had consisted of Campbell's cream of tomato and chicken noodle. I'd eaten in restaurants before, sure, but this was the first food I really noticed. It was the first food I enjoyed and, more important, remembered enjoying. I asked our patient British waiter what this delightfully cool, tasty liquid was.

'Vichyssoise,' came the reply, a word that to this day—even though it's now a tired old warhorse of a menu selection and one I've prepared thousands of times—still has a magical ring to it. I remember everything about the experience: the way our waiter ladled it from a silver tureen into my bowl, the crunch of tiny chopped chives he spooned on as garnish, the rich, creamy taste of leek and potato, the pleasurable shock, the surprise that it was cold.

I don't remember much else about the passage across the Atlantic. I saw *Boeing Boeing* with Jerry Lewis and Tony Curtis in the *Queen's* movie theater, and a Bardot flick. The old liner shuddered and groaned and vibrated terribly the whole way—barnacles on the hull was the official explanation—and from New York to Cherbourg, it was like riding atop a giant lawnmower. My brother and I quickly became bored, and spent much of our time in the 'Teen Lounge', listening to 'House of the Rising Sun' on the jukebox, or watching the water slosh around like a contained tidal wave in the below-deck salt-water pool.

But that cold soup stayed with me. It resonated, waking me up, making me aware of my tongue, and in some way, preparing me for future events.

My second pre-epiphany in my long climb to chefdom also came during that first trip to France. After docking, my mother, brother and I stayed with cousins in the small seaside town of Cherbourg, a bleak, chilly resort area in Normandy, on the English Channel. The sky was almost always cloudy; the water was inhospitably cold. All the neighborhood kids thought I knew Steve McQueen and John Wayne personally—as an American, it was assumed we were all pals, that we hung out together on the range, riding horses and gunning down miscreants—so I enjoyed a certain celebrity right away. The beaches, while no good for swimming, were studded with old Nazi blockhouses and gun emplacements, many still bearing visible bullet scars and the scorch of flamethrowers, and there were tunnels under the dunes—all very cool for a little kid to explore. My little French friends were, I was astonished to find, allowed to have a cigarette on Sunday, were given watered *vin ordinaire* at the dinner table, and best of all, they owned Velo Solex motorbikes. *This* was the way to raise kids, I recall thinking, unhappy that my mother did not agree.

So for my first few weeks in France, I explored underground passageways, looking for dead Nazis, played miniature golf, sneaked cigarettes, read a lot of Tintin and Asterix comics, scooted around on my friends' motorbikes and absorbed little life-lessons from observations that, for instance, the family friend Monsieur Dupont brought his mistress to some meals and his wife to others, his extended brood of children apparently indifferent to the switch.

I was largely unimpressed by the food.

The butter tasted strangely 'cheesy' to my undeveloped palate. The milk—a staple, no, a mandatory ritual in '60s American kiddie life—was undrinkable here. Lunch seemed always to consist of sandwich au jambon or croque-monsieur. Centuries of French cuisine had yet to make an impression. What I noticed about food, French style, was what they *didn't* have.

After a few weeks of this, we took a night train to Paris, where we met up with my father, and a spanking new Rover Sedan Mark III, our touring car. In Paris, we stayed at the Hotel Lutetia, then a large, slightly shabby old pile on Boulevard Haussmann. The menu selections for my brother and me expanded somewhat, to include steak-frites and steak haché (hamburger). We did all the predictable touristy things: climbed the Tour Eiffel, picnicked in the Bois de Boulogne, marched past the Great Works at the Louvre, pushed toy sailboats around the fountain in the Jardin de Luxembourg—none of it much fun for a nine-year-old with an already developing criminal bent. My principal interest at this time was adding to my collection of English translations of Tintin adventures. Hergé's crisply drafted tales of drug-smuggling, ancient temples, and strange and faraway places and cultures were *real* exotica for me. I prevailed on my poor parents to buy hundreds of dollars-worth of these stories at W. H. Smith, the English bookstore, just to keep me from whining about the deprivations of France. With my little short-shorts a permanent affront, I was quickly becoming a sullen, moody, difficult little bastard. I fought constantly with my brother, carped about everything, and was in every possible way a drag on my mother's Glorious Expedition.

My parents did their best. They took us everywhere, from restaurant to restaurant, cringing, no doubt, every time we

insisted on steak haché (with ketchup, no less) and a 'Coca.' They
endured silently my gripes about cheesy butter, the seemingly
endless amusement I took in advertisements for a popular soft
drink of the time, Pschitt. 'I want shit! I want shit!' They managed
to ignore the eye-rolling and fidgeting when they spoke French,
tried to encourage me to find something, *anything*, to enjoy.

And there came a time when, finally, they *didn't* take the kids
along.

I remember it well, because it was such a slap in the face. It
was a wake-up call that food could be important, a challenge to
my natural belligerence. By being denied, a door opened.

The town's name was Vienne. We'd driven miles and miles of
road to get there. My brother and I were fresh out of Tintins and
cranky as hell. The French countryside, with its graceful, tree-
lined roads, hedgerows, tilled fields and picture-book villages
provided little distraction. My folks had by now endured weeks
of relentless complaining through many tense and increasingly
unpleasant meals. They'd dutifully ordered our steak haché,
crudités variés, sandwich au jambon and the like long enough.
They'd put up with our grousing that the beds were too hard,
the pillows too soft, the neck-rolls and toilets and plumbing
too weird. They'd even allowed us a little watered wine, as it
was clearly the French thing to do—but also, I think, to shut
us up. They'd taken my brother and me, the two Ugliest Little
Americans, everywhere.

Vienne was different.

They pulled the gleaming new Rover into the parking lot of
a restaurant called, rather promisingly, La Pyramide, handed us
what was apparently a hoarded stash of Tintins … *and then left us
in the car!*

It was a hard blow. Little brother and I were left in that car
for over three hours, an eternity for two miserable kids already
bored out of their minds. I had plenty of time to wonder: *What
could be so great inside those walls?* They were eating in there. I
knew that. And it was certainly a Big Deal; even at a witless age
nine, I could recognize the nervous anticipation, the excitement,

the near-reverence with which my beleaguered parents had approached this hour. And I had the Vichyssoise Incident still fresh in my mind. Food, it appeared, could be *important*. It could be an event. It had secrets.

I know now, of course, that La Pyramide, even in 1966, was the center of the culinary universe. Bocuse, Troisgros, *everybody* had done their time there, making their bones under the legendarily fearsome proprietor, Ferdinand Point. Point was the Grand Master of cuisine at the time, and La Pyramide was Mecca for foodies. This was a pilgrimage for my earnestly francophile parents. In some small way, I got that through my tiny, empty skull in the back of the sweltering parked car, even then.

Things changed. *I* changed after that.

First of all, I was furious. Spite, always a great motivating force in my life, caused me to become suddenly adventurous where food was concerned. I decided then and there to outdo my foodie parents. At the same time, I could gross out my still uninitiated little brother. I'd show *them* who the gourmet was!

Brains? Stinky, runny cheeses that smelled like dead man's feet? Horsemeat? Sweetbreads? Bring it on!! Whatever had the most shock value became my meal of choice. For the rest of that summer, and in the summers that followed, I ate *everything*. I scooped gooey Vacherin, learned to love the cheesy, rich Normandy butter, especially slathered on baguettes and dipped in bitter hot chocolate. I sneaked red wine whenever possible, tried fritures—tiny whole fish, fried and eaten with persillade—loving that I was eating heads, eyes, bones and all. I ate ray in beurre noisette, saucisson à Pail, tripes, rognons de veau (kidneys), boudin noir that squirted blood down my chin.

And I had my first oyster.

Now, *this* was a truly significant event. I remember it like I remember losing my virginity—and in many ways, more fondly.

August of that first summer was spent in La Teste sur Mer, a tiny oyster village on the Bassin d'Arcachon in the Gironde (Southwest France). We stayed with my aunt, Tante Jeanne, and my uncle, Oncle Gustav, in the same red tile-roofed, white stuccoed house where my father had summered as a boy. My Tante Jeanne was a frumpy, bespectacled, slightly smelly old woman, my Oncle Gustav, a geezer in coveralls and beret who smoked hand-rolled cigarettes until they disappeared onto the tip of his tongue. Little had changed about La Teste in the years since my father had vacationed there. The neighbors were still all oyster fishermen. Their families still raised rabbits and grew tomatoes in their backyards. Houses had two kitchens, an inside one and an outdoor 'fish kitchen'. There was a hand pump for drinking water from a well, and an outhouse by the rear of the garden. Lizards and snails were everywhere. The main tourist attractions were the nearby Dune of Pyla (Europe's Largest Sand Dune!) and the nearby resort town of Arcachon, where the French flocked in unison for *Les Grandes Vacances*. Television was a Big Event. At seven o'clock, when the two national stations would come on the air, my Oncle Gustav would solemnly emerge from his room with a key chained to his hip and cere-moniously unlock the cabinet doors that covered the screen.

My brother and I were happier here. There was more to do. The beaches were warm, and closer in climate to what we knew back home, with the added attraction of the ubiquitous Nazi blockhouses. There were lizards to hunt down and exterminate with readily available *pétards*, firecrackers which one could buy legally (!) over-the-counter. There was a forest within walking distance where an actual hermit lived, and my brother and I spent hours there, spying on him from the underbrush. By now I could read and enjoy comic books in French and of course I was eating—*really* eating. Murky brown soupe de poisson, tomato salad, moules marinieres, poulet basquaise (we were only a few miles from the Basque country). We made day trips to Cap Ferret, a wild, deserted and breathtakingly magnificent Atlantic beach with big rolling waves, taking along baguettes and saucissons and wheels of cheese, wine and Evian (bottled water was at that time unheard of back home). A few miles west was Lac Cazeaux, a fresh-water lake where my brother and I could rent *pédalo* watercraft and pedal our way around the deep.

We ate gaufres, delicious hot waffles, covered in whipped cream and powdered sugar. The two hot songs of that summer on the Cazeaux jukebox were 'Whiter Shade of Pale' by Procol Harum, and 'These Boots Were Made for Walkin' by Nancy Sinatra. The French played those two songs over and over again, the music punctuated by the sonic booms from French air force jets which would swoop over the lake on their way to a nearby bombing range. With all the rock and roll, good stuff to eat and high-explosives at hand, I was reasonably happy.

So, when our neighbor, Monsieur Saint-Jour, the oyster fisherman, invited my family out on his *pinasse* (oyster boat), I was enthusiastic.

At six in the morning, we boarded Monsieur Saint-Jour's small wooden vessel with our picnic baskets and our sensible footwear. He was a crusty old bastard, dressed like my uncle in ancient denim coveralls, espadrilles and beret. He had a leathery, tanned and windblown face, hollow cheeks, and the tiny broken blood vessels on nose and cheeks that everyone seemed to have from drinking so much of the local Bordeaux. He hadn't fully briefed his guests on what was involved in these daily travails. We put-putted out to a buoy marking his underwater oyster *parc*, a fenced-off section of bay bottom, and we sat ... and sat ... and sat, in the roaring August sun, waiting for the tide to go out. The idea was to float the boat over the stockaded fence walls, then sit there until the boat slowly sank with the water level, until it rested on the *bassin* floor. At this point, Monsieur Saint-Jour, and his guests presumably, would rake the oysters, collect a few good specimens for sale in port, and remove any parasites that might be endangering his crop.

There was, I recall, still about two feet of water left to go before the hull of the boat settled on dry ground and we could walk about the *parc*. We'd already polished off the Brie and baguettes and downed the Evian, but I was still hungry, and characteristically said so.

Monsieur Saint-Jour, on hearing this—as if challenging his American passengers—inquired in his thick Girondais accent, if any of us would care to try an oyster.

My parents hesitated. I doubt they'd realized they might actually have to *eat* one of the raw, slimy things we were currently floating over. My little brother recoiled in horror.

But I, in the proudest moment of my young life, stood up smartly, grinning with defiance, and volunteered to be the first.

And in that unforgettably sweet moment in my personal history, that one moment still more alive for me than so many of the other 'firsts' which followed—first pussy, first joint, first day in high school, first published book, or any other thing—I attained glory. Monsieur Saint-Jour beckoned me over to the gunwale, where he leaned over, reached down until his head nearly disappeared underwater, and emerged holding a single silt-encrusted oyster, huge and irregularly shaped, in his rough, claw-like fist. With a snubby, rust-covered oyster knife, he popped the thing open and handed it to me, everyone watching now, my little brother shrinking away from this glistening, vaguely sexual-looking object, still dripping and nearly alive.

I took it in my hand, tilted the shell back into my mouth as instructed by the by now beaming Monsieur Saint-Jour, and with one bite and a slurp, wolfed it down. It tasted of seawater ... of brine and flesh ... and somehow ... of the future.

Everything was different now. Everything.

I'd not only survived—I'd *enjoyed*.

This, I knew, was the magic I had until now been only dimly and spitefully aware of. I was hooked. My parents' shudders, my little brother's expression of unrestrained revulsion and amazement only reinforced the sense that I had, somehow, become a man. I had had an *adventure*, tasted forbidden fruit, and everything that followed in my life—the food, the long and often stupid and self-destructive chase for *the next thing*, whether it was drugs or sex or some other new sensation—would all stem from this moment.

I'd learned something. Viscerally, instinctively, spiritually even in some small, precursive way, sexually—and there was no turning back. The genie was out of the bottle. My life as a cook, and as a chef, had begun.

Food had *power*.

It could inspire, astonish, shock, excite, delight and *impress*. It had the power to please me ... and others. This was valuable information.

For the rest of that summer, and in later summers, I'd often slip off by myself to the little stands by the port, where one could buy brown paper bags of unwashed, black-covered oysters by the dozen. After a few lessons from my new soul-mate, blood brother and bestest buddy, Monsieur Saint-Jour—who was now sharing his after-work bowls of sugared *vin ordinaire* with me too—I could easily open the oysters by myself, coming in from behind with the knife and popping the hinge like it was Aladdin's cave.

I'd sit in the garden among the tomatoes and the lizards and eat my oysters and drink Kronenbourgs (France was a wonderland for under-age drinkers), happily reading *Modesty Blaise* and the *Katzenjammer Kids* and the lovely hard-bound *bandes dessinées* in French, until the pictures swam in front of my eyes, smoking the occasional pilfered Gitane. And I still associate the taste of oysters with those heady, wonderful days of illicit late-afternoon buzzes. The smell of French cigarettes, the taste of beer, that unforgettable feeling of doing something I shouldn't be doing.

I had, as yet, no plans to cook professionally. But I frequently look back at my life, searching for that fork in the road, trying to figure out where, exactly, I *went bad* and became a thrill-seeking, pleasure-hungry sensualist, always looking to shock, amuse, terrify and manipulate, seeking to fill that empty spot in my soul with something new.

I like to think it was Monsieur Saint-Jour's fault. But of course, it was me all along.

# Abdulrazak Gurnah

## 2001

## *By the Sea*

And my name is Rajab Shaaban. It is not my real name, but a name I borrowed for the occasion of this life-saving trip. It belonged to someone I knew for many years. Shaaban is also the name of the eighth month of the year, the month of division, when the destinies of the coming year are fixed and the sins of the truly penitent are absolved. It precedes the month of Ramadhan, the month of the great heat, the month of fasting. Rajab is the month which precedes both, the seventh month, the revered month. It was during Rajab that the night of the Miraj occurred, when the Prophet was taken through the seven heavens to the Presence of God. How we loved that story when we were young. On the night of the 27th of Rajab, the Prophet was sleeping when the Angel Jibreel woke him and made him mount the winged beast Burakh, who took him through the sky to al-Quds, Jerusalem. There, in the ruins of the Temple Mount, he prayed with Abraham, Moses and Jesus and then ascended in their company to the Lote Tree of the Uttermost Limit, sidrat al-muntaha, which was the nearest that any being could approach the Almighty. The Prophet received God's injunction that Muslims were to pray fifty times in a day. On his way back, Moses advised him to return and haggle. He had been in the business a lot longer than the Prophet, and guessed that God would probably come down a bit. The Almighty came down to five times a day. In the telling of the story, a great sigh would issue from the congregation at this point. Imagine praying fifty times every single day. Then the Prophet returned to al-Quds and mounted the beast Burakh again, who flew him back to Makka before morning. There he had to face the inevitable carping and doubting from the benighted jahals of that town, but to the believers the miracle of the Miraj is an event of joyous cele-bration. Rajab preceded Shaaban which preceded Ramadhan, three holy months. Though God had only commanded that we fast during Ramadhan, the pious fasted throughout the three months. That was the holy joke my name-sake's parents played on him, calling him Rajab when his father's name was Shaaban, like calling him July when his father's name was August, and no doubt they had a good chuckle but he paid for it, the name. As I would have done, if my parents had really given me that name.

I didn't say any of this to Rachel Howard when she came to see me at the detention centre. I didn't say anything. To call it a detention centre is to be melodramatic. There were no locked gates or armed guards, not even a uniform in sight. It was an encampment in the countryside, which was run by a private company. There were three large structures that looked like sheds or warehouses, where they gave us a place to sleep and fed us. It was cold. The wind howled and wailed outside, gusting at times as if it would lift the whole building and hurl it away. I felt as if the blood in my veins had stopped flowing, had turned into sharp-edged crystals which bit into my inner flesh. When I stopped moving my limbs went numb. We slept in two of the buildings, twelve in one and ten in the other, our sleeping spaces partitioned with boards but without doors. Each building had a toilet and a shower, and a separate tap labelled 'Drinking Water'. I wondered about that, and whether it meant I should use the shower with circumspection, whether the water was safe. We ate in the third building, food delivered to us in a van in large square metal containers. It was served to us by a middle-aged Englishman of crumpled and gloomy appearance, not a specimen I had met yet in my travels at that point, but which I have seen in large numbers since. In fact many of the people I met in those early months surprised me in appearance. They seemed so unlike the straight-backed, unsmiling variety I remembered from years ago. Our Englishman was called Harold, and he served our food as well as cleaned the showers and the toilets in his own fashion. Another man sat in an office in a small building which also contained a public telephone, a dispensary and a consulting-room. He usually went home at night, whereas Harold slept in the building where we had our meals and seemed to be nearby at all times. There was yet another man who came to relieve Harold for a night or two, but he only came once while I was there, and kept himself out of the way, avoiding us. Harold provoked endless teasing from the detainees, which he lugubriously ignored, ticking his tasks off silently, as if consulting a list in his head. He must have seen many others like us passing through, whereas to us he was our first Englishman at such close quarters.

The sheds that accommodated us could once just as easily have contained sacks of cereals or bags of cement or some other valuable commodity that needed to be kept secure and out of the rain. Now they contained us, a casual and valueless nuisance that had to be kept in restraint. The man in the office took away our money and our papers, and told us we could take a walk in the countryside if we needed exercise, so long as we stayed within sight of the camp, in case we got lost. 'If you got lost, there'd be no one to come and find you,' he said, 'and it gets cold out there at night, and some of you lads aren't used to that.' It would get colder, I had known that all along. Napoleon's retreat from Moscow was not until February or March, and everything was frozen then. General Winter at the head of the Russian offensive. I arrived in November, three months before February, and it was already unbearably cold with months of deepening winter still ahead of us. It would get colder.

There were twenty-two men in the camp. The twelve in our building were four Algerians, three Ethiopians, two Iranian brothers just out of their teens, who clung to each other and whispered and sobbed in the night before they fell asleep in the same bed, a Sudanese and an Angolan, who was the dynamo and live-wire of our establishment, bursting with advice, with jokes, with politics, with deals, with the righteousness of Unita's cause in the war. No Nigerians here, the Angolan told us. Too many of them in detention and they're too much trouble, so they have to be kept under lock and key in an old castle in the frozen north, away from human habitation. Too many of them in the world altogether. His name was Alfonso, and he had a deep and unrelenting antipathy to Nigerians, which he did not explain but which illuminated every day of his life, it seemed. He had been in the camp, the barracks as he preferred to call it, for several weeks. He refused to be moved, saying he needed the seclusion and the rural air to finish the book he was writing. If he went and mingled with the English in the streets and spent all his evenings in their pubs watching football on TV, he would lose the edge of his recollections and there would be no point to anything he had done. He liked it there in the barracks among his rootless brethren, thank you. The detainees in the other building were all from south Asia, from India and Sri Lanka, and perhaps people of Indian origin from elsewhere. I don't know. They conducted their affairs separately from us, sat together as a group during meals, and seemed to have a language with which to speak to one another which was not comprehensible to the rest of us.

It was to the small building, which contained a dispensary, an office and some kind of consulting-room, that I was summoned to meet Rachel Howard.

'I understand you don't speak any English,' she said, consulting her papers and then smiling at me with an intense burst of goodwill, ardently requiring me to understand her despite my apparent lack of the language. It was early days, and I was not ready to be questioned and documented, and perhaps to be moved somewhere else. I had been in the camp two days and I liked it there despite the numbed feelings in my legs. I liked the spongy greenness of the countryside, which looked as if it had some give in it. I liked the drift of muffled rumbles and crashes in the sodden air, which made me slightly apprehensive at first because I thought they were the distant pounding of the sea but which I guessed only much later to have been the noise of traffic on a big road near by. I enjoyed Alfonso and his anarchic joy, the Ethiopians and their fragile silences, policing some secret under- standing between themselves, the Algerians and their mannered courtesies, their chortling mockery of each other, their endless whisperings, the Sudanese, serious and intimidated, and the two Iranian boys deep in their fertile miseries. I did not feel ready to be rescued yet from these only just visible lives.

They shuffled themselves to make room for me, calling me shebe, agha, old man, mister. What's brought you all this way so far from God and your loved ones, ya habibi? Don't you know the damp climate and the cold could damage someone with bones as fragile and ancient as your own? That is what I imagined them saying, because none of us apart from Alfonso spoke English to each other, and Alfonso didn't seem to care who listened to him or who understood him, waving his arms about, acting out his comedies, ignoring what sometimes felt to me like the unkind laughter of the others, especially the scorn- ful Algerians. I suspected they thought themselves nobler than this loquacious black man who carried himself with such confi- dence. Alfonso rattled on regardless, as if nothing could ever hurt him or molest him, as if he had no control over the mean little demons that kept him chattering so frantically.

I, on the other hand, was still not sure why the man who had sold me the ticket had advised that I did not speak English, or when it would be wise to admit that I did. And I was also unsure if the ignorance of English of my fellow camp-dwellers was similarly strategic, if they knew the reason for pretending not to speak it or if they too were acting on canny advice from another ticket-seller from elsewhere. Perhaps they feared that the one reckless English-speaker among us was some kind of informer, a thought that had occurred to me too, and they were sitting skut sakit until the danger was past. We were all fleeing places where authority required full submission and grovelling fear, and since this was not enforceable without daily floggings and public beheadings, its servants, its police and army and security appar- atus carried out repeated acts of petty malice to demonstrate the jeopardy of reckless insurrection. How could I guess the manner of infringement that would infuriate the doorkeepers of this estate? I did not wish to get caught out through lack of a proper exercise of cunning and find myself transferred to an old castle in the freezing north, or worse still, find myself on the plane making the return journey. It was altogether too soon to give up the deception, even though I would have enjoyed the drama of startling Rachel Howard's ardent smile from its attractive perch. Instead I shook my head and shrugged slowly, unaggressively, and smiled a helpless foreigner smile at her.

Her hair was black and curly, worn in a style that was deliberately unruly and tangled. It gave her appearance a touch of gaiety and youth, and made her look dark and a little foreign, both of which were no doubt intended. She frowned at her papers, leaning forward, while I sat silently in front of her. Then she looked up and smiled, and I thought that would be it until she could bring back an interpreter. She nodded vigorously to reassure me and then grabbed her hair with both hands and pulled it off her face. 'Now what?' she said, holding on to her hair with both hands and giving me a long look. I couldn't tell whether she was familiar with this ruse of not speaking English and wished to let me know that she was, or whether the look of cunning on her face was relish for a deepening intrigue. She stood up and walked away from the table, and turned to look back at me. I saw then that she had not really seen me, that the crafty look was turned inwards on the ways and means at her disposal. She was neither tall nor strongly built, but her movements had a supple assurance which suggested physical strength. Compact shoulders, probably a regular swimmer. 'We'll have to have you moved somewhere where you can have classes. Get you out of this detention centre, anyway. I don't think that will be too hard, because of your age, you see. That's the first thing we've got to do, arrange for you to be moved to the care of our area authority.'

She frowned, not seeing me, perhaps unsure what she should do next, unable to tell me in words what she was planning for me, concerned to make me feel that she was caring and that she was efficient. But she was not seeing me yet, she was looking inwards. I guessed she was the same age as my daughter, mid thirties, the same age as my daughter would have been. It seems absurd to call her mine. She didn't live long, she died. Rachel Howard came back to the table and sat down opposite me. I raised my eyes to hers, to let her know that I was there, and she did not become perturbed but sat silently taking me in. Then she reached out and put her hand on my arm. 'Sixty-five, that's a fine age to run away from home,' she said, smiling. 'What could you have been thinking of?'

I liked that she had made me think of my daughter, and that the thought had come not as a recollection of blame or pain but as a small pleasure amidst so much that was exotic and strange. Raiiya, that was what I called her, an ordinary citizen, a common indigene. Her mother thought the name a provocation, and certain to be an embarrassment to her when she grew up, so she called her Ruqiya after the Prophet's daughter with Khadija, his first wife and his benefactor. But she did not live long, she died. Rahmatullah alaiha.

'We'll have to see if we can find an interpreter,' Rachel Howard said, nodding encouragingly because I had spoken those last two words aloud, invoking God's mercy on her soul when it was God and his angels who took her away before she could even become a citizen, and then took her mother away too, may God have mercy on her soul, while I neither knew nor was there.

'Don't you understand *any* English? Never mind, we'll get you to school when we get you out of here. I think it's hard to learn when you're a certain age,' she said, smiling again at the thought of my age. 'Never mind, we'll get you out of here first of all. You'll like it there, where we're going. It's a small town by the sea. In a few days. We'll find you a bed and breakfast and get you fixed up with Social Security and all that. Then we'll find an interpreter. Do you have any relatives or friends? Oh I really hope so. It's hard enough as it is, but at your age.'

A small town by the sea. Yes, I'll like that, I thought. In a few days.

# Jeffrey Eugenides

## 2002

## *Middlesex*

I was born twice: first, as a baby girl, on a remarkably smogless Detroit day in January of 1960; and then again, as a teenage boy, in an emergency room near Petoskey, Michigan, in August of 1974. Specialized readers may have come across me in Dr. Peter Luce's study, "Gender Identity in 5-Alpha-Reductase Pseudohermaphrodites", published in the *Journal of Pediatric Endocrinology* in 1975. Or maybe you've seen my photograph in chapter sixteen of the now sadly outdated *Genetics and Heredity*. That's me on page 578, standing naked beside a height chart with a black box covering my eyes.

My birth certificate lists my name as Calliope Helen Stephanides. My most recent driver's license (from the Federal Republic of Germany) records my first name simply as Cal. I'm a former field hockey goalie, long-standing member of the Save-the-Manatee Foundation, rare attendant at the Greek Orthodox liturgy, and, for most of my adult life, an employee of the U.S. State Department. Like Tiresias, I was first one thing and then the other. I've been ridiculed by classmates, guinea-pigged by doctors, palpated by specialists, and researched by the March of Dimes. A redheaded girl from Grosse Pointe fell in love with me, not knowing what I was. (Her brother liked me, too.) An army tank led me into urban battle once; a swimming pool turned me into myth; I've left my body in order to occupy others—and all this happened before I turned sixteen.

But now, at the age of forty-one, I feel another birth coming on. After decades of neglect, I find myself thinking about departed great-aunts and -uncles, long-lost grandfathers, unknown fifth cousins, or, in the case of an inbred family like mine, all those things in one. And so before it's too late I want to get it down for good: this rollercoaster ride of a single gene through time. Sing now, O Muse, of the recessive mutation on my fifth chromosome! Sing how it bloomed two and a half centuries ago on the slopes of Mount Olympus, while the goats bleated and the olives dropped. Sing how it passed down through nine generations, gathering invisibly within the polluted pool of the Stephanides family. And sing how Providence, in the guise of a massacre, sent the gene flying again; how it blew like a seed across the sea to America, where it drifted through our industrial rains until it fell to earth in the fertile soil of my mother's own mid-western womb.

Sorry if I get a little Homeric at times. That's genetic, too.

Three months before I was born, in the aftermath of one of our elaborate Sunday dinners, my grandmother Desdemona Stephanides ordered my brother to get her silkworm box. Chapter Eleven had been heading toward the kitchen for a second helping of rice pudding when she blocked his way. At fifty-seven, with her short, squat figure and intimidating hairnet, my grandmother was perfectly designed for blocking people's paths. Behind her in the kitchen, the day's large female contingent had congregated, laughing and whispering. Intrigued, Chapter Eleven leaned sideways to see what was going on, but Desdemona reached out and firmly pinched his cheek. Having regained his attention, she sketched a rectangle in the air and pointed at the ceiling. Then, through her ill-fitting dentures, she said, "Go for *yia yia*, dolly *mou*."

Chapter Eleven knew what to do. He ran across the hall into the living room. On all fours he scrambled up the formal staircase to the second floor. He raced past the bedrooms along the upstairs corridor. At the far end was a nearly invisible door, wallpapered over like the entrance to a secret passageway. Chapter Eleven located the tiny doorknob level with his head and, using all his strength, pulled it open. Another set of stairs lay behind it. For a long moment my brother stared hesitantly into the darkness above, before climbing, very slowly now, up to the attic where my grandparents lived.

In sneakers he passed beneath the twelve damply newspapered birdcages suspended from the rafters. With a brave face he immersed himself in the sour odor of the parakeets, and in my grandparents' own particular aroma, a mixture of mothballs and hashish. He negotiated his way past my grandfather's book-piled desk and his collection of rebetika records. Finally, bumping into the leather ottoman and the circular coffee table made of brass, he found my grandparents' bed and, under it, the silkworm box.

Carved from olivewood, a little bigger than a shoe box, it had a tin lid perforated by tiny airholes and inset with the icon of an unrecognizable saint. The saint's face had been rubbed off, but the fingers of his right hand were raised to bless a short, purple, terrifically self-confident-looking mulberry tree. After gazing awhile at this vivid botanical presence, Chapter Eleven pulled the box from under the bed and opened it. Inside were the two wedding crowns made from rope and, coiled like snakes, the two long braids of hair, each tied with a crumbling black ribbon. He poked one of the braids with his index finger. Just then a parakeet squawked, making my brother jump, and he closed the box, tucked it under his arm, and carried it downstairs to Desdemona.

She was still waiting in the doorway. Taking the silkworm box out of his hands, she turned back into the kitchen. At this point Chapter Eleven was granted a view of the room, where all the women now fell silent. They moved aside to let Desdemona pass and there, in the middle of the linoleum, was my mother. Tessie Stephanides was leaning back in a kitchen chair, pinned beneath the immense, drum-tight globe of her pregnant belly. She had a happy, helpless expression on her face, which was flushed and hot. Desdemona set the silkworm box on the kitchen table and opened the lid. She reached under the wedding crowns and the hair braids to come up with something Chapter Eleven hadn't seen: a silver spoon. She tied a piece of string to the spoon's handle. Then, stooping forward, she dangled the spoon over my mother's swollen belly. And, by extension, over me.

Up until now Desdemona had had a perfect record: twenty-three correct guesses. She'd known that Tessie was going to be Tessie. She'd predicted the sex of my brother and of all the babies of her friends at church. The only children whose genders she hadn't divined were her own, because it was bad luck for a mother to plumb the mysteries of her own womb. Fearlessly, however, she plumbed my mother's. After some initial hesitation, the spoon swung north to south, which meant that I was going to be a boy.

Splay-legged in the chair, my mother tried to smile. She didn't want a boy. She had one already. In fact, she was so certain I was going to be a girl that she'd picked out only one name for me: Calliope. But when my grandmother shouted in Greek, "A boy!" the cry went around the room, and out into the hall, and across the hall into the living room where the men were arguing politics. And my mother, hearing it repeated so many times, began to believe it might be true.

As soon as the cry reached my father, however, he marched into the kitchen to tell his mother that, this time at least, her spoon was wrong. "And how you know so much?" Desdemona asked him. To which he replied what many Americans of his generation would have:

"It's science, Ma."

Ever since they had decided to have another child—the diner was doing well and Chapter Eleven was long out of diapers—Milton and Tessie had been in agreement that they wanted a daughter. Chapter Eleven had just turned five years old. He'd recently found a dead bird in the yard, bringing it into the house to show his mother. He liked shooting things, hammering things, smashing things, and wrestling with his father. In such a masculine household, Tessie had begun to feel like the odd woman out and saw herself in ten years' time imprisoned in a world of hubcaps and hernias. My mother pictured a daughter as a counterinsurgent: a fellow lover of lapdogs, a seconder of proposals to attend the Ice Capades. In the spring of 1959, when discussions of my fertilization got under way, my mother couldn't foresee that women would soon be burning their brassieres by the thousand. Hers were padded, stiff, fire-retardant. As much as Tessie loved her son, she knew there were certain things she'd be able to share only with a daughter.

On his morning drive to work, my father had been seeing visions of an irresistibly sweet, dark-eyed little girl. She sat on the seat beside him—mostly during stoplights—directing questions at his patient, all-knowing ear. "What do you call that thing, Daddy?" "That? That's the Cadillac seal." "What's the Cadillac seal?" "Well, a long time ago, there was a French explorer named Cadillac, and he was the one who discovered Detroit. And that seal was his family seal, from France." "What's France?" "France is a country in Europe." "What's Europe?" "It's a continent, which is like a great big piece of land, way, way bigger than a country. But Cadillacs don't come from Europe anymore, *kukla*. They come from right here in the good old U.S.A." The light turned green and he drove on. But my prototype lingered. She was there at the next light and the next. So pleasant was her company that my father, a man loaded with initiative, decided to see what he could do to turn his vision into reality.

Thus: for some time now, in the living room where the men discussed politics, they had also been discussing the velocity of sperm. Peter Tatakis, "Uncle Pete," as we called him, was a leading member of the debating society that formed every week on our black love seats. A lifelong bachelor, he had no family in America and so had become attached to ours. Every Sunday he arrived in his wine-dark Buick, a tall, prune-faced, sad-seeming man with an incongruously vital head of wavy hair. He was not interested in children. A proponent of the Great Books series—which he had read twice—Uncle Pete was engaged with serious thought and Italian opera. He had a passion, in history, for Edward Gibbon, and, in literature, for the journals of Madame de Staël. He liked to quote that witty lady's opinion on the German language, which held that German wasn't good for conversation because you had to wait to the end of the sentence for the verb, and so couldn't interrupt. Uncle Pete had wanted to become a doctor, but the "catastrophe" had ended that dream. In the United States, he'd put himself through two years of chiro-practic school, and now ran a small office in Birmingham with a human skeleton he was still paying for in installments. In those days, chiropractors had a somewhat dubious reputation. People didn't come to Uncle Pete to free up their kundalini. He cracked necks, straightened spines, and made custom arch supports out of foam rubber. Still, he was the closest thing to a doctor we had in the house on those Sunday afternoons. As a young man he'd had half his stomach surgically removed, and now after dinner always drank a Pepsi-Cola to help digest his meal. The soft drink had been named for the digestive enzyme pepsin, he sagely told us, and so was suited to the task.

It was this kind of knowledge that led my father to trust what Uncle Pete said when it came to the reproductive timetable. His head on a throw pillow, his shoes off, *Madame Butterfly* softly playing on my parents' stereo, Uncle Pete explained that, under the microscope, sperm carrying male chromosomes had been observed to swim faster than those carrying female chromo-somes. This assertion generated immediate merriment among the restaurant owners and fur finishers assembled in our living room. My father, however, adopted the pose of his favorite piece of sculpture, *The Thinker*, a miniature of which sat across the room on the telephone table. Though the topic had been brought up in the open-forum atmosphere of those postprandial Sundays, it was clear that, notwithstanding the impersonal tone of the discussion, the sperm they were talking about was my father's. Uncle Pete made it clear: to have a girl baby, a couple should "have sexual congress twenty-four hours prior to ovula-tion." That way, the swift male sperm would rush in and die off.

The female sperm, sluggish but more reliable, would arrive just as the egg dropped.

My father had trouble persuading my mother to go along with the scheme. Tessie Zizmo had been a virgin when she married Milton Stephanides at the age of twenty-two. Their engagement, which coincided with the Second World War, had been a chaste affair. My mother was proud of the way she'd managed to simultaneously kindle and snuff my father's flame, keeping him at a low burn for the duration of a global cataclysm. This hadn't been all that difficult, however, since she was in Detroit and Milton was in Annapolis at the U.S. Naval Academy. For more than a year Tessie lit candles at the Greek church for her fiancé, while Milton gazed at her photographs pinned over his bunk. He liked to pose Tessie in the manner of the movie magazines, standing sideways, one high heel raised on a step, an expanse of black stocking visible. My mother looks surprisingly pliable in those old snapshots, as though she liked nothing better than to have her man in uniform arrange her against the porches and lampposts of their humble neighborhood.

She didn't surrender until after Japan had. Then, from their wedding night onward (according to what my brother told my covered ears), my parents made love regularly and enjoyably. When it came to having children, however, my mother had her own ideas. It was her belief that an embryo could sense the amount of love with which it had been created. For this reason, my father's suggestion didn't sit well with her.

"What do you think this is, Milt, the Olympics?"

"We were just speaking theoretically," said my father.

"What does Uncle Pete know about having babies?"

"He read this particular article in *Scientific American*," Milton said. And to bolster his case: "He's a subscriber."

"Listen, if my back went out, I'd go to Uncle Pete. If I had flat feet like you do, I'd go. But that's it."

"This has all been verified. Under the microscope. The male sperms are faster."

"I bet they're stupider, too."

"Go on. Malign the male sperms all you want. Feel free. We don't want a male sperm. What we want is a good old, slow, reliable female sperm."

"Even if it's true, it's still ridiculous. I can't just do it like clockwork, Milt."

"It'll be harder on me than you."

"I don't want to hear it."

"I thought you wanted a daughter."

"I do."

"Well," said my father, "this is how we can get one."

Tessie laughed the suggestion off. But behind her sarcasm was a serious moral reservation. To tamper with something as mysterious and miraculous as the birth of a child was an act of hubris. In the first place, Tessie didn't believe you could do it. Even if you could, she didn't believe you should try.

Of course, a narrator in my position (prefetal at the time) can't be entirely sure about any of this. I can only explain the scientific mania that overtook my father during that spring of '59 as a symptom of the belief in progress that was infecting everyone back then. Remember, *Sputnik* had been launched only two years earlier. Polio, which had kept my parents quarantined indoors during the summers of their childhood, had been conquered by the Salk vaccine. People had no idea that viruses were cleverer than human beings, and thought they'd soon be a thing of the past. In that optimistic, postwar America, which I caught the tail end of, everybody was the master of his own destiny, so it only followed that my father would try to be the master of his.

A few days after he had broached his plan to Tessie, Milton came home one evening with a present. It was a jewelry box tied with a ribbon.

"What's this for?" Tessie asked suspiciously.

"What do you mean, what is it for?"

"It's not my birthday. It's not our anniversary. So why are you giving me a present?"

"Do I have to have a reason to give you a present? Go on. Open it."

Tessie crumpled up one corner of her mouth, unconvinced. But it was difficult to hold a jewelry box in your hand without opening it. So finally she slipped off the ribbon and snapped the box open.

Inside, on black velvet, was a thermometer.

"A thermometer," said my mother.

"That's not just any thermometer," said Milton. "I had to go to three different pharmacies to find one of these."

"A luxury model, huh?"

"That's right," said Milton. "That's what you call a basal thermometer. It reads the temperature down to *a tenth of a degree.*" He raised his eyebrows. "Normal thermometers only read every two tenths. This one does it every tenth. Try it out. Put it in your mouth."

"I don't have a fever," said Tessie.

"This isn't about a fever. You use it to find out what your base temperature is. It's more accurate and precise than a regular fever-type thermometer."

"Next time bring me a necklace."

But Milton persisted: "Your body temperature's changing all the time, Tess. You may not notice, but it is. You're in constant flux, temperature-wise. Say, for instance"—a little cough—"you happen to be ovulating. Then your temperature goes up. Six tenths of a degree, in most case scenarios. Now," my father went on, gaining steam, not noticing that his wife was frowning, "if we were to implement the system we talked about the other day—just for instance, say—what you'd do is, *first,* establish your *base temperature.* It might not be ninety-eight point six. Everybody's a little different. That's another thing I learned from Uncle Pete. Anyway, once you established your *base temperature,* then you'd look for that six-tenths-degree rise. And that's when, if we were to go through with this, that's when we'd know to, you know, mix the cocktail."

My mother said nothing. She only put the thermometer into the box, closed it, and handed it back to her husband.

"Okay," he said. "Fine. Suit yourself. We may get another boy. Number two. If that's the way you want it, that's the way it'll be."

"I'm not so sure we're going to have anything at the moment," replied my mother.

Meanwhile, in the greenroom to the world, I waited. Not even a gleam in my father's eye yet (he was staring gloomily at the thermometer case in his lap). Now my mother gets up from the so-called love seat. She heads for the stairway, holding a hand to her forehead, and the likelihood of my ever coming to be seems more and more remote. Now my father gets up to make his rounds, turning out lights, locking doors. As he climbs the stairway, there's hope for me again. The timing of the thing had to be just so in order for me to become the person I am. Delay the act by an hour and you change the gene selection. My conception was still weeks away, but already my parents had begun their slow collision into each other. In our upstairs hallway, the Acropolis night-light is burning, a gift from Jackie Halas, who owns a souvenir shop. My mother is at her vanity when my father enters the bedroom. With two fingers she rubs Noxzema into her face, wiping it off with a tissue. My father had only to say an affectionate word and she would have forgiven him. Not me but somebody like me might have been made that night. An infinite number of possible selves crowded the threshold, me among them but with no guaranteed ticket, the hours moving slowly, the planets in the heavens circling at their usual pace, weather coming into it, too, because my mother was afraid of thunderstorms and would have cuddled against my father had it rained that night. But, no, clear skies held out, as did my parents' stubbornness. The bedroom light went out. They stayed on their own sides of the bed. At last, from my mother, "Night." And from my father, "See you in the morning." The moments that led up to me fell into place as though decreed. Which, I guess, is why I think about them so much.

★

The following Sunday, my mother took Desdemona and my brother to church. My father never went along, having become an apostate at the age of eight over the exorbitant price of votive candles. Likewise, my grandfather preferred to spend his mornings working on a modern Greek translation of the "restored" poems of Sappho. For the next seven years, despite repeated strokes, my grandfather worked at a small desk, piecing together the legendary fragments into a larger mosaic, adding a stanza here, a coda there, soldering an anapest or an iamb. In the evenings he played his bordello music and smoked a hookah pipe.

In 1959, Assumption Greek Orthodox Church was located on Charlevoix. It was there that I would be baptized less than a year later and would be brought up in the Orthodox faith. Assumption, with its revolving chief priests, each sent to us via the Patriarchate in Constantinople, each arriving in the full beard of his authority, the embroidered vestments of his sanctity, but each wearying after a time—six months was the rule—because of the squabbling of the congregation, the personal attacks on the way he sang, the constant need to shush the parishioners who treated the church like the bleachers at Tiger Stadium, and, finally, the effort of delivering a sermon each week twice, first in Greek and then again in English. Assumption, with its spirited coffee hours, its bad foundation and roof leaks, its strenuous ethnic festivals, its catechism classes where our heritage was briefly kept alive in us before being allowed to die in the great diaspora. Tessie and company advanced down the central aisle, past the sand-filled trays of votive candles. Above, as big as a float in the Macy's Thanksgiving Day Parade, was the Christ Pantocrator. He curved across the dome like space itself. Unlike the suffering, earthbound Christs depicted at eye level on the church walls, our Christ Pantocrator was clearly transcendent, all-powerful, heaven-bestriding. He was reaching down to the apostles above the altar to present the four rolled-up sheepskins of the Gospels. And my mother, who tried all her life to believe in God without ever quite succeeding, looked up at him for guidance.

The Christ Pantocrator's eyes flickered in the dim light. They seemed to suck Tessie upward. Through the swirling incense, the Savior's eyes glowed like televisions flashing scenes of recent events ...

First there was Desdemona the week before, giving advice to her daughter-in-law. "Why you want more children, Tessie?" she had asked with studied nonchalance. Bending to look in the oven, hiding the alarm on her face (an alarm that would go unexplained for another sixteen years), Desdemona waved the idea away. "More children, more trouble ... "

Next there was Dr. Philobosian, our elderly family physician. With ancient diplomas behind him, the old doctor gave his verdict. "Nonsense. Male sperm swim faster? Listen. The first person who saw sperm under a microscope was Leeuwenhoek. Do you know what they looked like to him? Like worms ... "

And then Desdemona was back, taking a different angle: "God decides what baby is. Not you ... "

These scenes ran through my mother's mind during the interminable Sunday service. The congregation stood and sat. In the front pew, my cousins, Socrates, Plato, Aristotle, and Cleopatra, fidgeted. Father Mike emerged from behind the icon screen and swung his censer. My mother tried to pray, but it was no use. She barely survived until coffee hour.

From the tender age of twelve, my mother had been unable to start her day without the aid of at least two cups of immoderately strong, tar-black, unsweetened coffee, a taste for which she had picked up from the tugboat captains and zooty bachelors who filled the boardinghouse where she had grown up. As a high school girl, standing five foot one inch tall, she had sat next to auto workers at the corner diner, having coffee before her first class. While they scanned the racing forms, Tessie finished her civics homework. Now, in the church basement, she told Chapter Eleven to run off and play with the other children while she got a cup of coffee to restore herself.

She was on her second cup when a soft, womanly voice sighed in her ear. "Good morning, Tessie." It was her brother-in-law, Father Michael Antoniou.

"Hi, Father Mike. Beautiful service today," Tessie said, and immediately regretted it. Father Mike was the assistant priest at Assumption. When the last priest had left, harangued back to Athens after a mere three months, the family had hoped that Father Mike might be promoted. But in the end another new, foreign-born priest, Father Gregorios, had been given the post. Aunt Zo, who never missed a chance to lament her marriage, had said at dinner in her comedienne's voice, "My husband. Always the bridesmaid and never the bride."

By complimenting the service, Tessie hadn't intended to compliment Father Greg. The situation was made still more delicate by the fact that, years ago, Tessie and Michael Antoniou had been engaged to be married. Now she was married to Milton and Father Mike was married to Milton's sister. Tessie had come down to clear her head and have her coffee and already the day was getting out of hand.

Father Mike didn't appear to notice the slight, however. He stood smiling, his eyes gentle above the roaring waterfall of his beard. A sweet-natured man, Father Mike was popular with church widows. They liked to crowd around him, offering him cookies and bathing in his beatific essence. Part of this essence came from Father Mike's perfect contentment at being only five foot four. His shortness had a charitable aspect to it, as though he had given away his height. He seemed to have forgiven Tessie for breaking off their engagement years ago, but it was always there in the air between them, like the talcum powder that sometimes puffed out of his clerical collar.

Smiling, carefully holding his coffee cup and saucer, Father Mike asked, "So, Tessie, how are things at home?"

My mother knew, of course, that as a weekly Sunday guest at our house, Father Mike was fully informed about the thermometer scheme. Looking in his eyes, she thought she detected a glint of amusement.

"You're coming over to the house today," she said carelessly. "You can see for yourself."

"I'm looking forward to it," said Father Mike. "We always have such interesting discussions at your house."

Tessie examined Father Mike's eyes again but now they seemed full of genuine warmth. And then something happened to take her attention away from Father Mike completely.

Across the room, Chapter Eleven had stood on a chair to reach the tap of the coffee urn. He was trying to fill a coffee cup, but once he got the tap open he couldn't get it closed. Scalding coffee poured out across the table. The hot liquid splattered a girl who was standing nearby. The girl jumped back. Her mouth opened, but no sound came out. With great speed my mother ran across the room and whisked the girl into the ladies' room.

No one remembers the girl's name. She didn't belong to any of the regular parishioners. She wasn't even Greek. She appeared at church that one day and never again, and seems to have existed for the sole purpose of changing my mother's mind. In the bath-room the girl held her steaming shirt away from her body while Tessie brought damp towels. "Are you okay, honey? Did you get burned?"

"He's very clumsy, that boy," the girl said.

"He can be. He gets into everything."

"Boys can be very obstreperous."

Tessie smiled. "You have quite a vocabulary."

At this compliment the girl broke into a big smile. "'Obstreperous' is my favorite word. My brother is very obstrep-erous. Last month my favorite word was 'turgid'. But you can't use 'turgid' that much. Not that many things are turgid, when you think about it."

"You're right about that," said Tessie, laughing. "But obstrep-erous is all over the place."

"I couldn't agree with you more," said the girl.

★

Two weeks later. Easter Sunday, 1959. Our religion's adherence to the Julian calendar has once again left us out of sync with the neighborhood. Two Sundays ago, my brother watched as the other kids on the block hunted multicolored eggs in nearby bushes. He saw his friends eating the heads off chocolate bunnies and tossing handfuls of jelly beans into cavity-rich mouths. (Standing at the window, my brother wanted more than anything to believe in an American God who got resurrected on the right day.) Only yesterday was Chapter Eleven finally allowed to dye his own eggs, and then only in one color: red. All over the house red eggs gleam in lengthening, solstice rays. Red eggs fill bowls on the dining room table. They hang from string pouches over doorways. They crowd the mantel and are baked into loaves of cruciform *tsoureki*.

But now it is late afternoon; dinner is over. And my brother is smiling. Because now comes the one part of Greek Easter he prefers to egg hunts and jelly beans: the egg-cracking game. Everyone gathers around the dining table. Biting his lip, Chapter Eleven selects an egg from the bowl, studies it, returns it. He selects another. "This looks like a good one," Milton says, choosing his own egg. "Built like a Brinks truck." Milton holds his egg up. Chapter Eleven prepares to attack. When suddenly my mother taps my father on the back.

"Just a minute, Tessie. We're cracking eggs here."

She taps him harder.

"What?"

"My temperature." She pauses. "It's up six tenths."

She has been using the thermometer. This is the first my father has heard of it.

"Now?" my father whispers. "Jesus, Tessie, are you sure?"

"No, I'm not sure. You told me to watch for any rise in my temperature and I'm telling you I'm up six tenths of a degree." And, lowering her voice, "Plus it's been thirteen days since my last you know what."

"Come on, Dad," Chapter Eleven pleads.

"Time out," Milton says. He puts his egg in the ashtray. "That's my egg. Nobody touch it until I come back."

Upstairs, in the master bedroom, my parents accomplish the act. A child's natural decorum makes me refrain from imagining the scene in much detail. Only this: when they're done, as if topping off the tank, my father says, "That should do it." It turns out he's right. In May, Tessie learns she's pregnant, and the waiting begins.

By six weeks, I have eyes and ears. By seven, nostrils, even lips. My genitals begin to form. Fetal hormones, taking chromosomal cues, inhibit Müllerian structures, promote Wolffian ducts. My twenty-three paired chromosomes have linked up and crossed over, spinning their roulette wheel, as my *papou* puts his hand on my mother's belly and says, "Lucky two!" Arrayed in their regiments, my genes carry out their orders. All except two, a pair of miscreants—or revolutionaries, depending on your view—hiding out on chromosome number 5. Together, they siphon off an enzyme, which stops the production of a certain hormone, which complicates my life.

In the living room, the men have stopped talking about politics and instead lay bets on whether Milt's new kid will be a boy or a girl. My father is confident. Twenty-four hours after the deed, my mother's body temperature rose another two tenths, confirming ovulation. By then the male sperm had given up, exhausted. The female sperm, like tortoises, won the race. (At which point Tessie handed Milton the thermometer and told him she never wanted to see it again.)

All this led up to the day Desdemona dangled a utensil over my mother's belly. The sonogram didn't exist at the time; the spoon was the next best thing. Desdemona crouched. The kitchen grew silent. The other women bit their lower lips, watching, waiting. For the first minute, the spoon didn't move at all. Desdemona's hand shook and, after long seconds had passed, Aunt Lina steadied it. The spoon twirled; I kicked; my mother cried out. And then, slowly, moved by a wind no one felt, in that unearthly Ouija-board way, the silver spoon began to move, to swing, at first in a small circle but each orbit growing gradually more elliptical until the path flattened into a straight line pointing from oven to banquette. North to south, in other words. Desdemona cried, *"Koros!"* And the room erupted with shouts of *"Koros, koros."*

That night, my father said, "Twenty-three in a row means she's bound for a fall. This time, she's wrong. Trust me."

"I don't mind if it's a boy," my mother said. "I really don't. As long as it's healthy, ten fingers, ten toes."

"What's this 'it'. That's my daughter you're talking about."

I was born a week after New Year's, on January 8, 1960. In the waiting room, supplied only with pink-ribboned cigars, my father cried out, "Bingo!" I was a girl. Nineteen inches long. Seven pounds four ounces.

That same January 8, my grandfather suffered the first of his thirteen strokes. Awakened by my parents rushing off to the hospital, he'd gotten out of bed and gone downstairs to make himself a cup of coffee. An hour later, Desdemona found him lying on the kitchen floor. Though his mental faculties remained intact, that morning, as I let out my first cry at Women's Hospital, my *papou* lost the ability to speak. According to Desdemona, my grandfather collapsed right after overturning his coffee cup to read his fortune in the grounds.

When he heard the news of my sex, Uncle Pete refused to accept any congratulations. There was no magic involved. "Besides," he joked, "Milt did all the work." Desdemona became grim. Her American-born son had been proven right and, with this fresh defeat, the old country, in which she still tried to live despite its being four thousand miles and thirty-eight years away, receded one more notch. My arrival marked the end of her baby-guessing and the start of her husband's long decline. Though the silkworm box reappeared now and then, the spoon was no longer among its treasures.

I was extracted, spanked, and hosed off, in that order. They wrapped me in a blanket and put me on display among six other infants, four boys, two girls, all of them, unlike me, correctly tagged. This can't be true but I remember it: sparks slowly filling a dark screen.

Someone had switched on my eyes.

# Donna Tartt

## 2002

## The Little Friend

Though Allison irritated Edie, the aunts adored her, considering tranquil and even poetic many of the qualities that Edie found so frustrating. In their opinion, Allison was not only The Pretty One but The Sweet One—patient, uncomplaining, gentle with animals and old people and children—virtues which, as far as the aunts were concerned, far outshone any amount of good grades or smart talk.

Loyally, the aunts defended her. *After all that child's been through,* Tat once said fiercely to Edie. It was enough to shut Edie up, at least temporarily. For no one could forget that Allison and the baby had been the only ones out in the yard on that terrible day; and though Allison was only four, there was little doubt that she'd seen something, something most likely so horrific that it had slightly unhinged her.

Immediately after, she had been questioned rigorously by both family and police. Was somebody in the yard, a grown-up, a man, maybe? But Allison—though she had begun, inexplicably, to wet her bed, and to wake screaming in the night with ferocious terrors—refused to say yes or no. She sucked her thumb, and hugged her stuffed dog close, and would not say even her name or how old she was. Nobody—not even Libby, the gentlest and most patient of her old aunts—could coax a word from her.

Allison didn't remember her brother, and she had never recalled anything about his death. When she was little, she had lain awake sometimes after everyone else in the house had gone to sleep, staring at the jungle of shadows on the bedroom ceiling and casting her mind back as far as she was able, but searching was useless, there was nothing to find. The sweet dailiness of her early life was always there—front porch, fish pond, kitty-cat, flower beds, seamless, incandescent, immutable—but if she cast her mind back far enough she invariably reached a strange point where the yard was empty, the house echoing and abandoned, signs of a recent departure evident (clothes hanging on the line, the dishes from lunch not yet cleared away) but her whole family gone, vanished, she didn't know where, and Robin's orange cat—still a kitten then, not yet the languid, heavy-jowled tomcat he would become—gone strange, empty-eyed, wild, skittering across the lawn to dart up a tree, as frightened of her as of a stranger. She wasn't quite herself in these memories, not when they went this far back. Though she recognized very well the physical setting in which they took place—George Street, number 363, the house she'd lived in all her life—she, Allison, was not recognizable, not even to herself: she was not a toddler nor yet a baby but only a gaze, a pair of eyes that lingered in familiar surroundings and reflected upon them without person-ality, or body, or age, or past, as if she was remembering things that had happened before she was born.

Allison thought about none of this consciously except in the most vague and half-formed way. When she was small, it did not occur to her to wonder what these disembodied impressions meant and it occurred to her still less now that she was older. She scarcely thought about the past at all, and in this she differed significantly from her family, who thought of little else.

No one in her family understood this. They could not have understood even had she tried to tell them. For minds like theirs, besieged constantly by recollection, for whom present and future existed solely as schemes of recurrence, such a view of the world was beyond imagining. Memory—fragile, hazy-bright, miracu-lous—was to them the spark of life itself, and nearly every sentence of theirs began with some appeal to it: "You remem-ber that green-sprigged batiste, don't you?" her mother and her aunts would insist. "That pink floribunda? Those lemon teacakes? Remember that beautiful cold Easter, when Harriet was just a little thing, when you hunted eggs in the snow and built a big snow Easter rabbit in Adelaide's front yard?"

"Yes, yes," Allison would lie. "I remember." In a way, she did. She'd heard the stories so often that she knew them by heart, could repeat them if she wanted, sometimes even dash in a detail or two neglected in the retelling: how (for instance) she and Harriet had used pink blossoms fallen from the frost-bitten crabapples for the snow bunny's nose and ears. The stories were familiar much as stories from her mother's girlhood were familiar, or stories from books. But none of them seemed connected with her in any fundamental way.

The truth was—and this was something she had never admitted to anyone—there were an awful lot of things Allison did not remember. She had no clear memories of being in kindergarten, or the first grade, or of anything at all that she could definitely place as happening before she was eight. This was a matter of great shame, and something she tried (successfully for the most part) to conceal. Her baby sister Harriet claimed to recall things that happened before she was a year old.

Though she'd been less than six months old when Robin died, Harriet said she could remember him; and Allison and the rest of the Cleves believed that this was probably the truth. Every now and then Harriet came out with some obscure but shockingly accurate bit of information—details of weather or dress, menus from birthday parties attended before she was two—that made everyone's jaw drop.

But Allison could not remember Robin at all. This was inexcusable. She had been nearly five years old when he died. Nor could she remember the period following his death. She knew about the whole interlude, in detail—about the tears, the stuffed dog, her silences; how the Memphis detective—a big, camel-faced man with prematurely white hair named Snowy Olivet—had shown her pictures of his own daughter, named Celia, and given her Almond Joy candy bars from a wholesale box he kept in his car; how he'd shown her other pictures, too, of colored men, white men with crewcuts and heavy-lidded eyes, and how Allison had sat on Tattycorum's blue velveteen loveseat—she had been staying with Aunt Tat then, she and the baby, too, their mother was still in bed—with the tears rolling down her face, picking the chocolate off the Almond Joy bars and refusing to say a word. She knew all this not because she remembered it but because Aunt Tat had told her about it, many times, sitting in her chair pulled up close to the gas heater when Allison went to see her after school on winter afternoons, her weak old sherry-brown eyes fixed on a point across the room and her voice fond, garrulous, reminiscent, as if she were relating a story about a third party not present.

Sharp-eyed Edie was neither as fond nor as tolerant. The stories she chose to tell Allison often had a peculiar allegorical tone.

"My mother's sister," Edie would begin as she was driving Allison home from piano lessons, her eyes never leaving the road and her strong, elegant falcon's beak of a nose high in the air, "my mother's sister knew a little boy named Randall Scofield whose family was killed in a tornado. He came home from school and what do you think he saw? His house was blown to pieces and the Negroes that worked on the place had pulled the bodies of his father and his mother and his three baby brothers out of the wreck and there they all lay, bloody as could be with not even a sheet over them, stretched out breast to breast beside each other like a xylophone. One of the brothers was missing an arm and his mother had an iron doorstop embedded in her temple. Well, do you know what happened to that little boy? He was *struck dumb*. And he never said another word for the next seven years. My father said he used to always carry around a stack of shirt cardboards and a grease pencil wherever he went and he had to write down every single word he said to anybody. The man who ran the dry cleaner's in town gave him the shirt cardboards for free."

Edie liked to tell this story. There were variations, children who had gone temporarily blind or bitten their tongues off or lost their senses when confronted with sundry horrific sights.

They had a slightly accusatory note that Allison could never quite put her finger on.

Allison spent most of her time by herself. She listened to records. She made collages of pictures cut from magazines and messy candles out of melted crayons. She drew pictures of ballerinas and horses and baby mice in the margins of her geometry notebook. At lunch she sat at a table with a group of fairly popular girls, though she seldom saw them outside school. In surface ways she was one of them: she had good clothes, clear skin, lived in a big house on a nice street; and if she was not bright or vivacious, neither was there anything about her to dislike.

"You could be so popular if you wanted," said Edie, who missed not a trick when it came to social dynamics, even on the tenth-grade scale. "The most popular girl in your class, if you felt like trying."

Allison didn't want to try. She didn't want kids to be mean to her, or make fun of her, but as long as nobody bothered her she was happy. And—except for Edie—nobody did bother her much. She slept a lot. She walked to school by herself. She stopped to play with dogs she saw on the way. At night she had dreams with a yellow sky and a white thing like a sheet billowing out against it, and these distressed her greatly, but she forgot all about them as soon as she woke up.

Allison spent a lot of time with her great-aunts, on the weekends and after school. She threaded needles for them and read to them when their eyes gave out, climbed stepladders to fetch things on high dusty shelves, listened to them talk about dead schoolmates and piano recitals sixty years before. Sometimes, after school, she made candy—fudge, seafoam, divinity—for them to take to their church bazaars. She used chilled marble, a thermometer, meticulous as a chemist, following the recipe step by step, scraping the ingredients level in the measuring cup with a butter knife. The aunts—girlish themselves, rouged cheeks, curled hair, full of fun—pattered back and forth and out and through, delighted with the activity in the kitchen, calling each other by their childhood nicknames.

What a good little cook, the aunts all sang. How pretty you are. You're an angel to come see us. What a good girl. How pretty. How sweet.

---

Harriet, the baby, was neither pretty nor sweet. Harriet was smart.

From the time she was old enough to talk, Harriet had been a slightly distressing presence in the Cleve household. Fierce on the playground, rude to company, she argued with Edie and checked out library books about Genghis Khan and gave her mother headaches. She was twelve years old and in the seventh grade. Though she was an A student, the teachers had never known how to handle her. Sometimes they telephoned her mother, or Edie—who, as anyone who knew anything about the Cleves was aware, was the one you wanted to talk to; she was both field marshal and oligarch, the person of greatest power in the family and the person most likely to act. But Edie herself was uncertain how to deal with Harriet. Harriet was not disobedient, exactly, or unruly, but she was haughty, and somehow managed to irritate nearly every adult with whom she came in contact.

Harriet had none of her sister's dreamy fragility. She was sturdily built, like a small badger, with round cheeks, a sharp nose, black hair bobbed short, a thin, determined little mouth. She spoke briskly, in a reedy, high-pitched voice that for a Mississippi child was oddly clipped, so that strangers often asked where on earth she had picked up that Yankee accent. Her gaze was pale, penetrating, and not unlike Edie's. The resemblance between her and her grandmother was pointed, and did not go unremarked; but the grandmother's quick, fierce-eyed beauty was in the grandchild merely fierce, and a trifle unsettling. Chester, the yard man, likened them in private to hawk and baby chickenhawk.

To Chester, and to Ida Rhew, Harriet was a source of exasperation and amusement. From the time she had first learned to talk, she had tagged along behind them as they went about their work, interrogating them at every step. How much money did Ida make? Did Chester know how to say the Lord's Prayer? Would he say it for her? She also amused them by stirring up trouble among the generally peaceful Cleves. More than once, she had been the cause of rifts very nearly grievous: telling Adelaide that neither Edie nor Tat ever kept the pillowcases she embroidered for them, but wrapped them up to give to other people; informing Libby that her dill pickles—far from being the culinary favorite she believed them—were inedible, and that the demand for them from neighbors and family was due to their strange efficacy as a herbicide. "Do you know that bald spot in the yard?" Harriet said. "Out by the back porch? Tatty threw some of your pickles there six years ago, and nothing has grown there since." Harriet was all for the idea of bottling the pickles and selling them as weed killer. Libby would become a millionaire.

It was three or four days before Aunt Libby stopped crying over this. With Adelaide and the pillowcases it had been even worse. She, unlike Libby, enjoyed nursing a grudge; for two weeks she would not even speak to Edie and Tat, and coldly ignored the conciliatory cakes and pies they brought to her porch, leaving them out for neighborhood dogs to eat. Libby, stricken by the rift (in which she was blameless; she was the only sister loyal enough to keep and use Adelaide's pillowcases, ugly as they were), dithered back and forth trying to make peace. She had very nearly succeeded when Harriet got Adelaide stirred up all over again by telling her that Edie never even unwrapped the presents Adelaide gave her, but only took off the old gift tag and put on a new one before sending them out again: to charity organizations, mostly, some of them Negro. The incident was so disastrous that now, years later, any reference to it still prompted cattiness and subtle accusations and Adelaide, at birthdays and Christmas, now made a point of buying her sisters something demonstrably prodigal—a bottle of Shalimar, say, or a nightgown from Goldsmith's in Memphis—from which more often than not she forgot to remove the price tags. "I like a homemade gift myself," she would be overheard explaining loudly: to the ladies at her bridge club, to Chester in the yard, over the heads of her humiliated sisters as they were in the very act of unwrapping the unwanted extravagance.

"It means more. *It shows thought.* But all that matters to some people is how much money you've spent. They don't think a gift is worth anything unless it comes from the store."

"I like the things you make, Adelaide," Harriet would always say. She did, too. Though she had no use for aprons, pillowcases, tea towels, she hoarded Adelaide's garish linens and had drawers full of them in her room. It was not the linens but the designs she liked: Dutch girls, dancing coffee pots, snoozing Mexicans in sombrero hats. She coveted them to the point of stealing them out of other people's cupboards, and she had been extremely irritated that Edie was sending the pillowcases off to charity ("Don't be ridiculous, Harriet. What on *earth* can you want with that?") when she wanted them herself.

"I know *you* like them, darling," murmured Adelaide, her voice tremulous with self-pity, drooping to give Harriet a theatrical kiss as Tat and Edie exchanged looks behind her back. "Someday, when I'm gone, you may be glad you have those things."

"That one," said Chester to Ida, "loves to start a scrap."

Edie, who did not much mind a scrap herself, found in her youngest granddaughter a solid competitor. Despite, or perhaps because of this, they enjoyed each other's company and Harriet spent a good bit of time over at her grandmother's house. Edie often complained of Harriet's stubbornness and lack of manners, and grumbled about how she was always under foot, but though Harriet was exasperating Edie found her a more satisfying companion than Allison, who had very little to say. She liked having Harriet around, though she wouldn't have admitted it, and missed her on the afternoons when she didn't come.

Though the aunts loved Harriet, she was not as affectionate a child as her sister, and her pridefulness troubled them. She was too forthright. She did not at all understand reticence or diplomacy, and in this she resembled Edie more than Edie realized.

In vain, the aunts tried to teach her to be polite. "But don't you *understand*, darling," said Tat, "that if you don't like fruit-cake, it's better to eat it anyway instead of hurting your hostess's feelings?"

"But I don't like fruitcake."

"I know you don't, Harriet. That's why I used that example."

"But fruitcake is horrible. I don't know anybody that likes it. And if I tell her I like it she's just going to keep on giving it to me."

"Yes, dear, but that's not the point. The point is, if some-body has gone to the trouble to cook you something, it's good manners to eat it even if you don't want it."

"The Bible says not to lie."

"That's different. This is a white lie. The Bible's talking about another kind of lie."

"The Bible doesn't say black or white lies. It just says lies."

"Believe me, Harriet. It's true, Jesus tells us not to lie, but that doesn't mean we have to be rude to our hostess."

"Jesus doesn't say anything about our hostess. He says that lying is a sin. He says that the Devil is a liar and the prince of lies."

"But Jesus says Love Thy Neighbor, doesn't He?" said Libby, inspired, taking over for the now speechless Tat. "Doesn't that mean your hostess? Your hostess is your neighbor, too."

"That's right," said Tat gladly. "Not," she hastened, "that anybody is trying to say your hostess necessarily *lives next door* to you. All Love Thy Neighbor means is that you should eat what you're offered and be gracious about it."

"I don't see why loving my neighbor means telling him I love fruitcake. When I don't."

No one, not even Edie, had any idea how to respond to this grim pedantry. It could go on for hours. It didn't matter if you talked until you were blue in the face. Even more infuriating was that Harriet's arguments, preposterous as they were, usually had at bottom some more or less sound scriptural basis. Edie was unimpressed by this. Though she did charity and mission-ary work, and sang in the church choir, she did not actually believe that every word of the Bible was true any more than, in her heart, she actually believed some of her own favorite sayings: that, for example, everything that happened was always for the best or that, deep down, Negroes were exactly the same as white people. But the aunts—Libby, in particular—were troubled if they thought too much about some of the things Harriet said. Her sophisms were grounded undeniably in the Bible, yet flew in the face of common sense and everything that was right. "Maybe," Libby said uneasily after Harriet had stumped off home to supper, "maybe the Lord doesn't see a difference between a white lie and a wicked lie. Maybe they're all wicked in His eyes."

"Now, Libby."

"Maybe it takes a little child to remind us of that."

"I'd just as soon go to Hell," snapped Edie—who had been absent during the earlier exchange—"as have to go around all the time letting everybody in town know exactly what I thought of them."

"Edith!" cried all her sisters at once.

"Edith, you don't mean that!"

"I do. And I don't care to know what everybody in town thinks of me, either."

"I can't imagine what it is you've done, Edith," said self-righteous Adelaide, "that makes you believe everyone thinks so badly of you."

Odean, Libby's maid—who pretended to be hard of hearing—listened to this stolidly as she was in the kitchen warming some creamed chicken and biscuits for the old lady's supper. Not much exciting happened at Libby's house, and the conversation was usually a little more heated on the days when Harriet visited.

Unlike Allison—whom other children accepted vaguely, without quite knowing why—Harriet was a bossy little girl, not particularly liked. The friends she did have were not lukewarm or casual, like Allison's. They were mostly boys, mostly younger than herself, and fanatically devoted, riding their bicycles halfway across town after school to see her. She made them play Crusades, and Joan of Arc; she made them dress up in sheets and act out pageantry from the New Testament, in which she herself took the role of Jesus. The Last Supper was her favorite. Sitting all on one side of the picnic table, à la Leonardo, under the muscadine-draped pergola in Harriet's back yard, they all waited eagerly for the moment when—after dispensing a Last Supper of Ritz crackers and grape Fanta—she would look around the table at them, fixing and holding each boy, for a matter of seconds, with her cold gaze. "And yet one of you," she would say, with a calm that thrilled them, "one of you here tonight will betray me."

"No! No!" they would shriek with delight—including Hely, the boy who played Judas, but then Hely was Harriet's favorite and got to play not only Judas but all the other plum disciples: Saint John, Saint Luke, Saint Simon Peter. "Never, Lord!"

Afterwards, there was the procession to Gethsemane, which was located in the deep shade beneath the black tupelo tree in Harriet's yard. Here Harriet, as Jesus, was forced to undergo capture by the Romans—violent capture, more boisterous than the version of it rendered in the Gospels—and this was exciting enough; but the boys mainly loved Gethsemane because it was played under the tree her brother was murdered in. The murder had happened before most of them were born but they all knew the story, had patched it together from fragments of their parents' conversation or grotesque half-truths whispered by their older siblings in darkened bedrooms, and the tree had thrown its rich-dyed shadow across their imaginations ever since the first time their nursemaids had stooped on the corner of George Street to clasp their hands and point it out to them, with hissed cautions, when they were very small.

# Khaled Hosseini

## 2003

## *The Kite Runner*

"Let's do it," I said.

Hassan's face brightened. "Good," he said. He lifted our kite, red with yellow borders, and, just beneath where the central and cross spars met, marked with Saifo's unmistakable signature. He licked his finger and held it up, tested the wind, then ran in its direction—on those rare occasions we flew kites in the summer, he'd kick up dust to see which way the wind blew it. The spool rolled in my hands until Hassan stopped, about fifty feet away. He held the kite high over his head, like an Olympic athlete showing his gold medal. I jerked the string twice, our usual signal, and Hassan tossed the kite.

Caught between Baba and the mullahs at school, I still hadn't made up my mind about God. But when a Koran *ayat* I had learned in my *diniyat* class rose to my lips, I muttered it. I took a deep breath, exhaled, and pulled on the string. Within a minute, my kite was rocketing to the sky. It made a sound like a paper bird flapping its wings. Hassan clapped his hands, whistled, and ran back to me. I handed him the spool, holding on to the string, and he spun it quickly to roll the loose string back on.

At least two dozen kites already hung in the sky, like paper sharks roaming for prey. Within an hour, the number doubled, and red, blue, and yellow kites glided and spun in the sky. A cold breeze wafted through my hair. The wind was perfect for kite flying, blowing just hard enough to give some lift, make the sweeps easier. Next to me, Hassan held the spool, his hands already bloodied by the string.

Soon, the cutting started and the first of the defeated kites whirled out of control. They fell from the sky like shooting stars with brilliant, rippling tails, showering the neighborhoods below with prizes for the kite runners. I could hear the runners now, hollering as they ran the streets. Someone shouted reports of a fight breaking out two streets down.

I kept stealing glances at Baba sitting with Rahim Khan on the roof, wondered what he was thinking. Was he cheering for me? Or did a part of him enjoy watching me fail? That was the thing about kite flying: Your mind drifted with the kite.

They were coming down all over the place now, the kites, and I was still flying. I was still flying. My eyes kept wandering over to Baba, bundled up in his wool sweater. Was he surprised I had lasted as long as I had? *You don't keep your eyes to the sky, you won't last much longer.* I snapped my gaze back to the sky. A red kite was closing in on me—I'd caught it just in time. I tangled a bit with it, ended up besting him when he became impatient and tried to cut me from below.

Up and down the streets, kite runners were returning triumphantly, their captured kites held high. They showed them off to their parents, their friends. But they all knew the best was yet to come. The biggest prize of all was still flying. I sliced a bright yellow kite with a coiled white tail. It cost me another gash on the index finger and blood trickled down into my palm. I had Hassan hold the string and sucked the blood dry, blotted my finger against my jeans.

Within another hour, the number of surviving kites dwindled from maybe fifty to a dozen. I was one of them. I'd made it to the last dozen. I knew this part of the tournament would take a while, because the guys who had lasted this long were good—they wouldn't easily fall into simple traps like the old lift-and-dive, Hassan's favorite trick.

By three o'clock that afternoon, tufts of clouds had drifted in and the sun had slipped behind them. Shadows started to lengthen. The spectators on the roofs bundled up in scarves and thick coats. We were down to a half dozen and I was still flying.

My legs ached and my neck was stiff. But with each defeated kite, hope grew in my heart, like snow collecting on a wall, one flake at a time.

My eyes kept returning to a blue kite that had been wreaking havoc for the last hour.

"How many has he cut?" I asked.

"I counted eleven," Hassan said.

"Do you know whose it might be?"

Hassan clucked his tongue and tipped his chin. That was a trademark Hassan gesture, meant he had no idea. The blue kite sliced a big purple one and swept twice in big loops. Ten minutes later, he'd cut another two, sending hordes of kite runners racing after them.

After another thirty minutes, only four kites remained. And I was still flying. It seemed I could hardly make a wrong move, as if every gust of wind blew in my favor. I'd never felt so in command, so lucky. It felt intoxicating. I didn't dare look up to the roof. Didn't dare take my eyes off the sky. I had to concentrate, play it smart. Another fifteen minutes and what had seemed like a laughable dream that morning had suddenly become reality: It was just me and the other guy. The blue kite.

The tension in the air was as taut as the glass string I was tugging with my bloody hands. People were stomping their feet, clapping, whistling, chanting, *"Boboresh! Boboresh!"* Cut him! Cut him! I wondered if Baba's voice was one of them. Music blasted. The smell of steamed *mantu* and fried *pakora* drifted from rooftops and open doors.

But all I heard—all I willed myself to hear—was the thudding of blood in my head. All I saw was the blue kite. All I smelled was victory. Salvation. Redemption. If Baba was wrong and there *was* a God like they said in school, then He'd let me win. I didn't know what the other guy was playing for, maybe just bragging rights. But this was my one chance to become someone who was looked at, not seen, listened to, not heard. If there was a God, He'd guide the winds, let them blow for me so that, with a tug of my string, I'd cut loose my pain, my longing. I'd endured too much, come too far. And suddenly, just like that, hope became knowledge. I was going to win. It was just a matter of when.

It turned out to be sooner than later. A gust of wind lifted my kite and I took advantage. Fed the string, pulled up. Looped my kite on top of the blue one. I held position. The blue kite knew it was in trouble. It was trying desperately to maneuver out of the jam, but I didn't let go. I held position. The crowd sensed the end was at hand. The chorus of "Cut him! Cut him!" grew louder, like Romans chanting for the gladiators to kill, kill!

"You're almost there, Amir agha! Almost there!" Hassan was panting.

Then the moment came. I closed my eyes and loosened my grip on the string. It sliced my fingers again as the wind dragged it. And then ... I didn't need to hear the crowd's roar to know. I didn't need to see either. Hassan was screaming and his arm was wrapped around my neck.

"Bravo! Bravo, Amir agha!"

I opened my eyes, saw the blue kite spinning wildly like a tire come loose from a speeding car. I blinked, tried to say something. Nothing came out. Suddenly I was hovering, looking down on myself from above. Black leather coat, red scarf, faded jeans. A thin boy, a little sallow, and a tad short for his twelve years. He had narrow shoulders and a hint of dark circles around his pale hazel eyes. The breeze rustled his light brown hair. He looked up to me and we smiled at each other.

Then I was screaming, and everything was color and sound, everything was alive and good. I was throwing my free arm around Hassan and we were hopping up and down, both of us laughing, both of us weeping. "You won, Amir agha! You won!"

"We won! We won!" was all I could say. This wasn't happening. In a moment, I'd blink and rouse from this beautiful dream, get out of bed, march down to the kitchen to eat breakfast with no one to talk to but Hassan. Get dressed. Wait for Baba. Give up. Back to my old life. Then I saw Baba on our roof. He was standing on the edge, pumping both of his fists. Hollering and clapping. And that right there was the single greatest moment of my twelve years of life, seeing Baba on that roof, proud of me at last.

But he was doing something now, motioning with his hands in an urgent way. Then I understood. "Hassan, we—"

"I know," he said, breaking our embrace. "*Inshallah,* we'll celebrate later. Right now, I'm going to run that blue kite for you," he said. He dropped the spool and took off running, the hem of his green *chapan* dragging in the snow behind him.

"Hassan!" I called. "Come back with it!"

He was already turning the street corner, his rubber boots kicking up snow. He stopped, turned. He cupped his hands around his mouth. "For you a thousand times over!" he said. Then he smiled his Hassan smile and disappeared around the corner. The next time I saw him smile unabashedly like that was twenty-six years later, in a faded Polaroid photograph.

I began to pull my kite back as people rushed to congratulate me. I shook hands with them, said my thanks. The younger kids looked at me with an awestruck twinkle in their eyes; I was a hero. Hands patted my back and tousled my hair. I pulled on the string and returned every smile, but my mind was on the blue kite.

Finally, I had my kite in hand. I wrapped the loose string that had collected at my feet around the spool, shook a few more hands, and trotted home. When I reached the wrought-iron gates, Ali was waiting on the other side. He stuck his hand through the bars. "Congratulations," he said.

I gave him my kite and spool, shook his hand. "*Tashakor,* Ali jan."

"I was praying for you the whole time."

"Then keep praying. We're not done yet."

I hurried back to the street. I didn't ask Ali about Baba. I didn't want to see him yet. In my head, I had it all planned: I'd make a grand entrance, a hero, prized trophy in my bloodied hands. Heads would turn and eyes would lock. Rostam and Sohrab sizing each other up. A dramatic moment of silence. Then the old warrior would walk to the young one, embrace him, acknowledge his worthiness. Vindication. Salvation. Redemption. And then? Well ... happily ever after, of course. What else?

The streets of Wazir Akbar Khan were numbered and set at right angles to each other like a grid. It was a new neighborhood then, still developing, with empty lots of land and half-constructed homes on every street between compounds surrounded by eight-foot walls. I ran up and down every street, looking for Hassan. Everywhere, people were busy folding chairs, packing food and utensils after a long day of partying. Some, still sitting on their rooftops, shouted their congratulations to me.

Four streets south of ours, I saw Omar, the son of an engineer who was a friend of Baba's. He was dribbling a soccer ball with his brother on the front lawn of their house. Omar was a pretty good guy. We'd been classmates in fourth grade, and one time he'd given me a fountain pen, the kind you had to load with a cartridge.

"I heard you won, Amir," he said. "Congratulations."

"Thanks. Have you seen Hassan?"

"Your Hazara?"

I nodded.

Omar headed the ball to his brother. "I hear he's a great kite runner." His brother headed the ball back to him. Omar caught it, tossed it up and down. "Although I've always wondered how he manages. I mean, with those tight little eyes, how does he *see* anything?"

His brother laughed, a short burst, and asked for the ball. Omar ignored him.

"Have you seen him?"

Omar flicked a thumb over his shoulder, pointing southwest. "I saw him running toward the bazaar awhile ago."

"Thanks." I scuttled away.

By the time I reached the marketplace, the sun had almost sunk behind the hills and dusk had painted the sky pink and purple. A few blocks away, from the Haji Yaghoub Mosque, the mullah bellowed *azan*, calling for the faithful to unroll their rugs and bow their heads west in prayer. Hassan never missed any of the five daily prayers. Even when we were out playing, he'd excuse himself, draw water from the well in the yard, wash up, and disappear into the hut. He'd come out a few minutes later, smiling, find me sitting against the wall or perched on a tree. He was going to miss prayer tonight, though, because of me.

The bazaar was emptying quickly, the merchants finishing up their haggling for the day. I trotted in the mud between rows of closely packed cubicles where you could buy a freshly slaughtered pheasant in one stand and a calculator from the adjacent one. I picked my way through the dwindling crowd, the lame beggars dressed in layers of tattered rags, the vendors with rugs on their shoulders, the cloth merchants and butchers closing shop for the day. I found no sign of Hassan.

I stopped by a dried fruit stand, described Hassan to an old merchant loading his mule with crates of pine seeds and raisins. He wore a powder blue turban.

He paused to look at me for a long time before answering. "I might have seen him."

"Which way did he go?"

He eyed me up and down. "What is a boy like you doing here at this time of the day looking for a Hazara?" His glance lingered admiringly on my leather coat and my jeans—*cowboy pants*, we used to call them. In Afghanistan, owning anything American, especially if it wasn't secondhand, was a sign of wealth.

"I need to find him, Agha."

"What is he to you?" he said. I didn't see the point of his question, but I reminded myself that impatience wasn't going to make him tell me any faster.

"He's our servant's son," I said.

The old man raised a pepper grey eyebrow. "He is? Lucky Hazara, having such a concerned master. His father should get on his knees, sweep the dust at your feet with his eyelashes."

"Are you going to tell me or not?"

He rested an arm on the mule's back, pointed south. "I think I saw the boy you described running that way. He had a kite in his hand. A blue one."

"He did?" I said. *For you a thousand times over,* he'd promised. Good old Hassan. Good old reliable Hassan. He'd kept his
promise and run the last kite for me.

"Of course, they've probably caught him by now," the old
merchant said, grunting and loading another box on the mule's
back.

"Who?"

"The other boys," he said. "The ones chasing him. They were
dressed like you." He glanced to the sky and sighed. "Now, run
along, you're making me late for *namaz.*"

But I was already scrambling down the lane.

For the next few minutes, I scoured the bazaar in vain. Maybe
the old merchant's eyes had betrayed him. Except he'd seen the
blue kite. The thought of getting my hands on that kite ... I
poked my head behind every lane, every shop. No sign of Hassan.

I had begun to worry that darkness would fall before I
found Hassan when I heard voices from up ahead. I'd reached
a secluded, muddy road. It ran perpendicular to the end of the
main thoroughfare bisecting the bazaar. I turned onto the rutted
track and followed the voices. My boot squished in mud with
every step and my breath puffed out in white clouds before me.
The narrow path ran parallel on one side to a snow-filled ravine
through which a stream may have tumbled in the spring. To my
other side stood rows of snow-burdened cypress trees peppered
among flat-topped clay houses—no more than mud shacks in
most cases—separated by narrow alleys.

I heard the voices again, louder this time, coming from one of
the alleys. I crept close to the mouth of the alley. Held my breath.
Peeked around the corner.

Hassan was standing at the blind end of the alley in a defiant
stance: fists curled, legs slightly apart. Behind him, sitting on piles
of scrap and rubble, was the blue kite. My key to Baba's heart.

Blocking Hassan's way out of the alley were three boys, the
same three from that day on the hill, the day after Daoud Khan's
coup, when Hassan had saved us with his slingshot. Wali was
standing on one side, Kamal on the other, and in the middle,

Assef. I felt my body clench up, and something cold rippled up my spine. Assef seemed relaxed, confident. He was twirling his brass knuckles. The other two guys shifted nervously on their feet, looking from Assef to Hassan, like they'd cornered some kind of wild animal that only Assef could tame.

"Where is your slingshot, Hazara?" Assef said, turning the brass knuckles in his hand. "What was it you said? 'They'll have to call you One-Eyed Assef.' That's right. One-Eyed Assef. That was clever. Really clever. Then again, it's easy to be clever when you're holding a loaded weapon."

I realized I still hadn't breathed out. I exhaled, slowly, quietly. I felt paralyzed. I watched them close in on the boy I'd grown up with, the boy whose harelipped face had been my first memory.

"But today is your lucky day, Hazara," Assef said. He had his back to me, but I would have bet he was grinning. "I'm in a mood to forgive. What do you say to that, boys?"

"That's generous," Kamal blurted, "Especially after the rude manners he showed us last time." He was trying to sound like Assef, except there was a tremor in his voice. Then I understood: He wasn't afraid of Hassan, not really. He was afraid because he had no idea what Assef had in mind.

Assef waved a dismissive hand. "*Bakhshida*. Forgiven. It's done." His voice dropped a little. "Of course, nothing is free in this world, and my pardon comes with a small price."

"That's fair," Kamal said.

"Nothing is free," Wali added.

"You're a lucky Hazara," Assef said, taking a step toward Hassan.

"Because today, it's only going to cost you that blue kite. A fair deal, boys, isn't it?"

"More than fair," Kamal said.

Even from where I was standing, I could see the fear creeping into Hassan's eyes, but he shook his head. "Amir agha won the tournament and I ran this kite for him. I ran it fairly. This is his kite."

"A loyal Hazara. Loyal as a dog," Assef said.

Kamal's laugh was a shrill, nervous sound.

"But before you sacrifice yourself for him, think about this: Would he do the same for you? Have you ever wondered why he never includes you in games when he has guests? Why he only plays with you when no one else is around? I'll tell you why, Hazara. Because to him, you're nothing but an ugly pet. Something he can play with when he's bored, something he can kick when he's angry. Don't ever fool yourself and think you're something more."

"Amir agha and I are friends," Hassan said. He looked flushed.

"Friends?" Assef said, laughing. "You pathetic fool! Someday you'll wake up from your little fantasy and learn just how good of a friend he is. Now, *bas!* Enough of this. Give us that kite."

Hassan stooped and picked up a rock.

Assef flinched. He began to take a step back, stopped. "Last chance, Hazara."

Hassan's answer was to cock the arm that held the rock.

"Whatever you wish." Assef unbuttoned his winter coat, took it off, folded it slowly and deliberately. He placed it against the wall.

I opened my mouth, almost said something. Almost. The rest of my life might have turned out differently if I had. But I didn't. I just watched. Paralyzed.

Assef motioned with his hand, and the other two boys separated, forming a half circle, trapping Hassan in the alley.

"I've changed my mind," Assef said. "I'm letting you keep the kite, Hazara. I'll let you keep it so it will always remind you of what I'm about to do."

Then he charged. Hassan hurled the rock. It struck Assef in the forehead. Assef yelped as he flung himself at Hassan, knocking him to the ground. Wali and Kamal followed.

I bit on my fist. Shut my eyes.

# Barbara Trapido

## 2003

## *Frankie & Stankie*

While both Dinah's parents think the government is raving mad, it's her dad who takes the matter more to heart. So the most direct effect of the Nationalist election victory upon Lisa and Dinah is that they wake up every morning to the sound of their dad shouting back at Foreign Minister Eric Louw on the early morning radio. Eric Louw, wartime Nazi enthusiast and our new liaison person at the UN, is doing his regular broadcast. It's his brief to enlighten the UN as to the beneficial nature of apartheid, especially for the black man, and to explain how we, in South Africa, are single-handedly carrying the torch for Western civilisation. Eric Louw's big friend at the UN is Eamon de Valera who, thanks to the Boer War, still thinks of the Afrikaner Nationalists, not as our newest and most ghoulish racist oppressors, but as fellow republican victims of British Imperialism. Eric and Eamon sort of wear the same hat – and not only metaphorically – because it's from the Boer leader, General de Wet, that Michael Collins and the Irish rebels got their photogenic hats: those fetching leather hats with the poppers on one side. The IRA call these de Wet hats and they wear them in a spirit of brotherhood. Meanwhile, Eric and Eamon are bonded. Eric and Eamon are friends.

After their dad has woken the household ranting back at Eric Louw on the radio, he gets up and goes stamping through the house in sandals, venting his rage on all the Venetian blinds, which he wrenches up with such force that their mum's family of ebony elephants regularly bounces off the living-room pelmet and bangs him on the head. The pelmet is one of several which are of his own making and they are the only item of wood-work that Dinah has ever seen him undertake. The pelmets are like three-sided wooden window boxes made of plywood that get screwed upside-down over the curtain rail to obscure the rufflette tape and the hooks. They are so much de rigueur at the time that even Dinah's dad, who is prodigiously non-DIY, is required to succumb to necessity and take up his tool kit in the cause of their construction.

While its main business is to make the lives of blacks even more of a waking nightmare than it was before the election, the new government is at the same time dealing with smaller swathes of English-speaking whites. It starts by pitching out numbers of high-profile top honchos in the armed services, the police and the civil service, especially those who might possibly have dossiers on the pro-Nazi activities undertaken during the Second World War by certain members of the present cabinet. It also puts the screws on any Afrikaner public servants that it suspects of having the wrong leanings. It sheds any English-speaking civil servants whose Afrikaans won't quite pass muster, in order that right-thinking Afrikaners can be moved into their jobs. Very soon the civil service and the armed forces are effectively the exclusive preserve of the *Volk*.

One of the government's main undertakings is to swipe the jobs off blacks and give them to poor white Afrikaners. This is what the Job Reservation Act is for, because it redefines whole categories of job as being for white people only. When Dinah and her mum go shopping in Stuttaford's, Dinah always likes the lift man whose name is Ephraim. He wears a smart khaki uniform with an epauletted drill-cloth shirt and matching trou-sers with very ironed creases and turn-ups. Ephraim has to move a shiny brass lever in a groove across a big brass disc to make the lift go up and down and to open and close the doors. All the shop assistants who get into the lift always start talking to Ephraim right away, because he's such a good listener.

One of the shop women will get in and say, 'You better make sure this lift doesn't break down today, Ephraim, because my feet is killing me this morning, honest-to-God. I'm telling you that, so help me.'

Then Ephraim will say, '*Hau*, madam, too much the foot is hurting today?'

'You can say that again,' the shop lady says. 'I went dancing last night, you know, Ephraim, and as true's God's my witness, my shoes was killing me all night long. Now I swear to God I've got bunions like I don't know what. Like nobody's business and that's for sure, I'm telling you.'

'*Hau*, madam,' Ephraim says again, after several sympathetic clicks. 'Too much the foot is hurting. Too much.'

Then, when that shop assistant gets out, another one will get in and she'll start right away as well.

'Well, I hope you aren't going to take so long to come when it's five o'clock, Ephraim. Because you might as well know that I'll have to be out of here like a bat out of hell tonight, as true's God's my witness,' she says.

'*Hau*, madam, too much busy tonight?' Ephraim will say.

'You not far wrong there, Ephraim, I swear to God,' the shop lady will say. 'Because *I've* only got my Ma and my fiancé's Ma and my Gran and my Auntie Hettie coming over – well, she's not *really* my auntie, but I call her my auntie – and anyway I've still got all my cooking to do and my greens to prepare and everything. And God only knows what there's going to be for dessert, so help me, plus I don't exactly want to look like I've been pulled through a bush backwards when they come, now do I, Ephraim?'

'*Hau*, madam,' Ephraim says. 'Too much busy tonight. Too much.'

'Well, I reckon it's lucky for you people that you just eat *mieliepap* and that's it, hey, Ephraim? I swear to God I'd eat it myself, so help me.'

All the shop ladies love talking to Ephraim, except for once when Dinah hears one of them say to another one, 'It really jives on my G-string the way that boy talks back all the time like that, you know? So help me, they not so cheeky where I come from on the farm. I'm not used to it.'

Then one day when Dinah and her mum get into the lift, Ephraim isn't there and a pinched-looking white girl with so-what body language is working Ephraim's brass lever. She's chewing gum while she's gabbling off her newly rote-learned lift patter and she's sniffing loudly in the pauses.

hardware-kitchenware-linenware-crockery
Go-wing-UP
lingerie-hoserie-ladies'fashions-tearoom-powder-room-
     accessories
Go-wing-UP

Dinah never sees Ephraim again, but when blacks disappear like that it's called going back to the farm. It means that the person has been sent back to the native reserve which is where the golf-ball oranges grow.

As an experiment in social engineering, it's amazing to see how successfully apartheid is working. Week by week, year by year, the white poor are getting richer and more skilled; the blacks are getting more invisible. Sanlam, the ever-expanding Afrikaner insurance company, has now taken over the building in the city square that housed the Maypole Tearoom and, at some point in the future, as repression creates defiance and its suppression creates an underground, the Special Branch ensconces itself there in brightly lit offices across the whole top floor. The offices are brightly lit because the Special Branch likes its enemies to see that their guys are keeping busy.

The university people on the Butcher Estate respond in different ways to the Nationalist election victory. There are those who shudder and leave at once, taking jobs in Toronto, Los Angeles, Glasgow, Salisbury and New South Wales. Harry Stent goes, the Pecks go, the Frankels and their three children go, Dr Lieberman goes, but of all those who go it's Peter Bullen whose departure is the hardest to accept – though he's left the girls with all his hard-back children's books, including his Cautionary Tales and his childhood A. A. Milne collection. And over the next few years, Lisa and Dinah fight a war of possession over these precious relics until the flyleaves are covered with their alternately written and scratched out names:

Lisa Sophia de Bondt
Dinah Louisa de Bondt

The handwriting gets gradually more and more mature and it goes on until there's no more space on which to write.

There are those among the Butcher residents who assert that the Nats can't possibly stay in power for more than one term. They say that we're in it for five years and that's it. *Finito.* The whole show will be over and all we need do is to fix our minds on damage limitation. These are the people who drain away later, because, come 1953, when Dinah and her sister are twelve and thirteen, the Nats romp home with a massively increased majority, not only because gerrymandering is paying hand-some dividends, not only because most wavering Afrikaners have by now been brought into the fold. It's also because lots of the English business people have discovered that they like the government's new laws, which make it even easier for them to regulate and control their black workers.

Anyway, in that same year, the English are focused on a happening which is vastly more exciting in their hierarchy of public goings-on than a general election, and the teachers and pupils at the Berea Road Government School for Girls are no exception. They are all preparing to celebrate the Coronation of Queen Elizabeth II. This is a very big occasion, but it's one that is not without its down side for Lisa and Dinah, much as they are enchanted by their free Coronation mugs. For weeks before-hand, the up-coming Coronation has ushered in a fever pitch of Durbanite royalism among the staff, and the girls' headmistress employs a non-stop three-line whip in the matter of peddling her stock of British flags. Every child is required to bring half a crown to school for the purpose of buying a small Union Jack on a stick. The flags are about the size of a standard school exercise book and they're selling at a brisk pace.

The problem for Lisa and Dinah is that their dad has a theory about flags and he says they're not to have them. Flags represent nationalism, he says, and nationalism is a Bad Thing. Nationalism, along with religion, is the root of all evil.

'Look what happened in Germany,' he says. 'Look at what's happening right here.'

Lisa and Dinah are unimpressed. They're sick of always being deviants at school and they're longing to wave their Union Jacks along with the rest of the herd.

'Oh plee-*eez*,' they whinge, but their dad is adamant.

'You go and tell Miss Marshall that I'd just as soon you waved the flag of the Transvaal Republic,' he says. 'Why not?' He is starting to get quite exercised about the flags and they can tell that he's really enjoying himself. 'Go on,' he says. 'Tell her. You go and tell her that you'll be happy to wave the *Vierkleur*.' The *Vierkleur* is the flag of the Transvaal's defunct Boer Republic.

Each day in the morning assembly, the head interrogates the children, who are seated before her in rows, cross-legged on the woodblock floor.

'Stand up all those girls who have not yet purchased their flags,' she says.

At first it's lots of children who stand up, because, even for normally coping little girls, it takes time to remember your half a crown. But each day, as the group of non-purchasers is smaller, it gets more and more embarrassing. It's especially awful for Lisa who is a prefect and in the top class. One day it's only Lisa and Dinah, plus the tiny smattering of neglected children whose parents can never get anything much together, let alone find half a crown. Then, finally, it's that terrible day when it's only Lisa and Dinah.

The girls are utterly mortified but the two possible options open to them have simply never crossed their minds. One would be to stop standing up in the assembly hall and the other would be to explain. Instead they carry their shame through the whole day and go home, where Lisa, thank goodness, breaks down over their mum and cries. Their mum promises to slip them each half a crown next morning and whispers that they're not to tell their dad. But the Coronation isn't over yet because, in addition to the flag waving, there's to be all-day feasting, singing, English country dancing and a fancy-dress parade. Your mum has got to make you a costume and she's also got to bake a cake for you to take to school for the party.

Dinah's mum throws herself into the fancy-dress project with enthusiasm. Lisa, who is now nearly as tall as a grown-up, has shed most of her puppy fat and can fit into her mother's clothes. Plus, she's newly besotted with Italian opera because the girls have recently been taken to a touring production of Verdi's *La Traviata*. For this reason, their mum conceives the idea that Lisa shall go as Violetta. She rakes through the *Klappkasten*, pulling out various numbers that date from her pre-marital dressy phase in Cape Town, and she settles on an ankle-length frilled white muslin garment which she has modified, complete with Born Arm sleeve, by Mrs van der Walt. With a camellia stuck in her auburn hair and a fan in her hand and a crewel-work scarf with a silk fringe, Lisa probably looks a lot more like Carmen than Violetta, but she certainly looks very nice. Dinah, thanks to her long blonde hair, is to go as Alice in Wonderland.

Among their fairly regular family book readings, the *Alice* books have always been big favourites of their dad's. He likes all the maths-y jokes and, since he's invariably the reader, he also gets to choose all the books. This means that until Peter comes along with his Hilaire Belloc Cautionary Tales, the girls are frequently subjected to the *Struwwelpeter* stories, which are read to them in German. Their parents think these stories are funny – though poor Lisa, the family's one-handed thumbsucker, is never much amused by the Dreaded Scissor Man who leaps on to the page in full colour, brandishing his giant's shears, and hacks off the small boy's thumbs. Lisa finds this upsetting, particularly as the picture shows his two copiously bleeding stumps in accurate close-up.

And Dinah, in turn, is wholly uncaptivated by the Fat Boy who suddenly becomes a non-eater and who – with repeated cries of '*Ich esse keine Suppe nein!*' – dwindles swiftly from Fat Boy to Matchstick Boy and then to Deceased Boy, over five graphic illustrations. The second to last picture shows the Fat Boy relegated, thread-like, to the sick bed with a futile clutter of medicine bottles alongside him on the bedside cabinet. The only thing Dinah likes about this picture is the carefully drawn chamber pot that is sitting underneath the Fat Boy's bed. The last picture is of the Fat Boy's tombstone which is planted on a sad little grassy knoll. The *Struwwelpeter* readings tend to be rotated with *Huckleberry Finn* and *Tom Sawyer*, both of which Lisa and Dinah think of as boys' books, and with the *Alice* books which tend to go way above their heads, but it's true that the books make a store of mental furniture which both girls come to relish later on.

In Sir John Tenniel's illustrations Alice has Dinah-length hair which exhibits the same kind of undulating crimp that Dinah gets when she unravels her school plaits. And Alice is wearing a full-skirted, puff-sleeved dress that happens to look very like Dinah's favourite party dress. So all Dinah needs for her fancy-dress costume is an Alice band and an apron which are both easily acquired. Then, Dinah's mum decides, she must have a flamingo: a full-sized model flamingo which is to be carried upside-down, just as Alice does in the croquet scene, when she uses the bird as a mallet. Dinah's mum has a lot of fun with the flamingo, because it's the first item of sculpture she's ever tried to make and it's also one of the few really challenging projects that's come her way in years. She starts by moulding a fine chicken-wire frame and covering it with strips of old blanket. Then she covers the whole thing with shades of flamingo-pink felt, detailing the creature's wings, beak and webbed feet with subtle artifice. The completed flamingo is a triumph and stands as tall as Dinah on wonderful spindly legs. And the crimped, loose Alice hair is rather enhancing. The girls' mum has just this once added a little blush of rouge to each daughter's cheeks, so they feel very satisfied with the way they look. There is a spring in their step as Violetta and Alice set out for school on Coronation Day.

At first they are merely slightly shaken when they meet five London Bobbies, two Beefeaters and one Grenadier Guard along the way, but by the time they are assembled in the playground for the parade, Lisa and Dinah have found themselves to be oddballs once again, in the company of two dozen crowned Lillibets and a dozen Dukes of Edinburgh. There are several more Beefeaters and a pair of Robin Hoods, four Admirals Lord Nelson, each with a cardboard telescope clamped to his blind eye, a smattering of square-mile City gents in bowler hats carrying rolled umbrellas and faked-up copies of the London *Times*, twenty-five redcoats, half a dozen khaki-clad British Tommies, three Sir Walter Raleighs and two ornately dressed Virgin Queens. One proud little girl is head to foot in yards of Union Jack. She has a Union Jack hat, a Union Jack dress and Union Jack ballet shoes with pompoms. But probably the most envied girl of all is a bronzed and tridented Britannia encircled by an ingenious, coin-like bronze hoop that miraculously says 'ONE PENNY' in apparently free-standing but discreetly wired bronze letters. The costume is a marvel and is shouting First Prize Winner before the procession so much as gets off the ground. In addition, there are a pair of Punch and Judys and one blue-painted Boadicea.

Nobody except for Lisa is dressed as a loose-living foreign consumptive and nobody, except for Dinah, is unaccountably wearing a pinny over her best party dress while carrying a large pink bird the wrong way up. Even before the parade has begun Dinah has heard poor Lisa try to explain herself twenty times.

'I'm Violetta. She's in *La Traviata*. No, it's a op'ra. I said *op'ra*.'

The listening children gawp and shrug. The nearest anyone in Lisa's class has got to knowing what an opera is comes from early evening Springbok Radio, where the Firestone Strings play excerpts from the overture to *The Flying Dutchman*. The excerpts are interrupted, roughly every fifty seconds, by the ad breaks which repeatedly remind listeners that the Firestone Strings come courtesy of the Firestone Rubber Company.

Through the gauntlet of the fancy-dress parade, Dinah's ordeal is punctuated by the onlookers' repeating refrain: 'Who's she?' 'Who's she?' 'Who's *she*?'

Only occasionally there's a variation as the more protective members of the crowd move forward to pluck her by the sleeve. 'Excuse me,' they whisper discreetly.

'Excuse me, lovey, but you're carrying that bird upside-down.'

So Dinah, succumbing to the consensus, starts to carry her flamingo the right way up.

After the procession is over, she and her bosom friend Angela Trevean abandon their accessories under a tree and run off to find the stash of home-made cakes that have been cut up and arranged on enormous platters.

'Look at that cake,' Angela says. 'Look at *that* one. Look at *those*.'

'Look at *that* one,' Dinah says.

They giggle as they point out what they take to be the funnier-looking cakes, though none of them is really that funny. It's just that everything makes them giggle and giggle-stoking has become a sort of etiquette between them. Meanwhile they are loading their plates with slices of chocolate Swiss roll and wedges of Victoria sponge. Some people's mothers have been so intensely patriotic they've done their cakes in three layers, red, white and blue.

'Look at *that* one,' Angela says.

'*Ugh*,' Dinah says, and she giggles and groans extra hard, because it's a slice of two-tone loaf cake, chocolate and plain.

It's been cut from her own mother's German marble cake and she's not at all keen to have Angela find this out. She knows that cakes should be Victoria sponge. They should be two rounds stuck together with jam. Angela's mother knows this because she comes from Cornwall. It's because she comes from Cornwall that she has a pixie on her door knocker. Angela can't remember being a baby in St Austell, but she knows that pixies are her heritage. Dinah's mum's marble loaf cake is called *Karierte Affe*, which means chequered monkey.

# Susanna Clarke

## 2004

## *Jonathan Strange & Mr Norrell*

A gentleman with thistledown hair

*October 1807*

There was no one there.

Which is to say there was someone there. Miss Wintertowne lay upon the bed, but it would have puzzled philosophy to say now whether she were someone or no one at all. They had dressed her in a white gown and hung a silver chain about her neck; they had combed and dressed her beautiful hair and put pearl-and-garnet earrings in her ears. But it was extremely doubtful whether Miss Wintertowne cared about such things any more. They had lit candles and laid a good fire in the hearth, they had put roses about the room, which filled it with a sweet perfume, but Miss Wintertowne could have lain now with equal composure in the foulest-smelling garret in the city.

"And she was quite tolerable to look at, you say?" said Mr Lascelles.

"You never saw her?" said Drawlight. "Oh! she was a heavenly creature. Quite divine. An angel."

"Indeed? And such a pinched-looking ruin of a thing now! I shall advise all the good-looking women of my acquaintance not to die," said Mr Lascelles. He leaned closer. "They have closed her eyes," he said.

"Her eyes were perfection," said Drawlight, "a clear dark grey, with long, dark eye-lashes and dark eye-brows. It is a pity you never saw her — she was exactly the sort of creature you would have admired." Drawlight turned to Mr Norrell. "Well, sir, are you ready to begin?"

Mr Norrell was seated in a chair next to the fire. The resolute, businesslike manner, which he had adopted on his arrival at the house, had disappeared; instead he sat with neck bowed, sighing heavily, his gaze fixed upon the carpet. Mr Lascelles and Mr Drawlight looked at him with that degree of interest appropriate to the character of each — which is to say that Mr Drawlight was all fidgets and bright-eyed anticipation, and Mr Lascelles all cool, smiling scepticism. Mr Drawlight took a few respectful steps back from the bed so that Mr Norrell might more conveniently approach it and Mr Lascelles leant against a wall and crossed his arms (an attitude he often adopted in the theatre).

Mr Norrell sighed again. "Mr Drawlight, I have already said that this particular magic demands complete solitude. I must ask you to wait downstairs."

"Oh, but, sir!" protested Drawlight. "Surely such intimate friends as Lascelles and I can be no inconvenience to you? We are the quietest creatures in the world! In two minutes' time you will have quite forgotten that we are here. And I must say that I consider our presence as absolutely essential! For who will broadcast the news of your achievement tomorrow morning if not Lascelles and myself? Who will describe the ineffable grandeur of the moment when your magicianship triumphs and the young woman rises from the dead? Or the unbearable pathos of the moment when you are forced to admit defeat? You will not do it half so well yourself, sir. You know that you will not."

"Perhaps," said Mr Norrell. "But what you suggest is entirely impossible. I will not, *cannot* begin until you leave the room."

Poor Drawlight! He could not force the magician to begin the magic against his will, but to have waited so long to see some magic and then to be excluded! It was almost more than he could bear. Even Mr Lascelles was a little disappointed for he had hoped to witness something very ridiculous that he could laugh at.

When they had gone Mr Norrell rose wearily from his seat and took up a book that he had brought with him. He opened it at a place he had marked with a folded letter and placed it upon a little table so that it would be to hand if he needed to consult it. Then he began to recite a spell.

It took effect almost immediately because suddenly there was something green where nothing green had been before and a fresh, sweet smell as of woods and fields wafted through the room. Mr Norrell stopped speaking.

Someone was standing in the middle of the room: a tall, handsome person with pale, perfect skin and an immense amount of hair, as pale and shining as thistledown. His cold, blue eyes glittered and he had long dark eye-brows, which terminated in an upward flourish. He was dressed exactly like any other gentleman, except that his coat was of the brightest green imaginable – the colour of leaves in early summer.

"*O Lar!*" began Mr Norrell in a quavering voice. "*O Lar! Magnum opus est mihi tuo auxilio. Haec virgo mortua est et familia eius eam ad vitam redire vult.*"[1] Mr Norrell pointed to the figure on the bed.

At the sight of Miss Wintertowne the gentleman with the thistledown hair suddenly became very excited. He spread wide his hands in a gesture of surprized delight and began to speak Latin very rapidly. Mr Norrell, who was more accustomed to seeing Latin written down or printed in books, found that he could not follow the language when it was spoken so fast, though he did recognize a few words here and there, words such as "*formosa*" and "*venusta*" which are descriptive of feminine beauty.

Mr Norrell waited until the gentleman's rapture had subsided and then he directed the gentleman's attention to the mirror above the mantelpiece. A vision appeared of Miss Wintertowne walking along a narrow rocky path, through a mountainous and gloomy landscape. "*Ecce mortua inter terram et caelum!*" declared

[1] "O Fairy. I have great need of your help. This virgin is dead and her family wish her to be returned to life."

Mr Norrell. "*Scito igitur, O Lar, me ad hanc magnam operam te vocare elegisse quia ...*"[2]

"Yes, yes!" cried the gentleman suddenly breaking into English. "You elected to summon *me* because my genius for magic exceeds that of all the rest of my race. Because I have been the servant and confidential friend of Thomas Godbless, Ralph Stokesey, Martin Pale *and* of the Raven King. Because I am valorous, chivalrous, generous and as handsome as the day is long! That is all quite understood! It would have been madness to summon anyone else! We both know who *I* am. The question is: who in the world are *you*?"

"I?" said Mr Norrell, startled. "I am the greatest magician of the Age!"

The gentleman raised one perfect eye-brow as if to say he was surprized to hear it. He walked around Mr Norrell slowly, considering him from every angle. Then, most disconcerting of all, he plucked Mr Norrell's wig from his head and looked underneath, as if Mr Norrell were a cooking pot on the fire and he wished to know what was for dinner.

"I ... I am the man who is destined to restore magic to England!" stammered Mr Norrell, grabbing back his wig and replacing it, slightly askew, upon his head.

"Well, obviously you are *that!*" said the gentleman. "Or I should not be here! You do not imagine that I would waste my time upon a three-penny hedge-sorcerer, do you? But *who* are you? That is what I wish to know. What magic have you done? Who was your master? What magical lands have you visited? What enemies have you defeated? Who are your allies?"

Mr Norrell was extremely surprized to be asked so many questions and he was not at all prepared to answer them. He wavered and hesitated before finally fixing upon the only one to which he had a sensible answer. "I had no master. I taught myself."

"How?"

---

[2] "Here is the dead woman between earth and heaven! Know then, O Fairy, that I have chosen you for this great task because ..."

"From books."

"Books!" (This in a tone of the utmost contempt.)

"Yes, indeed. There is a great deal of magic in books now-adays. Of course, most of it is nonsense. No one knows as well as I how much nonsense is printed in books. But there is a great deal of useful information too and it is surprizing how, after one has learnt a little, one begins to see …"

Mr Norrell was beginning to warm to his subject, but the gentleman with the thistledown hair had no patience to listen to other people talk and so he interrupted him.

"Am I the first of my race that you have seen?"

"Oh, yes!"

This answer seemed to please the gentleman with the thistledown hair and he smiled. "So! Should I agree to restore this young woman to life, what would be my reward?"

Mr Norrell cleared his throat. "What sort of thing …?" he said, a little hoarsely.

"Oh! That is easily agreed!" cried the gentleman with the thistledown hair. "My wishes are the most moderate things in the world. Fortunately I am utterly free from greed and sordid ambition. Indeed, you will find that my proposal is much more to your advantage than mine – such is my unselfish nature! I simply wish to be allowed to aid you in all your endeavours, to advise you upon all matters and to guide you in your studies. Oh! and you must take care to let all the world know that your greatest achievements are due in larger part to me!"

Mr Norrell looked a little ill. He coughed and muttered something about the gentleman's generosity. "Were I the sort of magician who is eager to entrust all his business to another person, then your offer would be most welcome. But unfortunately … I fear … In short I have no notion of employing you or indeed any other member of your race – ever again."

A long silence.

"Well, this is ungrateful indeed!" declared the gentleman, coldly. "I have put myself to the trouble of paying you this visit. I have listened with the greatest good nature to your dreary conversation. I have borne patiently with your ignorance of the proper forms and etiquette of magic. And now you scorn my offer of assistance. Other magicians, I may say, have endured all sorts of torments to gain my help. Perhaps I would do better to speak to the other one. Perhaps he understands better than you how to address persons of high rank and estate?" The gentleman glanced about the room. "I do not see him. Where is he?"

"Where is who?"

"The other one."

"The other what?"

"Magician!"

"Magici ..." Mr Norrell began to form the word but it died upon his lips. "No, no! There is no other magician! I am the only one. I assure you I am the only one. Why should you think that ...?"

"*Of course* there is another magician!" declared the gentleman, as if it were perfectly ridiculous to deny anything quite so obvious. "He is your dearest friend in all the world!"

"I have no friends," said Mr Norrell.

He was utterly perplexed. Whom might the fairy mean? Childermass? Lascelles? *Drawlight?*

"He has red hair and a long nose. And he is very conceited – as are all Englishmen!" declared the gentleman with the thistledown hair.

This was no help. Childermass, Lascelles and Drawlight were all very conceited in their ways, Childermass and Lascelles both had long noses, but none of them had red hair. Mr Norrell could make nothing of it and so he returned, with a heavy sigh, to the matter in hand. "You will not help me?" he said. "You will not bring the young woman back from the dead?"

"I did not say so!" said the gentleman with the thistledown hair, in a tone which suggested that he wondered why Mr Norrell should think *that.* "I must confess," he continued, "that in recent centuries I have grown somewhat bored of the society of my family and servants. My sisters and cousins have many virtues to recommend them, but they are not without faults. They are,

I am sorry to say, somewhat boastful, conceited and proud. This young woman," he indicated Miss Wintertowne, "she had, I dare say, all the usual accomplishments and virtues? She was graceful? Witty? Vivacious? Capricious? Danced like sunlight? Rode like the wind? Sang like an angel? Embroidered like Penelope? Spoke French, Italian, German, Breton, Welsh and many other languages?"

Mr Norrell said he supposed so. He believed that those were the sorts of things young ladies did nowadays.

"Then she will be a charming companion for me!" declared the gentleman with the thistledown hair, clapping his hands together.

Mr Norrell licked his lips nervously. "What exactly are you proposing?"

"Grant me half the lady's life and the deal is done."

"Half her life?" echoed Mr Norrell.

"Half," said the gentleman with the thistledown hair.

"But what would her friends say if they learnt I had bargained away half her life?" asked Mr Norrell.

"Oh! They will never know any thing of it. You may rely upon me for that," said the gentleman. "Besides, she has no life now. Half a life is better than none."

Half a life did indeed seem a great deal better than none. With half a life Miss Wintertowne might marry Sir Walter and save him from bankruptcy. Then Sir Walter might continue in office and lend his support to all Mr Norrell's plans for reviving English magic. But Mr Norrell had read a great many books in which were described the dealings of other English magicians with persons of this race and he knew very well how deceitful they could be. He thought he saw how the gentleman intended to trick him.

"How long is a life?" he asked.

The gentleman with the thistledown hair spread his hands in a gesture of the utmost candour. "How long would you like?"

Mr Norrell considered. "Let us suppose she had lived until she was ninety-four. Ninety-four would have been a good age.

She is nineteen now. That would be another seventy-five years. If you were to bestow upon her another seventy-five years, then I see no reason why you should not have half of it."

"Seventy-five years then," agreed the gentleman with the thistledown hair, "exactly half of which belongs to me."

Mr Norrell regarded him nervously. "Is there anything more we must do?" he asked. "Shall we sign something?"

"No, but I should take something of the lady's to signify my claim upon her."

"Take one of these rings," suggested Mr Norrell, "or this necklace about her neck. I am sure I can explain away a missing ring or necklace."

"No," said the gentleman with the thistledown hair. "It ought to be something ... Ah! I know!"

Drawlight and Lascelles were seated in the drawing-room where Mr Norrell and Sir Walter Pole had first met. It was a gloomy enough spot. The fire burnt low in the grate and the candles were almost out. The curtains were undrawn and no one had put up the shutters. The rattle of the rain upon the windows was very melancholy.

"It is certainly a night for raising the dead," remarked Mr Lascelles. "Rain and trees lash the window-panes and the wind moans in the chimney – all the appropriate stage effects, in fact. I am frequently struck with the play-writing fit and I do not know that tonight's proceedings might not inspire me to try again a tragi-comedy, telling of an impoverished minister's desperate attempts to gain money by any means, beginning with a mercenary marriage and ending with sorcery. I should think it might be received very well. I believe I shall call it, *'Tis Pity She's a Corpse*."

Lascelles paused for Drawlight to laugh at this witticism, but Drawlight had been put out of humour by the magician's refusal to allow him to stay and witness the magic, and all he said was: "Where do you suppose they have all gone?"

"I do not know."

"Well, considering all that you and I have done for them, I think we have deserved better than this! It is scarcely half an hour since they were so full of their gratitude to us. To have forgotten us so soon is very bad! And we have not been offered so much as a bit of cake since we arrived. I dare say it is rather too late for dinner – though I for one am famished to death!" He was silent a moment. "The fire is going out too," he remarked.

"Then put some more coals on," suggested Lascelles.

"What! And make myself all dirty?"

One by one all the candles went out and the light from the fire grew less and less until the Venetian paintings upon the walls became nothing but great squares of deepest black hung upon walls of a black that was slightly less profound. For a long time they sat in silence.

"That was the clock striking half-past one o'clock!" said Drawlight suddenly. "How lonely it sounds! Ugh! All the horrid things one reads of in novels always happen just as the church bell tolls or the clock strikes some hour or other in a dark house!"

"I cannot recall an instance of any thing very dreadful happening at half-past one," said Lascelles.

At that moment they heard footsteps on the stairs – which quickly became footsteps in the passageway. The drawing-room door was pushed open and someone stood there, candle in hand.

Drawlight grasped for the poker.

But it was Mr Norrell.

"Do not be alarmed, Mr Drawlight. There is nothing to be afraid of."

Yet Mr Norrell's face, as he raised up his candlestick, seemed to tell a different story; he was very pale and his eyes were wide and not yet emptied, it seemed, of the dregs of fear. "Where is Sir Walter?" he asked. "Where are the others? Miss Wintertowne is asking for her mama."

Mr Norrell was obliged to repeat the last sentence twice before the other two gentlemen could be made to understand him.

Lascelles blinked two or three times and opened his mouth as if in surprize, but then, recovering himself, he shut his mouth again and assumed a supercilious expression; this he wore for the remainder of the night, as if he regularly attended houses where young ladies were raised from the dead and considered this particular example to have been, upon the whole, a rather dull affair.

Drawlight, in the meantime, had a thousand things to say and I dare say he said all of them, but unfortunately no one had attention to spare just then to discover what they were.

Drawlight and Lascelles were sent to find Sir Walter. Then Sir Walter fetched Mrs Wintertowne, and Mr Norrell led that lady, tearful and trembling, to her daughter's room. Meanwhile the news of Miss Wintertowne's return to life began to penetrate other parts of the house; the servants learnt of it and were overjoyed and full of gratitude to Mr Norrell, Mr Drawlight and Mr Lascelles. A butler and two manservants approached Mr Drawlight and Mr Lascelles and begged to be allowed to say that if ever Mr Drawlight or Mr Lascelles could benefit from any small service that the butler or the manservants might be able to render them, they had only to speak.

Mr Lascelles whispered to Mr Drawlight that he had not realized before that doing kind actions would lead to his being addressed in such familiar terms by so many low people – it was most unpleasant – he would take care to do no more. Fortunately the low people were in such glad spirits that they never knew they had offended him.

It was soon learnt that Miss Wintertowne had left her bed and, leaning upon Mr Norrell's arm, had gone to her own sitting-room where she was now established in a chair by her fire and that she had asked for a cup of tea.

Drawlight and Lascelles were summoned upstairs to a pretty little sitting-room where they found Miss Wintertowne, her mother, Sir Walter, Mr Norrell and some of the servants.

One would have thought from their looks that it had been Mrs Wintertowne and Sir Walter who had journeyed across several supernatural worlds during the night, they were so grey-faced and drawn; Mrs Wintertowne was weeping and Sir Walter passed his hand across his pale brow from time to time like someone who had seen horrors.

Miss Wintertowne, on the other hand, appeared quite calm and collected, like a young lady who had spent a quiet, uneventful evening at home. She was sitting in a chair in the same elegant gown that she had been wearing when Drawlight and Lascelles had seen her last. She rose and smiled at Drawlight. "I think, sir, that you and I scarcely ever met before, yet I have been told how much I owe to you. But I fear it is a debt quite beyond any repaying. That I am here at all is in a large part due to your energy and insistence. Thank you, sir. Many, many thanks."

And she held out both her hands to him and he took them.

"Oh! Madam!" he cried, all bows and smiles. "It was, I do assure you, the greatest hon ..."

And then he stopped and was silent a moment. "Madam?" he said. He gave a short, embarrassed laugh (which was odd enough in itself – Drawlight was not easily embarrassed). He did not let go of her hands, but looked around the room as if in search of someone to help him out of a difficulty. Then he lifted one of her own hands and shewed it to her. She did not appear in any way alarmed by what she saw, but she did look surprized; she raised the hand so that her mother could see it.

The little finger of her left hand was gone.

# Russell Hoban

## 2005

## *Come Dance With Me*

### Christabel Alderton

21 January 2003. I read somewhere that a butterfly flapping its wings in Hong Kong could affect the course of a tornado in Texas. Sure, why not? Probably the first time I put on mascara I made it rain in Norwich three years later and Dick Turpin fall off a roof a year and a half after that. I don't need a scientist to tell me that everything's connected and a teentsy cause in one place can result in a big effect some other place. Chaos Theory is what they call it, which is the right name for any theory that concerns me. Life is full of problems, you have to expect that, but I have this extra thing that gives me trouble.

I was thirteen the first time it happened. We lived in High Hill Ferry by the River Lea, that's in Upper Clapton. Across the river the view is very wide. Over the Walthamstow Marshes the sky is big, everything else is small. Beyond the railway the sheds, pylons, gantries and distant buildings are all very small under the sky.

It was in August: 7 August 1962, I wrote the date in my diary. I was walking by the river. The banks were all purple with Michaelmas daisies and there were moorhens nesting in the reeds. The sky was blue, the sun was warm, the shadows were cool in the tunnel under the railway bridge. Beyond the bridge the river stretched away all calm and peaceful into the distance. A boat came along, a big cabin cruiser, the *Badroulbadour*. The name reminded me of a princess in *The Arabian Nights*, Badoura, but this name had a different feel to it. There were a lot of people on the boat and some of them waved to me. As I looked the action seemed to freeze for a moment and it was like a photograph of people waving. 'Better not,' I said. Not loud enough for them to hear me. Why did I say that? The picture unfroze and the boat and the people passed out of my view while I stood there shaking my head and feeling strange.

After tea my stepfather went to The Anchor & Hope for his usual four pints and later on I went out too. I liked that time of evening when the lamps were lit and the sky was still light, it sometimes gave me good ideas for the poems I wrote in my diary. I saw a bat flittering about and tossed up a pebble. The bat followed it down for a moment but its sonar must have told it pebbles are no good to eat so it flew off into the dusk.

I didn't ordinarily go near the pub in the evening when Ron, my stepdad, was there. But there were men on the benches outside The Anchor & Hope and I wanted to hear what they were talking about. They were all local and I knew some of them. When I got close enough to hear them Ted Wilmot was saying, 'I was at the marina when I heard it blow up. You could see the smoke and flames from half a mile away. Killed all nine people.'

Without thinking I said, 'The *Badroulbadour*?' Everybody turned to look at me.

'That's the one, Chrissy,' said Mr Wilmot. 'Did you know anybody on board?'

'No,' I said. I started to cry and I ran home. I knew that I was somehow connected to the deaths of those people, but how? When I said, 'Better not,' I wasn't foreseeing anything, the words just came out of my mouth. I went up to my room and wrote what happened in my diary but I had no poems in me that evening. When Ron got back from the pub he came stomping up the stairs so the whole house shook and it was about a six-pint smell that came ahead of him. He flung the door open without knocking as he always did but I was used to this and I was fully dressed. 'Piss off, Ron,' I said.

'I know for a fact you were in all afternoon,' he said. 'How'd you know about the *Badroulbadour*?'

'I've got second sight,' I said. 'Want me to tell you what's going to happen to you?'

His eyes got very big and he went pale and hurried out of the room. He died of a stroke a year later. I couldn't see his future, I was only trying to scare him because he was a creep and I hated him.

When school started again I asked the English teacher, Mr Burton, about the name Badroulbadour. He was a short man who wasn't fat but his shirts always seemed about to pop their buttons. He smelled of sweat and aftershave and when he talked to you his hands always seemed about to touch you in various places but he pulled them back before they did. I guess he was about forty.

'You're thinking about the boat that blew up?' he said.

'Yes.' I backed away a little because of his breath.

'It's a variant of the name of the *Arabian Nights* princess Budur or Badr-al-Budur,' he said, 'and it's from a poem by Wallace Stevens, "The Worms at Heaven's Gate".' He took a book out of his desk and read:

> Out of the tomb, we bring Badroulbadour,
> Within our bellies, we her chariot.
> Here is an eye. And here are, one by one,
> The lashes of that eye and its white lid.
> Here is the cheek on which that lid declined,
> And, finger by finger, here, the hand,
> The genius of that cheek. Here are the lips,
> The bundle of the body and the feet.
>
> Out of the tomb we bring Badroulbadour.

I almost said, 'That's gross,' but I didn't because it gave me goose pimples. There was nobody else in the room but the two of us. I remember the smell of the chalk dust and the distant voices and footsteps in the halls.

'Worms,' I said, 'carrying her off in their bellies.'

'That's it,' he said. 'This beauty who was the Moon of Moons, to this favour did she come at last. This book is his collected poems. There's a copy of it in the library.'

'Have you got a boat?' I said.

'No.'

'If you had one, would you call it *Badroulbadour*?'

'No. Are you thinking of naming a boat?'

'No,' I said. 'Thank you, I'll look for the book.' I got it out of the library and read the poem. It put horrible pictures in my mind, the worms bringing out an eye and the eyelashes one by one and the eyelid. I wished I hadn't read it but it gave me a kind of thrill that made me ashamed. I leafed through the book and page after page grabbed me with ideas and images I never would have thought of, like, 'The bird kept saying that birds had once been men, / Or were to be …' With my birthday money I bought a copy for myself and although a lot of it was way over my head and still is, the crazy reality of his poems seems to me a realer way of seeing the world than what you get on the 'Six O'Clock News'.

The main thing on my mind back then was the blowing up of the *Badroulbadour*. Is there such a thing as luck? Most people think so, you even hear it said that some are born lucky, and being lucky is better than being rich. Was *Badroulbadour* an unlucky name to give a boat? I thought it was. When I said, 'Better not,' what exactly did I mean? Better not stay on that boat? I guess so. So maybe I really *did* have second sight, and from then on every time I had a weird feeling of any kind I expected something awful to happen but it didn't work that way. Sometimes a bad thing happened and sometimes it didn't, so I was never sure and I was always uneasy. Still am. I came to think that maybe I was just bad luck. I kept it all to myself and hoped that it would go away. I made friends and tried to lead a normal life and nothing happened for a long time.

I didn't mean to get into all that right now. I should be getting my head around doing my thing yet again at the Hammersmith Apollo this Friday. I've never been very dignified but I'm getting too old to climb out of a body drawer while the crew do Hammer Horror effects with dry ice. Mobile Mortuary is the name of the band and I've climbed out of that drawer in a lot of places I wouldn't mind never seeing again. In some of them the dressing rooms smell about the same as the toilets and the sink is the safest place to pee. I have to knock back a little vodka to get my voice straight and the guys in the band use up the same amount of liniment, painkillers, and knee and elbow bandages as a football team but we still make money and they love us in Tirana. So it's hard to stop but it really isn't me any more, I'm not who I was when I started rocking around various clocks. What else is new.

When I'm not working my life is quieter than it used to be. Last year I became a patron of the Royal Academy of Arts and I've been buying art books. When I discovered Goya's etchings I felt like starting a new band and calling it Los Caprichos. I didn't though. Sometimes I find pictures that were already in my head or they seem to have been: various lithographs by Odilon Redon especially. There are all kinds of things it would be better not to see and he's drawn as many of them as he could. Sometimes when I look at those lithographs I feel a bit queasy. It's as if he knows something about me that he oughtn't to know. Crazy thought. He's been dead since 1918. So far I haven't read anything about his life but I think there must have been a lot of blackness in it. His lithographs are called The Blacks, *Les Noirs*. Up to the evening I'm about to describe I had only that one book of Redon's work.

Today I was at a private view of 'The Symbolists' at the Royal Academy and all of a sudden there was a painting by Redon, *The Cyclops*. I'd never seen any of his paintings, not even reproductions. Looking at this one I felt that I'd seen that cyclops before. Had I been to that place in dreams where I smell the salt wind and the sea? The naked woman lying there, maybe she's been left as a sacrifice – is it me? She has her arms raised as if to ward off the stare of this huge creature that's peeping over the edge of where she is, a monstrous misshapen head with one giant eye in the centre of it and a disgusting little mouth that you don't want to think about. Or maybe she's accepting it, opening her arms to it, I didn't know, I couldn't be sure about the woman and the cyclops.

There were a lot of people between me and the painting and I hadn't yet finished looking at it when I noticed a man watching me from about ten feet away. Not a Mobile Mortuary fan, I thought. He was tall, nice-looking, definitely interested, and about fifteen to twenty years older than I used to pull. Well, the years are going by faster all the time, aren't they. I had to smile, not at him, but because I was thinking that his taste in women was as unreliable as mine in men.

The people between me and *The Cyclops* were gone and I had a clear view of it again and stepped closer. It's only about two feet high but it suddenly opened up and became huge in front of me. I was in a big silence and then I thought I could hear the sea far below me. 'Oh,' I said, as if I suddenly knew something that I hadn't known before. Then the room started to spin and I just made it down to the ladies' in time to throw up.

I was still shaky when I went back to the exhibition. I didn't see Mr Interested but I wasn't really in the mood for making new friends anyhow so that was OK. I didn't look at *The Cyclops* again and I avoided Redon altogether. There were some good Bresdins that didn't make me vomit and of course Moreau and Böcklin and others that I now know as the usual suspects in Symbolist art.

There were drinks after the show and a lot of champagne was being put away by people with money to spend on the arts. The catering staff, all young and all in black, kept topping me up and I kept emptying my glass, so I was feeling pretty free and easy by the time I bumped into Mr Interested or he bumped into me. He'd had enough bubbly to put a little heart into him and this time he smiled at me.

I said to him, '*Komm tanze mit mir!*' What in the world made me say that? I remember that I had to grab his arm because I almost fell over. Champagne doesn't do that to me, it must have been the vodka I'd had before coming to the Royal Academy, although I'd have thought my session in the ladies' would have given me a clean slate. '*Komm tanze mit mir!*' Did I say it twice?

He seemed surprised. 'Are you German?' he said.

'No,' I said. 'Are you?'

'Half – my mother is. That's a line from "Herr Oluf". Why did you say it to me?'

'I don't know, I'm not responsible for everything I say.'

'Are you the Erlking's daughter?'

'Maybe, but I don't feel like dancing now. Anyhow, this is not a dancing situation, it's a Symbolists do and symbols refer to something else. Like me.'

'What do you refer to?'

'Different things at different times. I have to pee.' Off I went. I hung around the loo for a long time thinking about the line I'd quoted from 'Herr Oluf'. It's a Loewe ballad and 'Come dance with me' is what the Erlking's daughter says to Herr Oluf as he's riding late and far to summon guests to his wedding the next day. '*Komm tanze mit mir,*' she sings. He turns her down and on his wedding day he's dead. I heard that ballad for the first time in Vienna at Adam Freund's flat when he sang it to me stark naked. A weird guy, that Adam. What made me say those words to this stranger? It was as if there was a connection between us before we'd ever met. I was sort of spooked by that and I didn't know how I felt about talking to him again.

I thought I heard a man's footsteps approaching so I ducked into a cubicle. Mine was the only one that was occupied. There was a knocking at the door of the loo, and when he got no answer he came to my cubicle and said, 'Are you all right?'

I said, 'Yes, but I can't talk any more tonight.'

'When can I see you again?' he said.

You'll be sorry, I thought. 'Write down your name and slip it under the door,' I said. 'I'll call you.'

'I don't know *your* name,' he said.

'Not now,' I said. 'I'll call you.' Why was I doing this? I don't know, I do a lot of stupid things. A scrap of paper came under the door: 'Elias Newman' and his phone number.

'I'll leave you to it,' he said, and his footsteps walked away.

When I came out the lobby was pretty empty. I got my things and went outside. The air was cold and seemed heavy with snow that was almost ready to fall. I walked across the forecourt, under the arch, over the road and hailed a taxi. Piccadilly was full of lights and traffic, with a lot of blackness around the lights. When we turned into Park Lane the cars rushing through it looked as if they were emptying London; soon there'd be no more people, only driverless cars hurrying into the night. The trees in Hyde Park were pale under the lamps, with cold black shadows. Bayswater Road stared at me as if I were a foreigner. When we got to my place in Notting Hill the street was deserted, the lamps were dim. I'd left lights on in my house but they looked like lights in an empty house. I could hear a helicopter quite close, then farther away, then close again. My cat Stevo came out to meet me and we went inside together. Before I closed the door I looked back at the street and it was like a photograph of something that was gone. I shook my head and locked the door. I didn't think I'd be phoning Elias Newman.

# William Boyd

## 2006

## *Restless*

I was in London by six o'clock that evening. Jochen was safe
with Veronica and Avril and all I had to do was find my mother
before she killed Lucas Romer. I took the train to Paddington
and, from Paddington, a taxi delivered me to Knightsbridge. I
could remember the street that my mother had said Romer
lived on, but not the number of the house: Walton Crescent was
where I told the taxi driver to take me and drop me close to
one end. I could see from my street map of London that there
was a Walton Street – that seemed to lead to the very portals of
Harrods – and a Walton Crescent that was tucked away behind
and to one side. I paid the driver, a hundred yards off, and made
my way to the Crescent on foot, trying all the while to think
as my mother would think, to second-guess her *modus operandi*.
First things first, I said to myself: check out the neighbourhood.

Walton Crescent breathed money, class, privilege, confidence – but it did so quietly, with subtlety and no ostentation.
All the houses looked very much the same until you paid closer
attention. There was a crescent-shaped public garden facing the
gentle arc of four-storey, creamy stuccoed Georgian terraced
houses, each with small front gardens and each with – on the
first floor – three huge tall windows giving on to a wrought-
iron filigreed balcony. The small gardens were well tended and
defiantly green despite the hosepipe ban – I took in box hedges,
roses, varieties of clematis and a certain amount of mossy statu-
ary – as I began to walk along its curving length. Almost every
house had a burglar alarm and many of the windows were

shuttered or secured with sliding grilles behind the glass. I was almost alone on the street apart from a nanny wheeling a pram and a grey-haired gentleman who was cutting a low yew hedge with pedantic, loving care. I saw my mother's white Allegro parked across the street from number 29.

I bent down and rapped sharply on the window. She looked round but seemed very unsurprised to see me. She smiled and reached over to open the door to let me in beside her.

'You took your time,' she said. 'I thought you'd be here ages ago – still, well done.' She was wearing her pearl-grey trouser suit and her hair was combed and shiny as if she'd just left the hairdresser's. She was wearing lipstick and her eyelashes were dark with mascara.

I allowed a shudder of anger to pass through me before I clambered into the passenger seat. She offered me a sandwich before I could begin to reproach her.

'What is it?' I said.

'Salmon and cucumber. Not salmon out of a tin.'

'Mayonnaise?'

'Just a little – and some dill.'

I took the sandwich and wolfed down a couple of mouthfuls: I was suddenly hungry and the sandwich was very tasty.

'There's a pub in the next street,' I said. 'Let's go and have a drink and talk this over properly. I'm very worried, I have to say.'

'No, I might miss him,' she said. 'Sunday evening, coming back from the country somewhere – his house or a friend's – he should be here before nine.'

'I will not let you kill him. I warn you, I –'

'Don't be absurd!' She laughed. 'I just want to have a brief chat.' She put her hand on my knee. 'Well done, Ruth, darling, tracking me here. I'm impressed – and pleased. I thought it was best this way – to let you figure it out for yourself, you know? I didn't want to ask you to come, put pressure on you. I thought you would figure it out because you're so clever – but now I know you're clever in a different way.'

'I suppose I should take that as a compliment.'

'Look: if I'd asked you outright you'd have thought of a hundred ways of stopping me.' She smiled, almost gleefully. 'But, anyway, here we are, both of us.' She touched my cheek with her fingers – where was all this affection coming from? 'I'm glad you're here,' she said. 'I know I could see him on my own but it'll be so much better with you beside me.'

I was suspicious. 'Why?'

'You know: moral support and all that.'

'Where's the gun?'

'I'm afraid I rather buggered it up. The barrels didn't come off cleanly. I wouldn't dare use it – anyway, now you're here I feel safe.'

We sat on talking and eating our sandwiches as the evening light seemed to thicken dustily, peachily, in Walton Crescent, turning the cream stucco the palest apricot for a few moments. As the sky slowly darkened – it was a cloudy day but warm – I began to notice a small squirm of fear entering me: sometimes it seemed in my guts, sometimes my chest, sometimes in my limbs, making them achy and heavy – and I began to wish that Romer wouldn't come home, that he'd gone away for a holiday to Portofino or Saint Tropez or Inverness, or wherever types like him vacationed, and that this vigil of ours would prove fruitless and we could go home and try to forget about the whole thing. But at the same time I knew my mother and I knew it wouldn't simply end with Romer's non-appearance: she had to see him just once more, one last time. And I realised, as I thought further, that everything that had happened this summer had been designed – manipulated – to bring about this confrontation: the wheelchair nonsense, the paranoia, the memoir –

My mother grabbed my arm.

At the far end of the crescent the big Bentley nosed round the corner. I thought I might faint, the blood seemed to be rushing audibly from my head. I took a huge gulp of air as I felt my stomach acids seethe and climb my oesophagus.

'When he gets out of the car,' my mother said evenly, 'you go out and call his name. He'll turn to you – he won't see me at first. Keep him talking for a second or two. I want to surprise him.'

'What do I say?'

'How about: "Good evening, Mr Romer, can I have a word?" I only need a couple of seconds.'

She seemed very calm, very strong – whereas I thought I might burst into tears at any moment, might bawl and blub, I felt suddenly so insecure and inadequate – not like me at all, I realised.

The Bentley stopped, double-parking with the engine running, and the chauffeur opened the door and stepped out, walking round the car to the rear. He held the back door open on the pavement side and Romer climbed out with some difficulty, stooped a little, perhaps stiff from the journey. He had a few words with his driver, who then got back into the car and pulled away. Romer went to his front gate; he was wearing a tweed jacket and grey flannels with suede shoes. A light came on in the transom of number 29 and simultaneously the garden lights were illuminated, shining on the flagged path to the front door, a cherry tree, a stone obelisk in the hedge corner.

My mother gave me a shove and I opened the door.

'Lord Mansfield?' I called and stepped out on to the road. 'May I have a word?'

Romer turned very slowly to face me.

'Who are you?'

'I'm Ruth Gilmartin – we met the other day.' I crossed the road towards him. 'At your club – I wanted to interview you.'

He peered at me. 'I've nothing to say to you,' he said. His raspy voice even, unthreatening. 'I told you that.'

'Oh, but I think you have,' I said, wondering where my mother was – I had no sense of her presence, couldn't hear her, had no idea which way she'd gone.

He laughed and opened the gate to his front garden.

'Good-night, Miss Gilmartin. Stop bothering me. Go away.'

I couldn't think what to say next – I had been dismissed.

He turned to close his gate and I saw behind him someone open the door a few inches, left ajar for easy access, no bother with keys or anything as vulgar as that. He saw I had remained standing there and his eyes flicked automatically up and down the street. And then he became very still.

'Hello, Lucas,' my mother said from the darkness.

She seemed to materialise from around the box hedge, not moving – just suddenly standing there.

Romer seemed paralysed for a moment, then he drew himself erect, stiffly, like a soldier on parade, as if he might fall over otherwise.

'Who're you?'

Now she stepped forward and the dusky late evening light showed her face, caught her eyes. I thought: she looks very beautiful, as if some sort of miraculous rejuvenation were taking place and the intervening thirty-five years of ageing were being erased.

I looked at Romer – he knew who she was – and he kept himself very still, one hand gripping the gatepost. I wondered what this moment must have been like for him – the shock beyond all shocks. But he gave nothing away, just managing to produce a small erratic smile.

'Eva Delectorskaya,' he said, softly, 'who would have thought?'

# Georgina Harding

## 2007

## *The Solitude of Thomas Cave*

He begins to see bears frequently now, coming close up to
the tent but also in the distance as they cross the ice, the more
easily distinguishable as their fur shows stained and yellowish on
bright days against the snow. There are lone bears but often pairs,
mothers with their cubs, and when he hunts and kills a mother
he is both astonished and distressed to see the devotion with
which the cub stays by and must be killed itself rather than leave
its mother's side. Over the course of the winter he has developed
an admiration for these beasts which the harshest conditions
do not deter, and which seem to roam so far and wide, appear-
ing sometimes from across the ice as if they have skated across
oceans to reach the island. He sees that they move on the ice like
skaters, with long slipping steps, and as the ice begins to melt he
is amazed to observe how light they can be in motion, escaping
his gun at times by cutting across ice far thinner than he himself
would dare to walk on.

At last the thaw becomes a perceptible process although there
are days still, sometimes a week together, of blizzard and cold
equal to any that he has previously experienced. It is the sky
that first tells him that the ice has begun to break up out beyond
the bay, dark streaks of what Captain Duke had called water sky,
revealing by the intensity of its reflected colour wherever the
darkness of clear sea, rather than the paleness of ice, lies beneath.
Out there it is evident also that the sea has begun to move, for
daily he witnesses the effects of the tide as its flow and ebb varies
the pressure on the ice in the bay and causes it to creak and

move and in places to crack open. He sees that ice rots before it dissolves, its texture becoming soft and spongy before it disintegrates into porridge and slush. Where it breaks and pools are revealed, the exposed sea reeks steam into the sunlight as if it had boiled beneath.

With the melt a drab and dirty world which he had almost forgotten begins to re-emerge. There is seaweed, slimy and almost black in colour, which the bears claw up on the strand, and patches of anaemic moss. There is the carcase of a fox that must have frozen as the winter began and become buried in the snow. In the area around the tent the objects of the whale station once more show themselves, and also his own detritus: not only the bones and scraps but every sausage of faeces he has carried out that winter and dumped beside the path. He begins to be aware now as he approaches his lodging of its smell, a smell that has become a constant of his enclosed existence, a fetid and manly smell of smoke and blubber and long-hung meat.

As May reaches its close there are endless days of crystal clarity when the sun at its height feels hot on his face as if it would burn his skin through. He closes his eyes to its brightness, relishes the heat on his lids, on his temples and cheeks as if it touched the bone beneath. One of these days, a day that is fine as the warmest spring day in England, he does at last a thing he has been thinking to do for weeks. He takes off his clothes in the sun, not only the boots and hat and furs of which he often now divests himself, but jacket and breeches, and linen that is grey and stained and comes off like old fruit peel. The skin he exposes is extraordinarily naked beneath the sunlight, so white that it is almost blued where the shadows fall beneath angular bones, in parts coloured darker where clothing has rubbed and it has been chafed and hardened. He observes his body almost objectively: the pale stomach and ribbed chest, his legs like sticks with a wiry mass of hairs on them, his thin arms hollowed at the elbows, hands at their ends that look huge and black as he turns them before his eyes, the dark tidemarks at his wrists, the other tidemark of filth that he cannot see but can only feel where the skin on his neck beneath his beard is both greasy and engrained with dirt.

He wraps his naked body in a cloak and walks down to a hole in the ice close to the shore. There for the first time he washes, rubbing himself until every part of his body tingles, and it is an extraordinary hard pleasure. He takes up the cloak again and returns to the tent. In his cabin there is other linen, clean linen. But first he throws a broad plank down on the dazzling patch of snow before his door and lies on the smooth wood in the sunshine and basks himself dry.

When he lies on his back he must put a hand across his eyes to shield them from the brightness, to give himself a filtered view that is criss-crossed by the passage of birds overhead. There are so many birds now, moving in gigantic flocks, thousands of birds at a time that come in from the south forming a band in the sky that seems to reach to the very horizon; he sees them approach at first as so many black specks, like particles blown in the smoke from a fire, separating and weaving and drawn together again, hears then the distant uproar of their cries coming closer, long before he can distinguish the individuals, the beat of their wings. He remembers how astonished he had been when he saw the first flock of seabirds, a little flock sudden as an apparition, no more than half a score of birds twittering on a rock on the mountainside. Later that same day a second group arrived, then others in the days that followed, until after a week the mountain and the glacier behind were entirely covered with birds, and they remained two days and then as unexpectedly as they had come they were gone, and he did not know if it was a change in the weather that drove them away or some purpose, some instinct they had that they must move on and breed on some ground even farther north.

Soon as the weather cleared again other flocks came in their wake, eiders and guillemots and other birds he has known at sea, and an innumerable flock of some grey bird the size of a pigeon for which he had no name, and he was as strange to them as they to him, for the birds showed no fear of him or caution and he could almost pluck them out of the sky or off the ground with his hand. He walked among them where they went to nest on the rocks that were now bare of snow, and there were so many of them that they darkened the sky above his head and he could hear nothing beyond their clamour. The little pigeon birds in particular were not much to eat, so little flesh they had on them, but he used their carcases to bait his traps and caught the foxes that were now to be found in numbers surprising for animals of such solitary nature, attracted to the coast he guessed by the presence of the birds.

*Now that the winter is over,* he has written in his log, *there is such an abundance of creatures and species here that it altogether boggles the mind, such numbers coming off the sea that you had not thought so many creatures could have survived and reproduced themselves since Noah's Flood.*

There were reindeer coming in, coming up to the tent and looking at him without any appearance of fear, and they were lean as sticks after the winter and hardly worth the killing. He did not know from where they had come, and marvelled that they came at all for there was so little for them to feed on at first, the vegetation so recently stripped of snow that it had not even greenness to it yet every patch of pale moss on the mountain-side behind the shore was marked with the glossy piles of their droppings.

With such plenty about him he saw that he could choose what he might hunt, knowing that whatever he required for his survival was so infinitesimal that its loss could hardly be reckoned. He phrased a prayer of thanksgiving in his mind and remembered how Adam had lived alongside the beasts in Eden, and made it his rule to kill no more than he needed. Gulls dived so close to his head that their wingtips brushed his hair but he made no attempt to knock them down; their eggs alone were enough to feed five thousand. And then there were the seals that came soon as the ice had broken apart and given them passage, these too in huge herds that played together in the water and then drew themselves on to the beach, steaming and snorting and jostling one another like cattle crowded into a market. The company of the seals touched him as that of none of the other creatures had, some kinship about them that made him at once warm and alone. It was their great uncanny eyes, so redolent of human expression as they popped their heads out from the ice and watched him. They made him conscious of himself as he had not been since he had last seen men, as he had thought he could not be save before another human being.

He walked out on the ice as far as he dared and crouched down on his hunkers before the ice holes and gazed back at them, eye to eye, and at last he began to speak to them, beneath his breath, just for the relief of it, and then one day one of them popped up its head before him and fixed him with such a very human look that he spoke to it aloud. He greeted it and asked it from where it had come, and it turned its head around and looked at him again as if there were indeed words forming there behind its eyes. He laughed at himself then for his fantasy and took himself back to his cabin. Later he went down to the very same hole and this time he had brought his violin with him that he had at last taken down from its pegs on the wall, and he had prepared the bow and tuned its untouched strings as best he could. Seals loved music, the sailors said; there were seals in tales that had human souls and deep under water where men could not see them they danced.

He stood at the edge of the hole in the ice and played, softly, waveringly at first, the notes creaking out of disuse. It was so very long since he had played. So long since he had heard music of any kind. And yet it still existed, he could bring it out of himself. He played to the empty hole and as he did so the tears rose in him and flooded out from his eyes. He held the instrument tighter to his chest then and played the harder, played now from deep within him, played to rouse and exorcise. Suddenly there was a splash and a pop in the hole before him as a seal came up and blew out a spray of water. He played on until his fingers were sore, and took a bow in a second of silence, and not until that was done did the seal dip and disappear.

233

*With the presence of the seals it is as if I live once again in a popu-
lated world. Their barks fill the air, and the yelps of the pups that begin
to be born now and grow and play at their mothers' sides between the
rocks on the strand. The cry of a seal pup is more akin to the cry of a
human child than any voice I have otherwise known. Massed together
the sound is something like the yells of a mob of children playing, but
singly and in distress a man could not I think tell it from the call of fear
a human child makes to its parent. I know of no cry so plaintive to my
ear as the cry of a seal pup left by its mother alone among the mass. It
lies with just the narrow cleft, the idea of a space between itself and all
the rest that are strange to it, and reaches up its head and calls that very
human and personal cry that seems directed precise as a name, to its
mother and to no other. I think that the sense of hearing owned by these
beasts must be very acute, for they seem to react to music and even to
hear it and be drawn to it from under water, and come then to the surface
and crane their necks to listen.*

# David Park

## 2008

## *The Truth Commissioner*

The lake is still, with only the gentlest of swells pushing half-heartedly through the reeds. Far out, sky and water like lifelong friends seem inseparable. A little breeze plays with the smoke of his dying cigarette. He wonders if Arnie is somewhere out there on his boat, casting his lines. Sitting waiting patiently for a catch. The sky feels so low he could almost stretch out a hand and touch it. He lights another cigarette – there seems no point any more. Arnie says the water is always cold, cold even in the heat of the day. Soon it will be time. In his broken, shallow sleep, words had slipped like eels through his mind but when he tried to trap the truth of what he must say this morning, and how he must tell her, they slipped into the shadows. A bird skims the surface of the water, a black arrowhead in the slowly strengthening light. He thinks of ever more elaborate lies then blows them away through the purse of his lips with the smoke of the cigarette. He tries to tell himself that there'll be a release in truth, that after all this time the weight of deception will be lifted from his shoulders. He walks to the end of the jetty and throws the cigarette away. It's almost time. He narrows his eyes and stares out into the sleeping heart of the lake. For the next hour or so it is able to wear its own face and does not have the luminous insistence of the sky pressed relentlessly against it. Then he bends down and scoops a handful of water and splashes his face with its coldness.

The walk back to the house is weighted with the words in his head arranged all wrong like the flowers he bought for her birthday and cack-handedly tried to shape in a vase. How many layers of their life will be pulled away by what he has to tell her? And what will be left when he has finished? He thinks of the stillness at the heart of the lake and tries to tell himself that love can endure. Even this. But he's no longer sure of anything he tells himself, of what he can believe and what is just another deception, designed to smooth his way, so it feels as if he knows nothing any more and that everything he wants to hold tightly slips through his fingers like water.

He hesitates at the door then goes in. Maybe she will stretch out her arms to him. Maybe she will tell him that he's cold and enfold him in the embrace of her sleep-stirred warmth. Then after a while she will say, 'What does a girl have to do around here to get a cup of coffee?' and he will slip reluctantly from her side.

She looks at him as he stands in the doorway of the bedroom watching her.

'Well, Danny, is the lake still there?'

He doesn't answer and she sits up in the bed, shaking the black shock of her hair away from her face.

'What's wrong, Danny?'

He looks into her eyes and takes a single step into the room.

'My name isn't Danny.'

She's looking at him and then she starts to smile but stops. No other way. It's the price that must be paid. The water is cold against his skin. He steps further into the room and each slow step is weighted with fear. More fear than he's ever felt and he knows there are no words.

# Kamila Shamsie

## 2009

## *Burnt Shadows*

From a distance, it looked as if they were praying.

Harry Burton and Hiroko Ashraf knelt on either side of a rock pool, hands on their knees, neither looking left towards seagulls gliding above the water's surface nor right towards the beach life on the sand: families sitting on shawls, eating oranges to counter the salty air; a group of boys rolling a tennis ball towards a group of girls, a piece of paper taped to the ball with something written on it which made the girls giggle and cluster together; camels with heavily mirror-worked seats eliciting screams from young passengers as they dipped forward and back in the see-saw of standing; Raza constructing an elaborate sand fort, because that's what Harry said he used to enjoy doing at the beach in his youth, while Sajjad inscribed Urdu verses on the fort's walls with the sharp end of a cuttlebone.

'Sometimes you only know the salamanders are there because they stir up the mud. Their camouflage is slightly more effective than yours.' Hiroko waved a hand in the direction of Harry's hennaed hair, several shades brighter than its natural colour.

Harry laughed.

'Don't mock. Even the Pathans think I'm Pathan when I'm wearing a shalwar kameez. I tell them my name is Lala Buksh, and then my inability to say very much more in Pashto gives me away. Any idea what happened to him? The real Lala Buksh?'

Hiroko shook her head. Turning her face towards the sea, she closed her eyes and smiled.

'It's such a pleasure to be here. We live so far inland I sometimes forget this is also a coastal city.'

'Also?'

'Like Nagasaki.'

She looked towards the three wooden fishing boats progressing
in a line towards the horizon, no sails, and at this distance no sound
of motors, so that they seemed to be propelled by the will of the
sea. Nagasaki to Bombay. Bombay to Istanbul. Istanbul to Karachi.
All that sea-travel in a single year, made more extraordinary by
the fact that in the years preceding she'd never left Japan, and in
the years that followed she had never left Pakistan. Rarely left
Karachi, in fact – Sajjad sometimes took Raza to Lahore to see his
brother Iqbal, or to Peshawar to see his sister, and once a decade
or so they'd cross the border to visit the family that remained
in Delhi, though those were always dispiriting trips. But Hiroko
didn't accompany them on these family trips, and Sajjad had long
ago recognised that his Japanese wife would always be an outsider
to his family, her presence reason for discomfort on every side, and
he'd finally stopped asking her to come along. So every so often
she would have these days alone in Karachi, and always there'd be
a secret thrill of imagining she might dip into their savings and
board a flight to somewhere – Egypt, Hong Kong, New York –
returning in time to welcome her husband and son home.

'Do you still think about it a lot? About Nagasaki?' It was not
the kind of question he would usually ask of someone he had
first met only a couple of months earlier, but already Hiroko
seemed like someone who had been in his life a very long time.

She touched her back, just above the waist.

'It's always there.'

Harry nodded, and looked down into the clear water of the
rock pool, seeing his face with sea plants growing out of it.

'How did you explain it to Raza? With Kim – the first time
she asked about Konrad, I made an excuse and left the room. My
mother told her something – I still don't know what, except that
it made her look terrifyingly grown-up when she walked out of
the room. She was eight.'

Hiroko glanced over to Raza, his concentration intent upon his fort. In this moment, he was a child.

'Fairy tales,' she said. 'I made up fairy tales.'

Harry shook his head, not understanding.

She took a deep breath.

'I'll tell you,' she said, and he knew by her voice that he was going to hear something that she would speak of to almost no one else. 'There was the one about the girl whose dying father slithers towards her in the shape of a lizard; she is so horrified by his grotesqueness it takes her years to understand that his final act was to come towards her, after a lifetime of walking away. The one about the boy shaken out of his life and told that was a dream, and so was everyone he loved in it – this charred world, this prison, this aloneness is reality. The one about the purple-backed book creatures with broken spines who immolate themselves rather than exist in a world in which everything written in them is shown to be fantasy. The woman who loses all feeling, fire entering from her back and searing her heart, so it's possible for her to see a baby's corpse and think only, There's another one. The men and women who walk through shadow-worlds in search of the ones they loved. Monsters who spread their wings and land on human skin, resting there, biding their time. The army of fire demons, dropped from the sky, who kill with an embrace. The schoolteacher in a world where textbooks come to life; she cannot escape from the anatomy text, its illustrations following her everywhere – bodies without skin, bodies with organs on display, bodies that reveal what happens to bodies when nothing in them works any more.'

'God. Hiroko.'

When he had applied to work at the CIA's Directorate of Operations he had anticipated running into trouble over his foreign birth and the question of divided allegiances; but the India and England years rated little mention in his interview, and the only sticky moment occurred when he was asked his views on the dropping of the bombs on Hiroshima and Nagasaki. Acutely aware of the polygraph machine attached to him, he had said, 'Like President Eisenhower, I believe we should not have done that.'

Now Pakistan was developing its nuclear programme. The CIA knew. And as far as Harry could make out all they were doing in response was gathering information that confirmed this was so and then funnelling more money into the country, making possible the huge expenditure that such a programme required. Harry had no memory of Konrad, but that hadn't prevented him from dreaming of mushroom clouds on a regular basis since the day in 1945 when he found the magazine his mother had brought home with its pictures of atomic-bomb victims – he had looked from the photographs of burnt lumps of humanity to the picture of Uncle Konrad as a young boy, just a little older than Harry was himself, smiling at the camera with Harry's own smile.

It was Ilse Weiss, not any of the CIA psychologists, who had suggested that at the very root of Harry's determination to join the CIA at the height of the Cold War was the terror of nuclear war, the threat of which could only be eliminated by conclusively ending the battle between America and Russia. Harry had laughed dismissively – he always refused to acknowledge to his mother that he worked for the CIA, though she had somehow managed to work it out while he was still in training at the Farm; but ever since he had read a colleague's report to Langley about the Pakistan nuclear project there had been times, while sitting across from the ISI officials, when Harry felt a rage that went beyond the usual mistrust and annoyances and anger that accompanied every step of the ISI–CIA alliance, and then he couldn't help wondering if his mother might have had a point.

'But I never told Raza the fairy tales,' Hiroko said. 'Not any of them. I kept thinking, One day he'll be old enough. But why should I ever let my child imagine all that?' She cupped water in her hand and drizzled it on Harry's scalp, which was beginning to turn red in the sun. 'He knows there was a bomb. He knows it was terrible, and that my father died, and the man I was engaged to died. He once received a history book for a birthday present which had a full page about Hiroshima, with a paragraph appended about Nagasaki. It showed a picture of an old Japanese man looking sad, and holding a bandage against his bloodied head. It looked as if he'd scraped it falling off the low branch of a tree. Raza showed it to me, nodded his head, and never said anything about it again.'

'And the burns on your back?'

He was unprepared for the anger streaking across her face, the bite in her voice as she said, 'Your mother had no business telling you about that.'

'I'm so sorry.' He found he was actually frightened of her displeasure, shaken by the unfamiliarity of her features without their customary good humour.

She brushed a hand over her face, as though wiping away the unpleasantness that had settled there, and reached out to pat Harry's wrist.

'Forgive my vanity. Sajjad is the one person in the world who I allow ...' She stopped, smiled in a way that told Harry that to continue would reveal details of intimacy between husband and wife, and added, 'Actually, Raza's never seen them.'

'He hasn't seen them?' Impossible to keep the shock out of his voice.

'Oh, he knows they're there. He knows there are places without feeling. When he was a child he liked to sneak up behind me and tap against my back with a fork or a pencil, laughing when I carried on doing whatever I was doing, unaware. It made Sajjad so angry, but I was grateful he could approach it with such lightness.' She looked amused by Harry's continued expression of amazement. 'This is not a world in which young boys see their mother's bare backs, you know. I never made a conscious choice for him not to see it – I simply didn't think I needed to go out of my way to show him what was done to me. And yes, Harry Burton, they're ugly. And I am vain.'

He wanted – strangely, wildly – to apologise to her, to beg her forgiveness. The only thing that stopped him was the certainty that whatever he said would be inadequate, and embarrassing to her.

'But I don't want you to think my life is haunted by the past,' Hiroko continued. 'I'm told most hibakusha have survivor's guilt. Believe me, I don't. Here I am, breathing in the sea air, watching for salamanders and hermit crabs with a Weiss while my husband and son build forts on the sand. Yesterday, I picked up the ringing telephone and heard my old friend Ilse's voice for the first time in thirty-five years.' She smiled with a deep pleasure. It had been extraordinary, the way the intervening years had compressed into nothing, and they had talked without constraint for over an hour, Ilse's voice happy in a way it had never been during the days of her marriage to James. 'And tomorrow morning I will walk into the schoolyard with my neighbour and friend, Bilqees, who teaches with me, and my students will crowd around to tell me about their school trip to the zoo, so many of them chattering at the same time that I won't understand a word any of them is saying. Yes, I know everything can disappear in a flash of light. That doesn't make it any less valuable.'

She leaned back and sank her feet into the rock pool. She didn't know how to tell him – without making him uncomfortable – that he had become part of all that was valuable in her life. The way he had entered their house in Nazimabad, entered their daily lives – there was something simply amazing in it. Earlier, watching Harry play cricket on the sand with Raza and a group of young boys, she realised that while Konrad would have determinedly wandered into parts of town which his sister stayed far from he would have done it self-consciously, aware of his own transgression. And Ilse, for all her years in New York, mingling with 'people of all kinds', as she put it, would still not be able to enter Sajjad's presence without remembering he had been only one rung up from a servant – this much was obvious in the only stilted moment of their conversation, when Ilse said, 'And how is your husband?' But Harry's attitude was simply one of gratitude for being welcomed.

Americans! she thought, watching Harry remove a tube of sunblock from the pocket of his shorts and apply some to the

top of his head. In Tokyo, thirty-five years ago, she had decided
their snobbery was not of class but of nation ('The bomb saved
American lives!' Even now, even now, she could feel her face
burning at the memory). But around Harry Burton she felt
herself relent. He was a consular officer – Konrad's nephew, a
consular officer. It seemed entirely right. He was the gatekeeper
between one nation and the next, and all she had seen of him
these last weeks led her to believe he swung the gate open, wide.

'Partition and the bomb,' Harry said, interrupting her. 'The
two of you are proof that humans can overcome everything.'

*Overcome.* Such an American word. What really did it mean?
But she knew he meant it generously, so it seemed discourteous
to throw the word back in his face with stories of a 'not right'
foetus which her body had rejected, or the tears Sajjad wept
after his first visit to his collapsed world in Delhi.

# Patti Smith

2010

## Just Kids

It was a Monday morning on July 3. I maneuvered the tearful goodbyes and walked the mile to Woodbury and caught the Broadway bus to Philadelphia, passing through my beloved Camden and nodding respectfully to the sad exterior of the once-prosperous Walt Whitman Hotel. I felt a pang abandoning this struggling city, but there was no work for me there. They were closing the great shipyard and soon everyone would be looking for jobs.

I got off at Market Street and stopped in Nedick's. I slipped a quarter in the jukebox, played two sides by Nina Simone, and had a farewell doughnut and coffee. I crossed over to Filbert Street to the bus terminal across from the bookstall that I had haunted for the last few years. I paused before the spot where I had pocketed my Rimbaud. In its place was a battered copy of *Love on the Left Bank* with grainy black-and-white shots of Paris nightlife in the late fifties, taken by Ed van der Elsken. The photographs of the beautiful Vali Myers, with her wild hair and kohl-rimmed eyes, dancing on the streets of the Latin Quarter deeply impressed me. I did not swipe the book, but kept her image in mind.

It was a big blow that the fare to New York had nearly doubled since last I'd traveled. I was unable to buy my ticket. I went into a phone booth to think. It was a real Clark Kent moment. I thought of calling my sister although I was too ashamed to return home. But there, on the shelf beneath the telephone, lying on thick yellow pages, was a white patent purse. It contained a locket and thirty-two dollars, almost a week's paycheck at my last job.

Against my better judgment, I took the money but I left the purse on the ticket counter in the hopes that the owner would at least retrieve the locket. There was nothing in it that revealed her identity. I can only thank, as I have within myself many times through the years, this unknown benefactor. She was the one who gave me the last piece of encouragement, a thief's good-luck sign. I accepted the grant of the small white purse as the hand of fate pushing me on.

At twenty years old, I boarded the bus. I wore my dungarees, black turtleneck, and the old gray raincoat I had bought in Camden. My small suitcase, yellow-and-red plaid, held some drawing pencils, a notebook, *Illuminations*, a few pieces of clothing, and pictures of my siblings. I was superstitious. Today was a Monday; I was born on Monday. It was a good day to arrive in New York City. No one expected me. Everything awaited me.

I immediately took the subway from Port Authority to Jay Street and Borough Hall, then to Hoyt-Schermerhorn and DeKalb Avenue. It was a sunny afternoon. I was hoping my friends might put me up until I could find a place of my own. I went to the brownstone at the address I had, but they had moved. The new tenant was polite. He motioned toward a room at the rear of the flat and suggested that his roommate might know the new address.

I walked into the room. On a simple iron bed, a boy was sleeping. He was pale and slim with masses of dark curls, lying bare-chested with strands of beads around his neck. I stood there. He opened his eyes and smiled.

When I told him of my plight, he rose in one motion, put on his huaraches and a white T-shirt, and beckoned me to follow him.

I watched him as he walked ahead, leading the way with a light-footed gait, slightly bowlegged. I noticed his hands as he tapped his fingers against his thigh. I had never seen anyone like him. He delivered me to another brownstone on Clinton Avenue, gave a little farewell salute, smiled, and was on his way.

The day wore on. I waited for my friends. As fortune would have it, they did not return. That night, having nowhere to go, I fell asleep on their red stoop. When I awoke, it was Independence Day, my first away from home with the familiar parade, veterans' picnic, and fireworks display. I felt a restless agitation in the air. Packs of children threw firecrackers that exploded at my feet. I would spend that day much as I spent the next few weeks, looking for kindred souls, shelter, and, most urgently, a job. Summer seemed the wrong time to find a sympathetic student. Everyone was less than eager to provide me with a helping hand. Everyone was struggling, and I, the country mouse, was just an awkward presence. Eventually I went back to the city and slept in Central Park, not far from the statue of the Mad Hatter.

Along Fifth Avenue, I left applications at shops and bookstores. I would often stop before a grand hotel, an alien observer to the Proustian lifestyle of the privileged class, exiting sleek black cars with exquisite brown-and-gold-patterned trunks. It was another side of life. Horse-drawn carriages were stationed between the Paris Theatre and the Plaza Hotel. In discarded newspapers I would search out the evening's entertainment. Across from the Metropolitan Opera I watched the people enter, sensing their anticipation.

The city was a real city, shifty and sexual. I was lightly jostled by small herds of flushed young sailors looking for action on Forty-second Street, with its rows of X-rated movie houses, brassy women, glittering souvenir shops, and hot-dog vendors. I wandered through Kino parlors and peered through the windows of the magnificent sprawling Grant's Raw Bar filled with men in black coats scooping up piles of fresh oysters.

The skyscrapers were beautiful. They did not seem like mere corporate shells. They were monuments to the arrogant yet philanthropic spirit of America. The character of each quadrant was invigorating and one felt the flux of its history. The old world and the emerging one served up in the brick and mortar of the artisan and the architects.

I walked for hours from park to park. In Washington Square, one could still feel the characters of Henry James and the presence of the author himself. Entering the perimeters of the white arch, one was greeted by the sounds of bongos and acoustic guitars, protest singers, political arguments, activists leafleting, older chess players challenged by the young. This open atmosphere was something I had not experienced, simple freedom that did not seem to be oppressive to anyone.

I was beat and hungry, roaming with a few belongings wrapped in a cloth, hobo style, a sack without a stick—my suitcase stashed in Brooklyn. It was a Sunday and I took a day off from searching for work. Through the night I had gone back and forth to the end of the line at Coney Island, snatching bits of sleep when I could. I got off the F train at the Washington Square station and walked down Sixth Avenue. I stopped to watch the boys shooting hoops near Houston Street. It was there I met Saint, my guide, a black Cherokee with one foot in the street and the other in the Milky Way. He suddenly appeared, as vagabonds will sometimes find one another.

I swiftly clocked him, inside and out, and perceived he was okay. It seemed natural talking with him, though I didn't normally talk to strangers.

"Hey, sister. What's your situation?"

"On earth or in the universe?"

He laughed and said, "All right!"

I sized him up while he was looking at the sky. He had a Jimi Hendrix look, tall, slim, and soft-spoken, though a bit ragged. He posed no threat, uttered no sexual innuendos, no mention of the physical plane, except the most basic.

"You hungry?"

"Yes."

"Come on."

The street of cafés was just waking up. He stopped at a few places on MacDougal Street. He greeted the fellows setting up for the new day. "Hey, Saint," they would say, and he'd shoot the shit while I stood a few feet away. "Got anything for me?" he asked.

The cooks knew him well and gave him offerings in brown paper bags. He returned the favor with anecdotes of his travels from the heartland to Venus. We walked to the park, sat on a bench, and divided his take: loaves of day-old bread and a head of lettuce. He had me remove the top layers of the lettuce as he broke the bread in half. Some of the lettuce was still crisp inside.

"There's water in the lettuce leaves," he said. "The bread will satisfy your hunger."

We piled the best leaves on the bread and happily ate.

"A real prison breakfast," I said.

"Yeah, but we are free."

And that summed it up. He slept for a while in the grass and I just sat quietly with no fear. When he awoke, we searched around until he found a patch of earth without grass. He got a stick and drew a celestial map. He gave me some lessons on man's place in the universe, then the inner universe.

"You follow this?"

"It's normal stuff," I said.

He laughed for a long time.

Our unspoken routine filled my next few days. At night we'd go our separate ways. I would watch him stroll away. He would often be barefoot, his sandals slung over his shoulder. I marveled how anyone, even in summer, would have the courage and stealth to roam barefoot in the city.

We would go find our own sleep outposts. We never spoke about where we slept. In the morning I would find him in the park and we'd make the rounds, "getting vitals," as he said. We'd eat pita bread and celery stalks. On the third day I found two quarters embedded in the grass in the park. We had coffee, toast and jam, and split an egg at the Waverly Diner. Fifty cents was real money in 1967.

That afternoon, he gave me a long recap of man and the universe. He seemed content with me as a pupil, though he was more distracted than usual. Venus, he had told me, was more than a star. "I'm waiting to go home," he said.

It was a beautiful day and we sat in the grass. I guess I dozed off. He wasn't there when I awoke. There was a piece of red chalk he used for drawing on the sidewalk. I pocketed it and went my way. The next day I half waited for him to return. But he didn't. He had given me what I needed to keep going.

I wasn't sad, because every time I thought of him I'd smile. I imagined him jumping on a boxcar on a celestial course to the planet he embraced, appropriately named for the goddess of love. I wondered why he devoted so much time to me. I reasoned it was because we were both wearing long coats in July, the brotherhood of *La Bohème*.

I grew more desperate to find a job and started a second-level search in boutiques and department stores. I was quick to comprehend I wasn't dressed right for this line of work. Even Capezio's, a store for classic dance attire, wouldn't take me, though I had cultivated a good beatnik ballet look. I canvassed Sixtieth and Lexington and as a last resort left an application at Alexander's, knowing I would never really work there. Then I began to walk downtown, absorbed in my own condition.

It was Friday, July 21, and unexpectedly I collided with the sorrow of an age. John Coltrane, the man who gave us *A Love Supreme*, had died. Scores of people were gathering across from St. Peter's Church to say goodbye. Hours passed. People were sobbing as the love cry of Albert Ayler spirited the atmosphere. It was if a saint had died, one who had offered up healing music yet was not permitted to heal himself. Along with many strangers, I experienced a deep sense of loss for a man I had not known save through his music.

Later I walked down Second Avenue, Frank O'Hara territory. Pink light washed over rows of boarded buildings. New York light, the light of the abstract expressionists. I thought Frank would have loved the color of the fading day. Had he lived, he might have written an elegy for John Coltrane like he did for Billie Holiday.

I spent the evening checking out the action on St. Mark's Place. Long-haired boys scatting around in striped bell-bottoms and used military jackets flanked with girls wrapped in tie-dye. There were flyers papering the streets announcing the coming of Paul Butterfield and Country Joe and the Fish. "White Rabbit" was blaring from the open doors of the Electric Circus. The air was heavy with unstable chemicals, mold, and the earthy stench of hashish. The fat of candles burned, great tears of wax spilling onto the sidewalk.

I can't say I fit in, but I felt safe. No one noticed me. I could move freely. There was a roving community of young people, sleeping in the parks, in makeshift tents, the new immigrants invading the East Village. I wasn't kin to these people, but because of the free-floating atmosphere, I could roam within it. I had faith. I sensed no danger in the city, and I never encountered any. I had nothing to offer a thief and didn't fear men on the prowl. I wasn't of interest to anyone, and that worked in my favor for the first few weeks of July when I bummed around, free to explore by day, sleeping where I could at night. I sought door wells, subway cars, even a graveyard. Startled to awake beneath the city sky or being shaken by a strange hand. Time to move along. Time to move along.

When it got really rough, I would go back to Pratt, occasionally bumping into someone I knew who would let me shower and sleep a night. Or else I would sleep in the hall near a familiar door. That wasn't much fun, but I had my mantra, "I'm free, I'm free." Although after several days, my other mantra, "I'm hungry, I'm hungry," seemed to be in the forefront. I wasn't worried, though. I just needed a break and I wasn't going to give up. I dragged my plaid suitcase from stoop to stoop, trying not to wear out my unwelcome.

It was the summer Coltrane died. The summer of "Crystal Ship." Flower children raised their empty arms and China exploded the H-bomb. Jimi Hendrix set his guitar in flames in

Monterey. AM radio played "Ode to Billie Joe." There were riots in Newark, Milwaukee, and Detroit. It was the summer of *Elvira Madigan*, the summer of love. And in this shifting, inhospitable atmosphere, a chance encounter changed the course of my life.

It was the summer I met Robert Mapplethorpe.

# Howard Jacobson

## 2010

## *The Finkler Question*

Tyler did, as it turned out, watch a second of her husband's television programmes in Treslove's Hampstead apartment that wasn't in Hampstead. And, at decent intervals, further series after that. She saw it as a consolation for her husband doing so much television. The thing she and Julian had going never blossomed into an affair. Neither was looking for an affair – or at least Tyler wasn't and Treslove had grown wary of looking for anything – but they found a way of showing kindnesses to each other over and above the conventions of an afternoon adultery fuelled by anger and envy.

Her growing tired was not lost on Treslove.

'You look pale,' he told her once, smothering her face with kisses.

She submitted to them, laughing. Her quiet, not her raucous laugh.

'And you are subdued somehow,' he said, kissing her again.

'I'm sorry,' she said. 'I didn't come round to depress you.'

'You don't depress me. Your pallor becomes you. I like a woman to look tragic.'

'God – tragic now. Is it as bad as that?'

It was as bad as that, yes.

Treslove would have said *Come and die at my place* but he knew he couldn't. A woman must die in her own home and in her own husband's arms, no matter that her lover would mop her brow with more consideration than the husband ever could.

'I do love you, you know,' he told her on what they both in their hearts suspected would be their last tryst. He had told her he loved her the first time they slept together, watching Sam on the box. But this time he meant it. Not that he didn't mean it then. But this time he meant it differently. This time he meant it for her.

'Don't be silly,' she told him.

'I do.'

'You don't.'

'I truly do.'

'You truly don't, but I am touched by your wanting to. You have been lovely to me. I am under no illusions, Julian. I get men. I know the bizarre way masculine friendship works. I have never fooled myself that I am any different to other wives in this position – a means for you two to work out your rivalry. I told you that at the beginning. But I've been happy to take advantage of that for my own purposes. And I thank you for having made me feel it was me you wanted.'

'It was you I wanted.'

'I believe it was. But not as much as you wanted Samuel.'

Treslove was horrified. '*I*, want Sam?'

'Oh, not in the wanting to fuck him sense. *I've* never loved him in the wanting to fuck him sense. I doubt anybody has. He's not a fuckable man. Not that that's ever stopped him ... or them. But he has something, my husband, not a glow exactly, but some air of secrecy that you want to penetrate, a kind of fast track competence or knowhow that you would like to have rub off on you. He is one of those Jews to whom, in another age, even the most avidly Jew-hating emperor or sultan would have given high office. He appears connected, he knows how to get on, and you feel that if you are close to him he will get on for the both of you. But I don't have to tell you. You feel it. I know you feel it.'

'Well, I didn't know I felt it.'

'Trust me, you feel it. And that's where I come in. I'm the bit that rubs off on you. Through me you connect to him.'

'Tyler –'

'It's all right. I don't mind being the stolen stardust that sprinkles you with second-hand importance. I get my revenge on him and at the same time get to feel more cared for by you.'

She kissed him. A thank you kiss.

The kiss, Treslove thought, that a woman gives a man who doesn't shake her to her soul. For that was what his 'caring' for her denoted – that he was kind but not challenging, not a man of influence, not someone who gave her access to the fast track. Yes, she came round to his house, slid with angular infidelity into his bed and fucked him, but without ever truly noticing he was there. Even this kiss somehow glanced by him, as though she were really kissing a man standing in the room behind.

Was it true, what she had said? That sleeping with Sam's wife gave him temporary honorary entry to Sam's success? If it was true, why then didn't he feel more successful? He liked the idea of Sam being an unfuckable man, but what was that information worth if he was an unfuckable man himself. Poor Tyler, fucking two unfuckable men. No wonder she looked ill.

But poor me as well, Treslove thought.

A means to work out *their* rivalry, she had called herself. Their rivalry – implying that there was something in this for Sam too. Did that mean he knew? Was it possible that when she got home Tyler would tell her husband what an unfuckable man his friend was? And would Sam get off on that? Would they get off on it together?

Did Finklers do that?

For the first time, Treslove broke the rule all adulterers must obey or perish, and pictured them in bed together. Tyler, fresh from Treslove, turning to her husband smiling, facing him as she had never once faced Treslove, holding his penis in front of her like a bridal bouquet, not a problem to be solved behind her back like Treslove's. Looking at it even, perhaps giving it name, confronting it head on, admiring it, as she had never once confronted and admired his.

'In the meantime,' she said, looking at her watch, though she didn't mean 'this minute', 'he's got himself a new craze.'

Did Treslove care? 'What?' he wondered.

She waved the subject away as though, now he asked, she wished she hadn't brought it up, or as though she felt he would never understand the ins and outs of it.

'Oh, this Israel business. Sorry, Palestine, as he insists on calling it.'

'I know. I've heard him.'

'You heard him on *Desert Island Discs*?'

'Missed it,' Treslove lied. He hadn't *missed* it. He had gone to great lengths not to hear it or to be in contact with anyone who had. Watching Finkler on television while sleeping with his wife was one thing, but *Desert Island Discs* to which the whole country tuned in …

'Wise move. I wish I'd missed it. In fact I'd have come round here *in order* to miss it but he wanted me to listen to it with him. Which should have made me suspicious. How come no Ronit …?'

Again Treslove found himself thinking of Tyler and Sam in bed together, face to face, listening to *Desert Island Discs*, Tyler admiring Sam's penis, crooning over it while on the radio the man himself did his Palestine thing.

He said nothing.

'Anyway, that was where he came out with it.'

'Came out with what?'

'His confession of shame.'

'Shame about Ronit?'

'Shame about Israel, you fool.'

'Oh, that. I've heard him on the subject with Libor. It's nothing new.'

'It's new to announce it to the country. Do you know how many people listen to that programme?'

Treslove had a fair idea but didn't want to get into a discussion about numbers. Mention of millions hurt Treslove's ear. 'So does he regret it now?'

'Regret it! He's like the cat that got the cream. He has a whole new bunch of friends. The ASHamed Jews. They're a bit like the Lost Boys. It's all down to careless mothering if you ask me.'

Treslove laughed. Partly in appreciation of Tyler's joke, partly to dispel the idea of Finkler having new friends. 'Does he know you call them that?'

'The Lost Boys?'

'No, the ASHamed Jews.'

'Oh, they're not my invention. They call themselves that. They're a movement, inspired, would you believe, by my hubby. They write letters to the papers.'

'As ASHamed Jews?'

'As ASHamed Jews.'

'That's a bit disempowering, isn't it?'

'How do you mean?'

'Well, to make your shame your platform. Reminds me of the Ellen Jamesians.'

'Haven't heard of them. Are they anti-Zionists too? Don't tell Sam. If they're anti-Zionist *and* women he'll join in a shot.'

'They're the deranged feminists in *The World According to Garp*. John Irving – no? Garrulous American novelist. Wrestler. Writes a bit like one. I made one of my first radio programmes about the Ellen Jamesians. They cut out their tongues in solidarity with a young woman who was raped and mutilated. Something of a self-defeating action, since they couldn't thereafter effectively voice their anger. A good anti-feminist joke, I always thought, not that I'm, you know –'

'Well. I doubt there'll be any tongue cutting with this lot. They're a gobby bunch, used to the limelight and the sound of their own voices. Sam's on the phone to them every minute God sends. And then there are the meetings.'

'They have meetings?'

'Not public ones, as far as I know. Not yet, anyway. But they meet at one another's houses. Sounds disgusting to me. Like group confessionals. Forgive me, Father, for I have sinned. Sam's their father confessor. "I forgive you, my child. Say three *I am ashameds* and don't go to Eilat for your holidays." I won't allow them in my house.'

'And is that all they stand for – being ashamed of being Jewish?'

'Whoa!' She laid a hand on his arm. 'You're not allowed to say that. It's not Jews they're ashamed of being. It's Israel. Palestine. Whatever.'

'So are they Israelis?'

'You know Sam is not an Israeli. He won't even go there.'

'I meant the others.'

'I don't know about all of them, but they're actors and comedians and those I've heard of certainly aren't Israelis.'

'So how can they be ashamed? How can you be ashamed of a country that's not yours?' Treslove truly was puzzled.

'It's because they're Jewish.'

'But you said they're not ashamed of being Jewish.'

'Exactly. But they're ashamed *as* Jews.'

'Ashamed *as* Jews of a country of which they are not citizens ...?'

Tyler laid a hand on his arm again. 'Look,' she said, 'what do we know? I think you've got to be one to get it.'

'Be one what? One of the ASHamed?'

'A Jew. You've got to be a Jew to get why you're ashamed of being a Jew.'

'I always forget that you're not.'

'Well, I'm not. Except by adoption and hard work.'

'But at least that way you're not ashamed.'

'Indeed I'm not. If anything I'm rather proud. Though not of my husband. Of him I'm ashamed.'

'So you're both ashamed.'

'Yes, but of different things. He's ashamed because he's a Jew, I'm ashamed because he's not.'

'And the kids?'

Tyler became abrupt. 'They're at university, Julian, remember. Which means they're old enough to make up their own minds ... but I haven't brought them up Jewish only to be ashamed.' She laughed at her own words. 'Listen to me – *brought them up Jewish.*'

Treslove wanted to tell her he loved her again.

'And?' he asked.

'And what?'

'And what are they?'

'One is, one isn't, one's not sure.'

'You have three?'

She pretended to hit him, but with little force. 'You're the one who should be ashamed,' she said.

'Oh, I am, don't worry. I am ashamed of most things though none of them have anything to do with Jews. Unless I should be ashamed of *us*.'

She exchanged a long look with him, a look that spoke of the past, not the future. 'Don't you get sick of us?' she said, as though wanting to change the subject. 'I don't mean us us, I mean Jews. Don't you get sick of our, their, self-preoccupation?'

'I never get sick of you.'

'Stop it. Answer me – don't you wish they'd shut up about themselves?'

'ASHamed Jews?'

'All Jews. Endlessly falling out in public about how Jewish to be, whether they are or they aren't, whether they're practising or they're not, whether to wear fringes or eat bacon, whether they feel safe here or precarious, whether the world hates them or it doesn't, the fucking Holocaust, fucking Palestine ...'

'No. Can't say I notice. Sam, maybe, yes. I always feel when he talks about Palestine that he's paying his parents back for something. It reminds me of swearing for the first time when you're a kid – daring God to strike you down. And wanting to show you belong to the kids who already do swear. But I don't understand the politics. Only that if anyone's going to be ashamed then maybe we all should be.'

'Exactly. The arrogance of them – ASHamed Jews for God's sake, as though the world waits upon the findings of their consciences. That's what shames me –'

'As a Jewess.'

'I've warned you about that word.'

'I know,' said Treslove, 'but I get hot saying it.'

'Well, you mustn't.'

'My Jewess,' he said, 'my unashamed Jewess that isn't,' and took her to him and held her. She felt smaller in his arms than when he'd first tried to hold her a year ago or more. There was less spring in her flesh, he thought. And her clothes were less sharp. Literally sharp. He bled when he first held her. There was anger in her still, but no fight. That she would consent to enter his arms at all, let alone be still in them, proved her alteration. The less of her there was, the more of her was his.

'I meant it,' he said, 'I truly do love you.'

'And I meant it when I thanked you for your kindness.'

For a moment it seemed to Treslove that they were the outsiders, just the two of them in the darkness, excluded from the pack of others. Today he didn't want her to go home, back to Sam's bed, back to Sam's penis. Was Sam now ashamed of his penis, too? Treslove wondered.

He had flaunted his circumcision at school. 'Women love it,' he'd told Treslove in the shower room.

'Liar.'

'I'm not. It's true.'

'How do you know?'

'I've read. It gives them greater satisfaction. With one of these beauties you can go for ever.'

Treslove read up about it himself. 'You don't get the pleasure I get,' he told his friend. 'You've lost the most sensitive part.'

'It might be sensitive but it's horrible. No woman will want to touch yours. So what's the sensitivity worth? Unless you want to spend the rest of your life being sensitive with yourself.'

'You'll never experience what I experience.'

'With that thing you'll never experience anything.'

'We'll see.'

'We'll see.'

And now? Did Finkler's Jewish shame extend to his Jewish dick? Or was his dick the one part of him to enjoy exclusion from the slur? Could an ASHamed Jew go on giving women greater satisfaction than an unashamed Gentile, Palestine or no Palestine?

That's if there'd ever been a grain of truth in any of it. You never knew with Jews what was a joke and what wasn't, and Finkler wasn't even a Jew who joked much. Treslove longed for Tyler to tell him. Solve the mystery once and for all. Did women have a preference? She was in the best position to make the comparison. Yes or no? Could her Shmuelly go for ever? Was her willingness to look at her husband's penis but not her lover's attributable to the foreskin and the foreskin alone? Was Treslove uncut too ugly to look at? Had the Jews got that one right at least?

It would explain, wouldn't it, why she fiddled with him the way she did, behind her back. Was she unconsciously trying to screw off his prepuce?

He didn't ask her. Didn't have the courage. And in all likelihood didn't want to hear the answer. Besides, Tyler wasn't well enough to be questioned.

You take your opportunity when you have it. Treslove was never given another.

# Stephen Kelman

## 2011

### *Pigeon English*

Manik's papa showed me how to tie my tie. It was my first day at my new school. I hid my tie in my bag, I was going to tell them it got stolen. But when I got to school I got scared. Everybody was wearing a tie. Manik's papa was there with Manik. The whole thing was his idea.

Manik's papa walks to school with him every day. He has to guard Manik from the robbers. Manik had his trainers stolen one time. One of the Dell Farm Crew stole them. When they didn't fit they put them up a tree. Manik couldn't get them down again because he's too fat to climb the tree.

Manik's papa: 'Let them try it again. It'll be a different story next time, little bastards.' Manik's papa's quite hutious. He's always red-eyes. He knows swordfighting. Asweh, I'm glad I'm not Manik's enemy!

Manik's papa put my tie on for me and made the knot. He showed me how to take the tie off without untying it. You just make a hole big enough to get your head through then you take the tie off over your head. That way you don't have to tie the tie every day. It even works. Now I'll never have to tie my tie my whole life. I beat the tie at his own game!

There's no songs in my new school. The best bit about my old school was when Kofi Allotey made up his own words:

Kofi Allotey: '*Before our Father's throne*
*We pour our ardent prayers.*
*Please don't burn me on the stove*
*Or push me down the stairs.*'

Asweh, he caught so many blows we called it the Kofi Stick!

At first me and Lydia stayed together at breaktime. Now we stay with our friends. If we see each other we have to pretend we don't know each other. The first one to say hello is the loser. At breaktime I just play suicide bomber or zombies. Suicide bomber is when you run at the other person and crash them as hard as you can. If the other person falls over you get a hundred points. If they just move but don't fall over it's ten points. One person is always the lookout because suicide bomber is banned. If the teacher catches you playing you'll get a detention.

Zombies is just acting like a zombie. You get extra points for accuracy.

When you're not playing games you can swap things instead. The most wanted things to swap are football stickers and sweets but you can swap anything if somebody wants it. Chevon Brown and Saleem Khan swapped watches. Saleem Khan's watch tells the time on the moon, but Chevon Brown's is chunkier and it's made of real titanium. They're both bo-styles. Everybody was happy with the deal but then Saleem Khan wanted to swap back.

Saleem Khan: 'I changed my mind, that's all.'

Chevon Brown: 'But we shook on it, man.'

Saleem Khan: 'I had my fingers crossed, innit.'

Chevon Brown: 'Pussy clart. Two punches.'

Saleem Khan: 'No, man. One.'

Chevon Brown: 'On the head though.'

Saleem Khan: 'The shoulder, the shoulder.'

Chevon Brown: 'Rarse.'

Chevon Brown punched Saleem Khan proper hard and gave him a dead arm. It was his fault for going back on the deal. He was only scared for if his mamma got red-eyes.

I don't have a watch yet, I don't even need one. The bell tells you where to be and there's a clock in the classroom. When you're outside school you don't need to know the hour, your belly tells you when it's chop time. You just go home when you're hungry enough, that way you never forget.

I was the dead boy. X-Fire was teaching us about chooking. He didn't use a real knife, just his fingers. They still felt quite sharp. X-Fire says when you chook somebody you have to do it proper quick because you feel it as well.

X-Fire: 'When the knife goes in them you can feel where it hits. If it hits a bone or something it feels disgusting, man. You're best going for somewhere soft like the belly so it goes in nice and easy, then you don't feel nothing. The first time I shanked someone was the worst, man. All his guts fell out. It was well sick. I didn't know where to aim yet, I got him too low down, innit. That's why I go for the side now, near the love handles. Then you don't get no nasty stuff falling out.'

Dizzy: 'The first time I shanked someone the blade got stuck. I hit a rib or something. I had to pull like f— to get it out. I was like, give me my blade back, bitch!'

Clipz: 'Innit. You just wanna stick him and get the f— outta there. No messing around.'

Killa didn't join in. He was just quiet. Maybe he hasn't chooked anybody yet. Or maybe he's chooked so many people that he's bored by now. That must be why he's called Killa.

I was the dead boy because X-Fire picked me. I just had to stand still. X-Fire didn't like it when I moved. He kept pulling me. I felt quite sick but I had to keep listening. I even wanted to listen. It was like when I first tasted mushy peas: it was disgusting but I had to finish it because wasting food is a sin.

I could still feel his fingers in my ribs even after he was gone. It felt very crazy. X-Fire's breath smells like cigarettes and chocolate milk. I wasn't even scared.

We always go to the market on Saturday. It's all outside so you get proper cold waiting for Mamma to pay, you have to keep your mouth closed to stop your teeth escaping. It's only even worth it for all the dope-fine things you can look at like a remote-control car or a samurai sword (it's only made from wood but it's still proper hutious. If I had the means I'd buy it like that, I'd use it to chase the invaders away).

My favourite shop is the sweets shop. It sells every kind of Haribo you can think of. It's my ambition to try every style there is. So far I've tried about half. Haribo comes in a million different shapes. Whatever there is in the world, there's a chewy Haribo version of it. Asweh, it's true. They make cola bottles, worms, milkshakes, teddy bears, crocodiles, fried eggs, dummies, fangs, cherries, frogs, and millions more. Cola bottles are the best.

I only don't like the jelly babies. They're cruel. Mamma has seen a dead baby for real. She sees them every day at work. I never buy the jelly babies for if it would remind her.

Mamma was looking all over for a pigeon net. I said a prayer to myself that she never found one.

Me: 'It's not fair. Just because Lydia's scared of them.'

Lydia: 'Gowayou! I'm not scared!'

Mamma: 'We can't have pigeons flying in the house all the time, it's dirty, they'll mess everywhere.'

Me: 'It was only one time. He was hungry, that's all.'

Mamma: 'Don't make squeeze-eyes at me, Harrison, I'm not arguing with you.'

Some people put nets over their balcony to stop the pigeons getting in. I don't even agree with it, they're not hurting anybody. I want my pigeon to come back. I even hid some fufu flour in my pant drawer specially for him. I don't want to eat him, I want to make him tame so he'll go on my shoulder. In the end my prayer was answered: they don't even sell pigeon nets at the market. Asweh, it was a mighty relief!

Me: 'Don't worry. If he comes back I'll tell him to find another home.'

Mamma: 'Don't put any more food out for it. Don't think I haven't seen the flour all over the balcony, I'm not stupid.'

Me: 'I won't!'

I hate it when Mamma reads my mind! From today onward going I'll just wait till she's asleep.

I pretended like I didn't see when Jordan stole the lady's phone. I didn't want Mamma to think I agreed with it, she already hates Jordan because he spits on the stairs. I was at Noddy's clothes stall.

I saw the whole thing while Mamma was paying for my Chelsea shirt. It was X-Fire and Dizzy who actually got the lady's phone. They were very tricky: they waited until she was talking, then they bumped her to make her drop the phone. They made it look like an accident. The phone fell on the ground, then Jordan came from nowhere, picked the phone up and ran off with it. He squeezed into the crowd and was gone in one second. It was like he was a ghost, he just disappeared. The lady looked around for her phone but it was already gone, there was nothing she could do. It was a clean getaway. Jordan doesn't get paid for help-ing them, he just gets some cigarettes or one week of freedom where they don't try to kill him. It's not even a good deal. If it was me I'd want a tenner every time.

My new Chelsea shirt is a bit too scratchy. I had to put a plaster on my nipples to stop them getting rubbed off. It's still bo-styles though. The dead boy loved Chelsea as well. He had the proper shirt with Samsung on it, even the away kit. I hope Heaven has proper goals with nets on them, then you don't have to run miles to get the ball every time you score a goal.

# Richard Ford

## 2012

## *Canada*

One woman with her daughter passed me by where I was standing at the drugstore window, doing nothing more than looking wondrously in at the colored vessels and beakers and powders and mortars and pestles and brass scales on display—all items the Rexall in Great Falls had lacked and that made the Fort Royal store seem more serious. The woman turned and came back up the sidewalk and said to me, "Can I help you with something?" She was dressed in a red-and-white flowered dress with a white patent leather belt and matching white patent leather shoes. She didn't have an accent—I was acute to this because of what Mildred had told me. She was only being friendly, possibly had seen me before, knew I was not from there. I'd never been addressed this way—as a total stranger. Everything about me had always been known to the adults in my life.

"No," I said. "Thank you." I was aware that while she didn't sound different to me, I possibly sounded different from people she was used to hearing. Possibly I looked different, too—though I didn't think I did.

"Are you here visiting?" She smiled but seemed doubtful about me. Her daughter—who was my age and had blond ringlet curls and small, pretty blue eyes that were slightly bulgy—stood beside her, looking at me steadily.

"I'm here visiting my uncle," I said.

"Who is he, now?" Her blue eyes that matched her daughter's were shining expectantly.

"Mr. Arthur Remlinger," I said. "He owns the Leonard."

The woman's brows thickened and she seemed to grow concerned. Her posture stiffened, as if I was someone different because of the sound of Arthur Remlinger's name. "Is he going to put you into school in Leader?" she asked, as if it worried her.

"No," I said. "I live in Montana with my parents. I'll go back down there soon. I go to school there." I felt good to be able to say that any of these things were still true.

"We went to the fair in Great Falls, once," she said. "It was nice but it was very crowded." She smiled more broadly, put her arm around her daughter's shoulder, which made her smile, too. "We're LDS. If you'd ever like to attend."

"Thank you," I said. I knew LDS meant Mormons, because of things my father had said, and because of Rudy, who said they talked to angels and didn't like black people. I thought the woman would say something else to me, ask me something about myself. But she didn't. The two of them just walked along down the street and left me in front of the drugstore.

On the afternoons I didn't stay on in Fort Royal and conduct my investigations and keep myself occupied, I rode the Higgins back out to Partreau with a small lunch box of cold food in my basket. This I would eat in my dilapidated house before the daylight died off. It was miserable to eat alone in either of the two cold, lightless rooms of my shack, since both were cluttered to the ceiling with the dank-smelling cardboard boxes and the dry accumulation of years of being the Overflow House for goose hunters who came in the fall and would soon be there again. There was almost no room for me, only the iron cot I slept on and the one that had been reserved for Berner, and the "kitchen room," with the bumpy red linoleum and a single fluorescent ceiling ring and a two-burner hot plate where I boiled tar-smelling pump water in a pan to make my bath at night. Everything in the house smelled of old smoke and long-spoiled food and the privy, and other stinging human odors I couldn't find a source for and try to clean, but could taste in my mouth and smell on my skin and clothes when I left for work each day and that made me self-conscious. In the morn-ings I cleaned my teeth at the outside pump and washed my face with a Palmolive bar I'd bought at the drugstore. Though as the weather grew colder, the wind stung my arms and cheeks and made my muscles tense and ache until I was done. If Berner had been there, I knew she would've been despondent and run away again—and I'd have gone with her.

But bringing food back and waiting until dark to eat it under the deathly ceiling ring would send me straight to my cot where I would lie miserably, trying to read one of my chess maga-zines in the awful light, or wishing I could watch a show on the busted television, while I listened to pigeons under the roof tins and the wind working the planks of the elevator across the highway, and the few cars and trucks that traveled the road at night, and sometimes Charley Quarters driving in late from the hotel bar, standing in the weeds in front of his trailer, talking to himself. (I'd by then looked up Métis in my *World Book* "M" volume and found out it meant half-breed between Indian and French.)

All of that would begin to conspire against me each night and swirl me up in abject thoughts of my parents and Berner, and of the certainty that I'd have been in better hands with the juvenile authorities who would at least have put me in a school, even if it had bars on its windows, but where I would have people to talk to, even if they were tough ranch boys and perverted Indians—instead of being here, where if I got sick as I sometimes did in the fall, no one would look after me or take me to the doctor. I was being left behind while everything else advanced beyond me. There'd been no mention—because no one talked to me except Charley, who I didn't like and who never paid atten-tion to me, and because I wasn't invited to talk to anyone and therefore knew nothing of my future—there'd been no mention that I would return to anything I'd known before or ever see my parents, or that they might come and find me. Therefore it seemed to me, cast off in the dark there in Partreau, that I was not exactly who I'd been before: a well-rounded boy on his way possibly to college, with a family behind him and a sister. I was now smaller in the world's view and insignificant, and possibly invisible. All of which made me feel closer to death than life. Which is not how fifteen-year-old boys should feel. I felt that by being where I was, I was no longer fortunate and was likely not going to be, although I'd always trusted that I was. My shack in Partreau was in fact what misfortune looked like. If I could've cried on those nights, I would've. But there was no one to cry to, and in any case I hated to cry and didn't want to be a coward.

And yet, if I didn't sink myself this way each day—becoming bitter, abandoned-feeling, corrupting the whole day following—if I simply pedaled back the four miles to Partreau and ate my cold lunch box by five rather than after dark, leaving time to assign myself an interest in things at hand, taking notice of what was present around me in Partreau (again, the way Mildred had advised—not to rule things out), *then* I could undertake a better view of my situation and feel I might sustain myself and endure.

Since, after all, it wasn't in my interest to be cast off. Even if I was visited each night by a vacant feeling of not knowing what or where I was in the world, or how things were, and how they might go for me—everything had already been worse! This was the truth Berner had understood and why she'd gone away and would likely never be back. Because she saw that anything was better than being the two left-behind children of bank robbers. Charley Quarters had told me you crossed borders to escape things and possibly to hide, and Canada in his view was a good place for that (though the border had hardly been an event I noticed). But it also meant you became someone different in the process—which was happening to me, and I needed to accept it.

And so on those long, cooling high-sky afternoons, when a person could see the moon in daylight, and before or after I ate my evening meal (a busted dinette table had been thrown away in the thistles, and I brought a broken chair from inside my shack and set these up outside the window by the lilac bush, where I could see to the north)—on those days I would make a second tour, around Partreau. This investigation seemed to me of a different nature. If my walks in Fort Royal were in pursuit of that town's difference from life I'd known, and to render myself reconciled to the new, then my inspections around Partreau, only four miles distant, were of a museum dedicated to the defeat of civilization—one that had been swept away to flourish elsewhere, or possibly never. There were only eight crumbling streets, lying north and south, and six going west and east.

There were actually eighteen empty, destitute houses, with windows out and doors off, and curtains flagging in the breeze, each house with its number, each street a sign—though only a few names remained up on their posts and identifiable. South Ontario Street. South Alberta Street (where my shack was). South Manitoba Street, where a tiny empty post office and Mrs. Gedins' house stood. And South Labrador Street, which ran the margin between the town and the cut-over wheat fields, along a three-sided, squared-off row of dead Russian olives and Lombardy poplars and caraganas and chokecherries, where prairie grouse perched in the branches watching the highway, and magpies squabbled in the underbrush for insects.

There had once been more than fifty houses, I calculated by walking each block and counting spaces and foundation squares. Back in the cluttered weeds and dooryards were rusted, burnt-out car relics and toppled appliance bodies and refuse pits full of cabinets and broken mirrors and patent medicine bottles and metal bed frames and tricycles and ironing boards and kitchen utensils and bassinets and bedpans and alarm clocks all half-buried and left behind. To the back of town, south and square to the fields and olive rows, stood the remains of an orchard, possibly apples, that had failed. The dried trunks were stacked husk on husk, as if someone had meant to burn them or save them for firewood, then had forgotten. Also, there I discovered the dismantled, rusted remnants of a carnival—red, mesh-hooded chairs of the Tilt-a-Whirl, the wire capsule of the Bullet, three Dodge-em cars and a Ferris wheel seat, all scattered and wrecked, with spools of heavy gear chain and pulleys, deep in the weeds with a wooden ticket booth toppled over and once painted bright green and red, with coils of yellow tickets still inside. There was no cemetery that I could see.

I took brief interest in two white bee hive boxes sitting solemnly in the volunteer wheatgrass outside the tree line where the sun caught their sides. These, I assumed, were Charley's and that he had tended them once. But the hives, which sat on bricks and lacked their important flat tops, were empty of bees. Their wood panels were loosed from their joinings; rot had taken over from below. Their thin paint was weathered and cracked, their beeswax frames (which I knew a good deal about by then) lay in the weeds beside a pair of rotted work gloves. Grasshoppers buzzed around them in the dust.

Farther—a hundred yards out in the field and beyond a dried pond bed—I investigated the lone pumping station, its motor humming in the breezy afternoon, exuding a stinging gassy odor as it sawed up and down, the hard, rounded earth saturated and black with oil that had been pumped and spilled. A pair of large, white-faced gauges attached to the motor mechanism measured what I didn't know. One day, from the distance of my shack, I watched a lone man drive through town in a pickup and out to the pumper site. He climbed out and fashioned around, consulting the gauges, inspecting various moving parts, and writing things on a pad of paper. Then he drove away in the direction of Leader and never (to my knowledge) came back.

Other days I simply walked up to the little commercial row, the businesses that had once thrived along the highway, facing across the hardtop to the pool elevator and the CP tracks. From my bed, I'd often heard freight cars late at night, the big diesels gathering and surging, the wheel springs squeaking, the brakes and sleepers crying out. It was much the way I'd experienced it in my bedroom in Great Falls. No trains stopped at Partreau. The elevator was long emptied. Though sometimes I'd be jolted awake and would step outside in the chill moonlit dark, barefoot, in my Jockeys, hoping I could view the northern lights, which my father had talked about but that I'd never seen in

RICHARD FORD

Great Falls—and never saw in Partreau. The blocky shadows of
the grain cars and tanker cars and gondolas swayed and bumped
along, sparks cracking off the brakes, lights dimmed and yellow
in the caboose. Often a man stood on the rear platform—the
way I'd seen photographs of politicians giving forceful speeches
to great crowds—staring back at the closing silence behind him,
the red tail-light not quite illuminating his face, unaware anyone
was watching.

But when I inspected the little commercial frontages—an
empty, pocket-size bank, a Masons' building of quarried stone
from 1909, the Atlas shoe store with shoes scattered inside, a
shadowy pool hall, a gas station with rusted, glass-top pumps,
an insurance office, a beauty parlor with two silver hair dryers
pushed over and broken apart, the floors littered with bricks and
broken furnishings and merchandise racks, the light dead and
cold, the busted back doors letting the damaging elements in,
all the establishments emptied of human uses—I found I always
thought of the life that had gone on there, not of life cast aside.
And not, as opposed to what I'd first thought, like a museum at
all. I had more positive views. Which made me feel that although
I hadn't been taught to assimilate, a person perhaps assimilated
without knowing it. I was doing it now. You did it alone, and
not with others or for them. And assimilating possibly wasn't so
hard and risky and didn't need to be permanent. This state of
mind conferred another freedom on me and was like starting
life over, or as I've already said, becoming someone else—but
someone who was not stalled but moving, which was the nature
of things in the world. I could like it or hate it, but the world
would change around me no matter how I felt.

# *Elizabeth Gilbert*

## 2013

## *The Signature of All Things*

The problem was that Alma had already spent her life studying the nature of White Acre, and she knew the place too well. She knew every tree and rock and bird and lady's slipper. She knew every spider, every beetle, every ant. There was nothing new here for her to explore. Yes, she could have studied the novel tropical plants that arrived at her father's impressive greenhouses every week—but that is not discovery! Somebody else had already discovered those plants! And the task of a naturalist, as Alma understood it, was to discover. But there would be no such chance for Alma, for she had reached the limits of her botanical borders already. This realization frightened her and made her unable to sleep at night, which, in turn, frightened her more. She feared the restlessness that was creeping upon her. She could almost hear her mind pacing within her skull, caged and bothered, and she felt the weight of all the years she had yet to live, bearing down upon her with heavy menace.

A born taxonomist with nothing new to classify, Alma kept her uneasiness at bay by setting other things into order. She tidied and alphabetized her father's papers. She smartened up the library, discarding books of lesser value. She arranged the collection jars on her own shelves by height, and she created ever more refined systems of superfluous filing, which is how it came to pass that—early one morning in June of 1822—Alma Whittaker sat alone in her carriage house, poring over all the research articles she had ever written for George Hawkes. She was trying to decide whether to organize these old issues of

*Botanica Americana* by subject or by chronology. It was an un-
necessary task, but it would fill an hour.

At the bottom of this pile, though, Alma found her earliest
article—the one she had written when she was only sixteen
years old, about *Monotropa hypopitys*. She read it again. The
writing was juvenile, but the science was sound, and her explanation of this shade-loving plant as a clever, bloodless parasite
still felt valid. When she looked closely at her old illustrations
of *Monotropa*, though, she almost had to laugh at their rudimen-
tary crudeness. Her diagrams looked as though they had been
sketched by a child, which, essentially, they had been. Not that
she had become a glittering artist over the past years, but these
early pictures were quite rough indeed. George had been kind
to publish them at all. Her *Monotropa* was meant to be depicted
growing out of a bed of moss, but in Alma's depiction, the plant
looked to be growing out of a lumpy old mattress. Nobody
would have been able to identify those dismal clumps at the
bottom of the drawing as moss at all. She ought to have shown
much more detail. As a good naturalist, she ought to have made
an illustration that depicted quite precisely in which variety of
moss *Monotropa hypopitys* grew.

On further consideration, though, Alma realized that she
herself did not know in which variety of moss *Monotropa hypopitys* grew. On still further consideration, she realized that she
was not entirely certain she could distinguish between different
varieties of moss at all. How many were there, anyway? A few? A
dozen? Several hundred? Shockingly, she did not know.

Then again, where would she have learned it? Who had
ever written about moss? Or even about Bryophyta in general?
There was no single authoritative book on the subject that she
knew of. Nobody had made a career out of it. Who would have
wanted to? Mosses were not orchids, not cedars of Lebanon.
They were not big or beautiful or showy. Nor was moss something medicinal and lucrative, upon which a man like Henry
Whittaker could make a fortune. (Although Alma did remember
her father telling her that he had packed his precious cinchona

seeds in dried moss, to preserve them during transport to Java.)
Perhaps Gronovius had written something about mosses? Maybe.
But the old Dutchman's work was nearly seventy years old by
now—very much out of date and terribly incomplete. What was
clear was that nobody paid much attention to the stuff. Alma
had even chinked up the drafty old walls of her carriage house
with wads of moss, as though it were common cotton batting.

She had overlooked it.

Alma stood up quickly, wrapped herself in a shawl, tucked a
large magnifying glass into her pocket, and ran outside. It was
a fresh morning, cool and somewhat overcast. The light was
perfect. She did not have to go far. At a high spot along the
riverbank, she knew there to be a large outcropping of damp
limestone boulders, shaded by a screen of nearby trees. There,
she remembered, she would find mosses, for that's where she had
harvested the insulation for her study.

She had remembered correctly. Just at that border of rock and
wood, Alma came to the first boulder in the outcropping. The
stone was larger than a sleeping ox. As she had suspected and
hoped, it was blanketed in moss. Alma knelt in the tall grass and
brought her face as near as she could to the stone. And there,
rising no more than an inch above the surface of the boulder, she saw a great and tiny forest. Nothing moved within this
mossy world. She peered at it so closely that she could smell
it—dank and rich and old. Gently, Alma pressed her hand into
this tight little timberland. It compacted itself under her palm
and then sprang back to form without complaint. There was
something stirring about its response to her. The moss felt warm
and spongy, several degrees warmer than the air around it, and
far more damp than she had expected. It appeared to have its
own weather.

Alma put the magnifying lens to her eye and looked again.
Now the miniature forest below her gaze sprang into majestic
detail. She felt her breath catch. This was a stupefying king-
dom. This was the Amazon jungle as seen from the back of a
harpy eagle. She rode her eye above the surprising landscape,

following its paths in every direction. Here were rich, abundant valleys filled with tiny trees of braided mermaid hair and minuscule, tangled vines. Here were barely visible tributaries running through that jungle, and here was a miniature ocean in a depression in the center of the boulder, where all the water pooled.

Just across this ocean—which was half the size of Alma's shawl—she found another continent of moss altogether. On this new continent, everything was different. This corner of the boulder must receive more sunlight than the other, she surmised. Or slightly less rain? In any case, this was a new climate entirely. Here, the moss grew in mountain ranges the length of Alma's arms, in elegant, pine tree-shaped clusters of darker, more somber green. On another quadrant of the same boulder still, she found patches of infinitesimally small deserts, inhabited by some kind of sturdy, dry, flaking moss that had the appearance of cactus. Elsewhere, she found deep, diminutive fjords—so deep that, incredibly, even now in the month of June—the mosses within were still chilled by lingering traces of winter ice. But she also found warm estuaries, miniature cathedrals, and limestone caves the size of her thumb.

Then Alma lifted her face and saw what was before her—dozens more such boulders, more than she could count, each one similarly carpeted, each one subtly different. She felt herself growing breathless. *This was the entire world.* This was bigger than a world. This was the firmament of the universe, as seen through one of William Herschel's mighty telescopes. This was planetary and vast. These were ancient, unexplored galaxies, rolling forth in front of her—and it was all right here! She could still see her house from here. She could see the familiar old boats on the Schuylkill River. She could hear the distant voices of her father's orchardmen working in the peach grove. If Hanneke had rung the bell for mealtime at that very instant, she would have heard it.

Alma's world and the moss world had been knitted together this whole time, lying on top of each other, crawling over each other. But one of these worlds was loud and large and fast, where the other was quiet and tiny and slow—and only one of these worlds seemed immeasurable.

Alma sank her fingers into the shallow green fur and felt a surge of joyful anticipation. This could belong to her! No botanist before her had ever committed himself uniquely to the study of this undervalued phylum, but Alma could do it. She had the time for it, as well as the patience. She had the competence. She most certainly had the microscopes for it. She even had the publisher for it—because whatever else had occurred between them (or had not occurred between them), George Hawkes would always be happy to publish the findings of A. Whittaker, whatever she might turn up.

Recognizing all this, Alma's existence at once felt bigger and much, much smaller—but a pleasant sort of smaller. The world had scaled itself down into endless inches of possibility. Her life could be lived in generous miniature. Best of all, Alma realized, she would never learn *everything* about mosses—for she could tell already that there was simply too much of the stuff in the world; they were everywhere, and they were profoundly varied. She would probably die of old age before she understood even half of what was occurring in this one single boulder field. *Well, huzzah to that!* It meant that Alma had work stretched ahead of her for the rest of her life. She need not be idle. She need not be unhappy. Perhaps she need not even be lonely.

She had a task.

She would learn mosses.

If Alma had been a Roman Catholic, she might have crossed herself in gratitude to God at this discovery—for the encounter did have the weightless, wonderful sensation of religious conversion. But Alma was not a woman of excessive religious passion. Even so, her heart rose in hope. Even so, the words she now spoke aloud sounded every bit like prayer:

"Praise be the labors that lie before me," she said. "Let us begin."

# Lucy Ellmann

## 2013

## *Mimi*

"Why do you look at my hands?"

"Because they charm me," I answered, kissing them, and it was true. I was now an advocate of Mimi's large hands and strong feet, and the well-rounded calves that sloped dramatically down to her unsprainable ankles. Mimi's feet seemed heroic to me, the kind of feet Liberty would need to man those barricades. *A mighty woman with a torch, whose flame was the imprisoned lightning.*

Mimi *was* heroic: heroic in the grocery store sniffing out the bargains, heroic on the subway pushing her way onto crowded trains, heroic when eating, when drinking, when sleeping, when laughing, just heroic all the time! Heroic in her beliefs, her angers and upsets, heroic when she dropped to her knees and took my cock in her mouth, heroic when I turned her to fuck her standing up, heroic coming and coming under the ceiling fan in her wide square bedroom. Heroic lying spoon-style behind me afterwards, calling me darling.

Is this not love?

When you first get together with someone, you hammer out a cosmos—through moments of discord as well as contentment. It's your Big Bang period. From then on, the way you interact has been established. Things evolve, sure, you can refine it. But the major accommodations have been made and met, parameters set, no-go zones delineated, and you'll pause before disturbing these balances and tilting the whole thing off course.

Mimi turned out to have a lot to say, but not in Gertrude's meandering megalomaniacal manner. Mimi had firm views, clear enemies, and battles to fight. None of it seemed aimed directly at me. It was exhilarating to watch, and had a strange erotic charge. Mimi was brash, she was brazen, I wasn't even sure she was completely *civilized*. And sometimes she'd lash out at me too, like a cornered animal: I was communing with nature at last.

"Where there's life, we can rail!" she declared one morning out on the roof, with the wind in her hair.

"Okay, but don't lean on the railing."

*Mimi on power suits:* "Power suits don't work. Power works."

*Mimi on jobs:* "Work's bad for you. It drives everybody nuts in the end! That's why I went freelance. If I wanna stay in bed, I stay there."

This wasn't exactly true—despite her fantasy of flexibility, Mimi always seemed to have to email somebody or Xerox something, frustrating all my endeavors to keep my own workload down to a minimum in order to be with her!

*Mimi on parenthood:* "You share your genetic defects with somebody, and then they get your crappy furniture when you die? Some deal." We were in total agreement on procreation: its unnecessariness.

*Mimi on male bonuses:* "They earn five times what women do, and still expect you to chip in for dinner!"

*Mimi on sports:* "What good's an Olympian to me?"

*Mimi on guys on the subway who spread their legs and their newspapers far and wide:* "We all paid the price of a ticket. And I like opening my legs too!" This she then demonstrated to me, in the most beguiling way.

*Mimi on the Hadron Collider* (which she insisted on calling the Hard-on Collider): "Who needs a big machine to re-create the chaos at the beginning of the universe? Chaos we got!"

"How about a Tippi Hedren Collider instead then?" I suggested. "You just throw birds at her until she flips."

*Mimi on the guy who claimed to have started an extramarital affair with a complete stranger, involuntarily, while sleepwalking as a result of taking an antidepressant:* "Yeah, sure."

*Mimi on a beer company promotion prize of a whole "caveman" weekend for five guys—free beer, video games, sports channels, and room service:* "Five drunks in a cheap hotel."

*Mimi on breast cancer campaigns:* "Them and their pink ribbons. It's sexual harassment! They never let you forget your breasts are a liability."

*Mimi on bras:* "Tit prisons. Who decided tits have to be this stiff and high anyway? The UN?"

"But without bras," I argued, "I'd have even more boob-jobs to do and I'm sick of them!"

"I didn't know men could get sick of breasts."

"Not of breasts maybe, but of altering them in accordance with their owner's latest caprice, or her husband's."

Mimi was pretty suspicious of my profession. We battled it out one day over Yankee bean soup and borscht at B & H Dairy on 2nd Avenue (even when you're in love, you still need soup!). I was admiring her lips, and made the mistake of saying they were beautiful.

"They're just my lips. Don't separate 'em off and compare them to other lips. You're not at work now, buddy."

"Well, shut up and kiss me then!"

She did, then resumed her rant. "Who decides what's beautiful anyway? It's all a matter of opinion, right?"

"Well, according to my partner Henry, beauty was decided *for* us by evolution. Hairiness in men, for instance, hairlessness in women. Sexual characteristics got exaggerated over time, since the people most universally recognized as desirable were the most likely to find mates. Youthfulness is another widely accepted beauty trait, because it implies fertility. Evolution decided it, and we just help it along."

"That's bullshit," declared Mimi.

"Look, Mimi. Imagine nature is the tailor, as a teacher of mine put it, and we're the invisible menders when the suit gets a bit worn out."

"Hmmm."

"Honey, it's just a job."

"Hmmm."

Those "hmmms" of hers.

"Some people really need help, Mimi, or their lives would be ruined! I had a woman in once who'd grown a *horn* on her forehead! Just an excess of keratin, easily removed—but in the Middle Ages she would have been dragged from town to town as an emblem of cuckoldry or something!"

"Or burnt as a witch," said Mimi, taking a big bite of challah bread. "But come on, Harrison—most people's lives aren't *in danger* if they don't have a nose-job."

"All I know is, a lot of middle-aged women come to me complaining they feel invisible."

"But being invisible's great!" Mimi said. "You can do whatever you want and nobody notices."

"I have this sudden twitch in my neck."

"That's 'cause you're talkin' through your hat!"

I quickly changed the subject to Haydn. "You know how Haydn was taught to play the drum? When he was three years old, they hung a drum on a hunchback's back and Haydn walked behind him with his drumsticks, tapping away. Later, he got the full drum kit with high hat and cymbal, requiring six hunchbacks and a midget who played the kazoo."

Mimi almost spat her borscht everywhere, something it's important not to do in such a small space. At B & H, you try to avoid any sudden movements, so as not to upset lethal quantities of hot soup. I moved on from midgets to a confession of my midget–maniac problem in childhood. Mimi had had similar mix-ups: she'd thought cirrus clouds were serious, and for a long time, to her mother's shame, called water "agooya", ravioli "ravaloli" and beef bouillon "Beef William."

"Did you know they've just invented a way of manufacturing sperm artificially?" I asked next, just to get a rise out of her.

"Isn't there enough of it around already?"

"Yeah, the thing would be to *de*-invent it," I said. "Everybody talks about recycling and hybrid cars but they never think seriously about overpopulation! If we could just stop having babies, we wouldn't need all these apocalypse scenarios." (Another bugbear of Mimi's.)

"But what would Hollywood do, without the end of the world?" she mused. "They aren't happy unless people are looting and drowning every place. And then a guy gets into his SUV and somehow saves the day, or at least his own stupid skin."

*Mimi on Cormac McCarthy*: "He writes about cowboys and the apocalypse. Enough said."

*Mimi on Branwell Brontë*: "Who cares?" She got mad about a million different things! But she could be easily charmed too.

*Mimi on generosity*: "Some people are so generous it breaks your heart. Pavarotti's generous. And that guy who had to land his plane in the Hudson. When they were all standing in the cold out on the wings, he gave his shirt to one of the freezing passengers. The shirt off his back! You're generous too. *You're* generous with your cock."

Forget the soup, cancel my appointments! Taxi!

Bubbles and Mimi had formed an instant rapport—almost as if they knew each other already. There was occasional competition between Bubbles and me over who got to sleep on top of Mimi. But most of the time our *ménage à trois* worked very well. When we all woke up entangled together on Valentine's Day, I started telling Mimi about the way my parents had incarcerated me in my bed as a kid, thereby putting me off bedtime for life (until now). She found my Berlioz problem funny so, getting bolder, I stood up to declaim, "It was in fact during those sleepless nights that I, like Edison, came up with my best stuff." Then I gave her some examples of my youthful "inventions" (so far unpatented):

1. Every sidewalk a conveyor belt.
2. Every basement a swimming pool.
3. Every attic a planetarium.

Mimi had invented the same stuff herself. Still, I had more!

4. Aquarium bathtub: translucent sides so you could have real fish in there—octopuses, sharks, baby alligators, whatever you want (Bee always wanted sea horses).

5. The Tornado Room-Tidier: a machine you place in the middle of your room and it spins faster and faster, blowing all your toys and clothes and shit into the corners and under the bed. Instant appearance of order.

6. The Yuck-Suck Machine: this consists of a pump, a disposable "reservoir" (plastic baggie), and a tube going down your sleeve, ending in a discreet nozzle. When you're presented with unfamiliar food at a friend's house (like Beef William, for instance), the Yuck-Suck secretly siphons it all up. Particularly good on cabbage and gravy.

7. The Nickel-Stick Shooter: this contraption divides your Kraft Karamel Nickel Stick into individual pieces, or shoots them at your friends in a mild, harmless way your mother can't object to—your mother who, by banning you from all toy-gun ownership, even water pistols, has relegated you to a life of insecurity and social ostracism.

"The musings of a kid who felt trapped in his bed, in his room, in his family, in his town, in his universe," I said in summation, before noticing I was much too far away from Mimi and rejoining her on the bed. "I was imprisoned at *school* too. Locked in the playpen: a sort of solitary confinement for hardened class scapegoats. I had to eat my lunch in there all on my own! ... Unless Bee came."

"Bee got into trouble too?" asked Mimi, reaching over to stroke my thigh.

"No, she just came to keep me company. She never got caught for anything. But she was a bit of an outlaw too. It was Bee who taught me how to squirt toothpaste at people from the top floor of the library. They thought it was bird shit. That was great! Later, she became the town's only graffiti artist."

I grabbed Mimi and forced her to bestraddle me so I could caress her hips and stomach and look up at her breasts while we talked. "Happy Valentine's Day, Mimi."

"Happy Valentine's Day," she returned, and bent to kiss me.

Possessiveness suddenly struck me as the sexiest thing in the world. I held her tight. "Be mine," I said, and meant it.

She *was* mine.

"Tell me you love me."

"I love you," she murmured. I already knew it. The girl was crazy about me!

# Esther Freud

## 2014

## Mr Mac and Me

Mother sends me over to the Kipperdrome for fish. I walk down to the river, and find I don't have to queue for the ferry, for there are so many herring boats jammed up in the harbour I can step from one to the next until I reach the other side.

The Kipperdrome is new. Newer even than the lighthouse, and inside its octagonal walls the stalls are heaped with every kind of fish. Sole and bass and whiting, mackerel, dogfish, cod. I look around for Betty and her sister but they are out on the river, gutting, and the herring that are here, gleaming shoals of them, are being sold by other, older women who have paid their dues.

It is cool inside the Kipperdrome with light that filters sideways through small high windows in the roof. If I close my eyes and breathe in deep I can imagine I am underwater, the shuffle and murmur of women, with hats tipped forward on their heads, making the same shimmery sound as the current. I squeeze my way between them and wait while they open their purses and close them again, while the fishmongers in their white aprons hold their knives ready to strip away the scales and slice open the bellies of whatever they might choose. I buy three skate. That is what my mother wants. She has a way of roasting them in the stove so that the meat falls lightly off the great sharp bone tasting of fennel and woodsmoke, and when I have my package wrapped and folded, I wander back along the beach, counting the longshore fishing boats dragged up on to the sand. The bathing huts have been rolled in, the boys offering goat rides have deserted, and the strip of high shingle is crowded with men at work, children climbing in and out of skiffs, dogs sniffing for a scrap of food.

I'm wanted back. I know it. But instead I walk along the harbour, one eye out for Danky. There is talk that he's been night fishing, trudging home by moonlight to his house, and for certain I've not seen him any morning this last week.

'And here's your friend, walking forward, come to pay us a call.' It's the sharp laughing voice of Betty's sister Meg, and I feel myself redden and I squeeze my package of fish until the squelch of it reminds me what it is.

'This one here's done,' the tall girl calls as she lays a last fish in the barrel, and a cooper comes and rolls it away. I step forward. The sisters will surely stop and stretch, but they are paid by the barrel, and they must begin again.

'Yes,' I hold up my packet of fish, 'I came out for my mother.' And I see a smile curl over Betty's face, a girl already three days' journey from her home, and no older than me.

'I'd best be getting back then.' My face is blazing, and to save myself I pick up a pebble and skim it out across the river. Its blunt edge chips the surface and it skips three times before it sinks.

'Bye then.' I can speak again, and with their eyes on me, I turn and hurry back the way I've come.

I've had Mac's pamphlet for so long I've almost forgotten it's not mine. I have my favourites now. The library in the School of Art with its soaring windows and its lamps. The Willow Tea Rooms, dark wood and bright white tablecloths, lit up by a cauldron of white flowers. It's on a street the name of which I can't pronounce. Sauchiehall. And I add that to my list.

I study Mrs Mac's work too. Her roses, which are Glasgow roses, wound about like balls of string. And her mysterious women, most of whom are clothed. But the picture that I look at till I have it off by heart is of a girl shrouded in a cloak so wide she could hide herself inside it. *The Mysterious Garden*, it is called. And along the top, as if they were trees, are the white faces of women. Are they ghosts? Or is the girl inside the cloak a ghost? And I have to turn over the page to keep from shuddering. But here, waiting, on the next page, are the tortured women Frances Macdonald paints. Naked or not, I fear them. Although the heat in my body rises if I look too long, and I calm myself by staring at *The Sleeping Princess*, a girl as beautiful as anything I've seen. As beautiful as Betty. She is lying in a silver frame, meshed around with spiderwebs and leaves, and moulded into it are the words, *Love, if thy tresses be so dark, how dark those hidden eyes must be.* I trace my fingers down the length of her hair, hanging far below her waist, and for all Frances Macdonald's insistence that she is sleeping, it's hard not to think she's dead.

I wait till both Mac and Mrs Mac are in their studio, checking on them downriver of the ferry where I can't be seen, and then, taking the muddy track that appears only at low tide, I cut past the Japanese bridge, until I'm in their lane. I don't waste time unlatching the Lea House gate, but climb over it, and scattering the rabbits with the thump of my landing, I streak up through the garden.

It's peaceful here in their house. I stand and breathe. There is a jug on the table filled with rosehip, and on the mantel are brambles thick with berries. The pile of books is still there, stacked and orderly, the spines lined up against the table's edge. They are the same books as before but in a different order and I slide my pamphlet in amongst them. I feel myself lighten, my conscience clear. I can go. But as I turn away I catch sight of an oblong purple box at the far end of the mantelpiece. There is a card tucked behind it and as I approach I get a whiff of that same sweet smell of liquor that seeped through the paper of the parcel I delivered.

*Dear Herr Rennie Mackintosh*, the card says. *Here is a small gift for you and your wife. I hope it gives you some pleasure in these difficult times. And that you do not see it as a bribe. As you know I await eagerly news of more flower drawings so that I may collect them together for a book. There are twelve you have been kind enough to show me, including*

*those you did on Holy Island, but if I am to publish I will need consider-*
*ably more as each one adds to and reflects the beauty of the others.*

*Do let me know how you are getting on. And never imagine that our*
*warring countries have altered my deep affection for you both. In hope*
*of better times.*

*With kind regards,*
*Your friend, Hermann Muthesius*

Hermann Muthesius. I struggle over the name, trying to find
the Gaelic in it, imagining it in one of Betty's songs. But I am
stopped by the double Herr of Hermann and Herr Mackintosh,
for I'm sure that it means Mr in German. 'Herr Mackintosh'. I
shouldn't say it. And I lift the top of the oblong box and find,
nestled there, six round chocolates resting in the paper.

They can't like them very much. Or maybe they like them so
much they are saving them for best, and I count the four dented
empty nests and imagine Mac and his wife limiting themselves
to one each week. I slide my fingers into the box and draw one
out. It sloshes hollowly, and the smell of the dark chocolate fills
my nose, but when I put it into my mouth the taste of cherry
brandy explodes there. I freeze, blowing my cheeks out like a
bloater to avoid the risk of swallowing, and step as carefully as
I can to the window where I force open the catch and spit it
out. A dribble of chocolate runs down the wall and I spit again,
leaking the syrupy mess over the sill. But all the time I'm cough-
ing and gagging I know that I'll have to take another of the evil
chocolates or they'll guess someone was here. If there are four,
they might forget from one long week to the next how many
they have eaten. But if there are five … And so with my nose
pinched up I take its twin, and looking round to check nothing
else is disturbed I slip out of the house, waiting until I'm in the
marshes before I hurl the black bomb with its liquid centre far
out into the grasses where a bittern might come across it and,
cracking it open with her beak, feed it to her young.

★

Our soldiers are being sent to France. Father slaps them on the back and stands them a drink, taking one himself, seeing as they're nearly gone. 'William,' Mother frowns across at him. But he ignores her.

I take out my copying. There are no boats in the margins now, not since I have my own sketchbook, and almost no crossing out and blots. Runnicles is pleased with me. He doesn't say so. But he's happy that I've stopped wasting my time with drawing and dreams of sailing off to sea, and I'm careful to keep the paper Mac gave me stored away out of sight.

'Thomas.' I don't realise at first it's my own name that's being called.

'Thomas!' Father's pint slams down on my table, sending a long pale splash of beer across my words. 'Tell these gentlemen about your friend old Mac. They've seen him in the village. Been wondering about him. Say he's out all hours.' There is a raised ridge of paper where the ale has settled and the ink I've used is bleeding from the words. 'Snooping around with those spyglasses of his.'

'Mr Charles Rennie Mackintosh', my heart is beating, 'is an architect from Glasgow. He built a school there.' I don't tell them it's a school of art. Because I'm not sure what that is. 'And a church. And he's made furniture too. Chairs taller than a man, and clocks like merry-go-rounds with the numbers upside down. And now he's here. Painting. He's taken over Thorogood's shed, down by the river. And he's made it into a studio.'

Father is staring at me. The soldiers too. And Gory, who is propped up in a corner, rolls his eyes. I drop my head and frown at the underwater writing like an inlet on my page.

'He uses the binoculars to examine things more clearly. Colours ... and shapes ...' I'm making this up now, 'so he'll know where the green of a leaf might change from one shade to the next.'

Father slurps his beer. 'We've had all sorts in here,' he turns to the men. 'Before the war. Artists and poets. A playwright even. All gone back to London now.'

'All gone,' Gory echoes him. 'Except old Mac.' And one of the soldiers spits, right there on the floor. He's a broad man with a meaty face. I don't like him. Or the other one either. 'Going about with his spyglass. A wonder no one's reported him.'

Mother says nothing and nor do I. Instead I run over the words I've used to check I've not betrayed him. *Hertz, Dekorative, Wiener, Rundschau.* No, I've not let any of these out. Nor have I told them about the requests from Hermann Muthesius to hurry up and send him more of our village's flowers.

'Ahh well,' the soldiers bend in to their beer. 'Probably harmless enough, although where there's smoke there's often as not fire,' and in the lull I rip out my page, and with my arm around the paper for protection I begin copying out my copying again.

I'm glad the next morning when the soldiers set off for their boat, their long cloth bags heaved across their shoulders like sorry-looking sows. When our first soldiers left we were down on the shore waving them off, and our second too, but today as we stand in the doorway of the Blue Anchor Mother says we can't spend our life on goodbyes. We'll have new men billeted with us by the end of the week and what will we do two weeks later when they leave?

Father catches hold of me as they walk away. 'You've been warned then?' He frowns down at my foot. I nod, although I don't know what he means. 'No more roaming about with your old Mac. You hear me?' And he thumps me hard on the shoulder, just because he can.

I was planning to do it anyway, but now I'm more determined than before. I take my paintbox, and after school I scoot along the river, ducking from one shed to the next till I come out by Thorogood's. There's no wind today, not even a breeze, and the sky lies crisp and blue above the boats. 'Hello,' Mrs Mac looks up, and I take a crate and sit myself in the shadow of their hut. I ease the lid off my squares of paint, the colours dancing, and I stare down at them, my brush hovering, too afraid of turning any one of them to sludge.

'What will you paint?' Mac swivels round, and when I hesitate, he shows me how to soak the board in a basin if the colours

need a wash. 'You can even clean your paints,' he eyes me, guess-
ing. 'Just take a cloth and wipe off the top layer.' And, relieved,
I tell him that I'm going to make a picture of HMS *Formidable*,
Jimmy Kerridge's boat.

'Has that not sailed?' Mrs Mac looks up. 'You'll not choose
something you can actually see?' And I smile, because I can see
it – Jimmy and his friends waving from the deck. I can see the
hats they wore and the scarves around their necks, and the wide
grins they had as their ship headed away, just as if I had been
there myself. I wet my brush and dip it into blue, and once I've
made the first line, it's easier to make another, so that soon my
page is streaked across with colour.

There's a thick, warm silence as we work. I've sensed that
silence, when I used to watch them, but now that I'm inside
it, it's as solid as a coat. If it was flax you could twist it into
rope, and I glance at Mac, growing the centre of an aster as if
he's God himself and just created it, the way he sits so still and
fierce in his dark suit. He is nothing like any of the artists that
I've seen, certainly not like the Miss Bishops, who wore cotton
smocks when they went out, and came home – at least the
younger of the two – with paint in their eyebrows and their
hair. But if Mac is neat then Mrs Mac is tidier still, standing,
so sure and precise that not a drop of colour falls on to her
clothes, not even on to the pale gloves she wears to protect her
hands from the sharp sting of the turps. I imagine her painting
on the white carpet of her Glasgow home, the white curtains
hanging at the window, a glow of embers smouldering in the
bed of the fire.

HMS *Formidable* has twenty-one sails. At least I imagine she
must if she's to carry seven hundred and fifty men, and supplies
for them all, and ammunition. I give her three masts, and a
multitude of rigging, so that soon my page is one big shimmery
mess of canvas, halyards and flags. There are portholes, cannons,
lifeboats, oars. I take the paper to the tin basin and I wash it
clean. Colours dribble off the page, but my boat remains there
in a mist, and rather than ask for Mac's old toothbrush to scrub

it off entirely, I take out the pencil I've brought and sketch in its shadowy shape.

When I next look up, the afternoon is gone. The sun, streaming downriver from the west, has turned the water turquoise and the sky is glittering with its last bright light. I stand up and squint behind me at the village. The inn will be about to open its doors, Mother may even now be standing on the street, waiting to give me a sharp word. And Father will be storming. Quickly I wash out my brush and taking the handkerchief from my pocket I wipe my hands, my arms, even my legs below the knee. 'There's a mark on your face,' Mrs Mac tells me, putting down her own tools, and when I clean it off, she laughs and points at my nose. 'Let me,' she shakes her head, and dipping the corner of the handkerchief in water she dabs at the smudge.

'Goodbye,' I say as I back away, but Mac is still working on his flower, his eyes boring into the paper, and he only grunts as I turn around and run.

# Hannah Rothschild

## 2015

## *The Improbability of Love*

Twenty minutes later, Annie was standing with Jesse and Agatha in the National Gallery's conservation studio considering the painting. It was just after 7.45 p.m., the sky outside had turned an inky black and the room was lit by one harsh tungsten bulb. Jesse tried to appear nonchalant and not look at Annie too often. Since their last meeting, she had, he decided, become more beautiful. Her hair settled like an auburn halo around her face and her white skin seemed to glow in the dark. Everything about her was fragile yet strong, energetic yet wistful. In the unflattering glare of the overhead light, he marvelled at her black lashes, the bluish hue of her eyelids, the pink curves of her earlobes and a tiny smattering of freckles, shaped like a crescent moon, on the back of her left hand.

'Though it is far too soon to make pronouncements,' Agatha told Annie, 'there is good evidence to suggest that your painting is from the early eighteenth century and is not a copy.'

'How can you be so sure?' Annie tried to swallow her excitement.

'There are several technical tricks we use. The first is a cleaning patch.' She pointed to a piece of sky and the treetops in the top left-hand corner. Compared to the dull yellows in the rest of the painting, this little area, about the size of a matchbox, had sprung into life; the foliage shimmered.

'Why didn't you go further?' Annie asked.

'Even that little patch test took about fifteen hours of painstaking work,' Jesse explained. 'It has to be done at a snail's pace to avoid accidental damage.'

'I'm sorry – I didn't mean to sound presumptuous.' Annie blushed, feeling brash and ungrateful. This woman was working for free and in her spare time.

Agatha smiled. 'As I said, this picture has brought Jesse back into my life, so it's a fair exchange.'

Jesse smiled gratefully at Agatha.

'The main problem is that the original paint had been covered with successive coats of thick brown varnish. Going forward, we will have to make a decision whether to take it all off or thin it out. Although the first is easier to achieve, it can remove the old patina. Thankfully the last few people to slap on a coat or two of varnish used a mastic resin base, which is the most reversible.'

Taking her torch, she beckoned for Annie to come close to the painting and, with her finger hovering over the surface, she pointed to the cleaned patch.

'Whoever did this was an extraordinarily skilled painter: just look at this foliage. Although it has all the depth and movement of a deep glade on a hot summer's day, though you can almost hear the birdsong and smell the sun's warmth on the leaves, he has made the whole thing with just a few dabs of brown and reddish brown.'

'But the effect is green and gold,' Annie said, staring in wonder.

'He prepared a blue and white ground and then flicked the colours over,' Agatha said, shining the torch over the area. 'It's also possible that he used a green or brown glaze of his own. If we take off too much varnish, we could wipe away his work.'

Putting down the torch, she went over to her worktable and returned with three large black-and-white photographs. Annie looked at one but could not really understand it – it was grainy and smudged but there was a ghost of a figure and a few high-lights in white, visible in one corner. Looking more closely, she recognised the outline of a clown. In the next photograph, she detected the woman and her admirer. The last photograph was unreadable, to her untrained eye; a series of squares and numerals.

'You are right to look nonplussed by this one,' Agatha said, smiling. 'Two of the X-rays are obvious but this one is of the back of the canvas. Those odd shapes hint at significant and revealing stamps hidden under different linings.'

'A bit like pass the parcel – you never know what you will find when you take off the wrapping,' Jesse said, and he and Agatha laughed.

'Stamps?' Annie asked, baffled by the conversation and failing to get the joke.

'In much the same way as a farmer stamps his cows, owners like to leave a proprietary mark,' Agatha explained before bringing out two photocopies of similar crests taken from a book and placing these next to the large photograph.

'This crest is undoubtedly the same insignia that Frederick the Great, King of Prussia, used but even more interestingly, this number, three hundred and twelve, is a cataloguing system that Louis XV put on pictures that entered his collection between March and September 1745.'

'How on earth do you know that?' Annie asked, studying the sequence of numbers.

'A colleague's life work has been cross-referencing contemporary sales catalogues and inventories from that period. Using his research we have been able to pinpoint when works went in and out of the royal collection.'

'Perhaps the gallery should start hanging paintings with their backs on show,' Jesse joked.

'You might laugh but we have often discussed doing just that,' Agatha said.

'What else did you discover?' Annie asked.

'There are two other numbers – here, at the bottom, two hundred and thirty-four, and in the top right-hand corner, you can just see the outline of an eighty – the latter looks a little bit like Catherine the Great's, but that would be far too exciting.'

'Why?'

'It would mean that your little picture has the most interesting history or provenance of any work I have ever come across,' Agatha said.

Annie, Jesse and Agatha looked at the painting. Annie thought back to the anvil-faced man at the British Museum: was this the answer to his riddle? She tried to remember the kings' and queens' names. What was it he had said? Louis, Catherine and Victoria? Annie tried to remember.

'Just imagine – you would be linked to some of the greatest rulers in history,' Jesse said to Annie.

'From king to queen to Miss Annie McDee, mistress of a small flat in Shepherd's Bush, four pairs of trousers, eleven shirts, three pairs of shoes, a black dress and a broken washing machine,' Annie said, with more than a trace of irony.

'Plus a masterpiece,' Jesse added.

'It partly explains why people want to own great works. It connects them to a glorious heritage and magnificent rulers,' Agatha said.

Annie made a fake royal wave at Jesse, who bowed deferentially.

'Actually there is more good news,' Agatha said, producing what to Annie looked like an X-ray. Just visible among the greys were the flowing white lines of the artist's preparatory sketch.

'We used infrared reflectography on the painting and if you look closely, you can see an underdrawing.'

'What does this mean?' Annie asked, confused.

'That it is highly unlikely to be a copy. Copyists don't need to work out where or how to place their figures – the original artist has done that for them.'

Agatha produced a handful of photocopies of the reflectographs taken from other pictures by Watteau as comparisons.

'I don't want to raise your hopes but these images are X-rays of other paintings by Watteau and you can see certain similarities.'

Annie looked closely, but to her the white marks could have been done by anyone.

'It's like spotting a person's handwriting,' Jesse explained. 'Different artists used different strokes and techniques.'

Picking up one example, Annie thought she could detect a faint pattern beneath the pastoral scene – a shield? Or a lance? 'What does this mean?' she asked.

'Watteau was often too poor to buy canvas so he painted on whatever came to hand. In this case it was the back of coach doors covered in heraldic signs. We know of another painting, *La Declaration*, that he painted over a copperplate engraving.'

'He was too poor to afford a piece of canvas?' Annie asked.

'That's what we assume. We found another clue about his financial circumstances. Follow me,' Agatha said, leading them through the door, along a narrow corridor and through two large doors. Beyond these were a series of rooms organised like a scientific laboratory.

The room was small and dark. There were several computers on the table and the walls were lined with shelves laden with test tubes and scientific paraphernalia. Annie looked at Jesse in amazement. She walked past the National Gallery twice a day and assumed that it was merely a repository for paintings.

Sitting at one screen was a man in a white coat, with wild grey hair and an irrepressibly cheerful expression.

'This is Dr Frears,' Agatha said.

'The lucky lady,' Dr Frears said, getting up from his computer and holding out his hand. 'Most of us can only dream of walking out of a junk shop with a lovely work of art.'

'Maybe it only happens to people who know nothing,' Annie said wryly.

'Would you like to see what I have been studying?'

Annie nodded. In spite of her scepticism and Delores's impending dinner, these engaging people and their extraordin-ary expertise were capturing her imagination. She followed Dr Frears to his computer and looked at an image of a mille-feuille gateau with layers of different-coloured cream and fruit.

'A cake?' she asked.

'This is a cross-section of a pinprick of paint taken from the side of your canvas multiplied several million times,' explained Dr Frears. 'While not visible to the human eye, that little spot can tell us many stories.'

Fascinated but entirely bewildered, Annie looked back at the image.

'The pigments used in your painting are identical to others in works by Antoine Watteau. What is fascinating is this tiny fragment of Prussian blue – we know that this pigment only arrived in Paris in early 1700. How your man could have afforded it is anyone's guess. In this lower section is an iron oxide that he often used and which we know came from a shop quite near to his lodgings.'

Annie and Jesse leaned in to the computer to inspect the layers of gradated colour and grain.

'So, as this young man suspected,' Dr Frears nodded at Jesse, 'we cannot discount that the picture was by Watteau's hand.'

'Surely it proves it?' Annie said.

'Unfortunately we can't conclude that. Our work is mainly to discount rather than prove,' Agatha said.

'Another absolutely fascinating discovery is here,' Dr Frears pointed to a tiny black mark. 'This turns out to be part of a brush bristle.'

Annie bit her lip – she wanted to giggle – what else would someone paint with?

Dr Frears ploughed on. 'There is also a trace of wine and blood and some kind of animal fat mixed in with the paint.'

'Perhaps we should send his DNA to our friends at King's College?' Agatha suggested.

'So they can clone the painter?' Annie asked.

Dr Frears smiled. 'You never know!'

An hour later, in a small pub off St James's Square, Annie and Jesse sat at the corner table drinking white wine.

'I'd love to have bought you champagne,' Jesse said apologetically.

'This is lovely, thank you,' Annie said.

'Here's to your painting.' Jesse raised his wine glass and Annie tapped hers against his. Having a drink with him was the least she could do. There was a clock on the wall behind the bar, it was 8.30 p.m.; Annie was tired and wanted to get home.

'You must be excited about the picture,' Jesse said.

'Excited? I don't understand this world. There is evidence to say that the picture is authentic. The restorer likes it and the scientist admires it. Age tests bear out. Paint tests stack up. There is even an engraving of the same work in a catalogue but yet none of this matters unless certain experts agree.'

'Art is subjective,' Jesse said.

'So is God.'

'Isn't it comforting that beauty can't be decided by science? That it is in the eye of the beholder?' Jesse asked.

'That is too random for me.'

'Isn't it like cooking – you can never quite tell how things will turn out?'

'At least there is a time frame with food – if you go on too long it spoils or burns.'

'We have found out so much in a relatively short time,' Jesse said. 'We know that the picture is old, that it was painted at the time Watteau lived. That it was owned by some swanky people and that it isn't a copy.'

'What next?'

I would like to kiss you, Jesse thought. I long to take you in my arms and brush the crossness and hurt out of your shoulders and kiss your eyelids. I want to stand next to you every minute of every day. I want to tell you how special and extraordinary you are to me.

Forcing these feelings aside, he said, 'Let's try and prove a strong line of ownership from the present day back to the early eighteenth century and make the case far more compelling.'

Annie looked across the pub at another couple sitting hand in hand looking at a holiday brochure. Something about the way that the woman leaned into the crook of the man's arm made her longing to be held almost overwhelming.

'Why?' Annie asked, forcing herself back to the present.

'Why what?' Jesse asked.

'Why are you helping me?'

'Isn't it obvious?' Jesse said. 'I like you. A lot. I was hoping that you might like me enough, a little bit enough, that is, to go on seeing me.'

Annie looked into her glass of wine, a feeling of panic welling up inside her. She could cope with meaningless encounters, but the prospect of real emotional involvement was terrifying.

'I don't feel the same way. I'm sorry.' She stood up, pulled on her coat, rushed out of the pub and on to the street. Walking away as fast as she could, she told herself: I must not fall for anyone again, it just leads to desolation. I must not.

Jesse sat for a few moments staring into his half-drunk glass of wine, unable to understand how he had misjudged the situation so badly. While it was true that Annie had never actively encouraged him, nor had she rejected him. He didn't feel angry, just abject. Jumping up, he ran after her.

Looking up and down King Street, he caught sight of her hunched figure heading towards St James's. Jesse sprinted down the road and caught up with Annie as she turned the corner.

'Wait, please,' he said panting, out of breath. 'I am not in the habit of making declarations to women – in fact, you are the first and, if you must know, I feel like an absolute idiot pursuing you like this, but I am overwhelmed, literally, by my feelings for you – I realise that this will probably be the death knell, the final straw, but even if you walk off now, even if I have got this completely wrong, at least if you ever change your mind, you know how to find me.'

With this, without giving Annie a moment to reply, he turned and walked quickly away.

# Ann Patchett

## 2016

## Commonwealth

Every year Beverly's second trip to the airport was worse because she always thought it was going to be better. She left her four stepchildren at home (first with her mother, then Bonnie, then Wallis, and now under Cal's supervision. They stayed home alone in Torrance after all, and Arlington was safer than Torrance) and drove back to Dulles to reclaim her girls. While Bert's children came east for the entire summer, Caroline and Franny traveled west for two short weeks: one with Fix and then one with her parents, just enough time to remind the girls how greatly they preferred California to Virginia. They shuffled off the plane looking like they were in an advanced state of dehydration from having cried for the entirety of their flight. Beverly dropped to her knees to hug them but they were nothing but ghosts. Caroline wanted to live with her father. She begged for it, she pleaded, and year after year she was denied. Caroline's hatred for her mother radiated through the cloth of her pink camp shirt as her mother pressed Caroline to her chest. Franny on the other hand simply stood there and tolerated the embrace. She didn't know how to hate her mother yet, but every time she left her father crying in the airport she came that much closer to figuring it out.

Beverly kissed their heads. She kissed Caroline again as Caroline pulled away from her. "I'm so glad you're home," she said.

But Caroline and Franny were not glad they were home. They were not glad at all. It was in this battered state that the Keating girls returned to Arlington to be reunited with their stepsiblings.

Holly was certainly friendly. She hopped up and down and actually clapped her hands when the girls came through the door. She said she wanted to put on another dance recital in the living room this summer. But Holly was also wearing Caroline's red T-shirt with the tiny white ribbon rosette at the neck, which her mother had made Caroline put in the Goodwill bag before she left because it was both faded and too small. Holly was not the Goodwill.

Caroline had the bigger room with two sets of bunk beds, and Franny, being smaller, had the smaller room with twin beds. The two sisters were connected by neither love nor mutual affinity but by a very small bathroom that could be entered from the bedroom on either side. Two girls and one bathroom was a workable situation from the beginning of September through the end of May, but in June when Caroline and Franny returned from California they found Holly and Jeanette had made themselves at home in one set of bunk beds while Franny had lost her room completely to the boys. It was four girls in one room and the two boys in the other with a bathroom the size of a phone booth for the six of them to share.

Caroline and Franny lugged their luggage up the stairs. Luggage: that which is to be lugged. They passed the open door of the master bedroom where Cal was lying across their mother's bed, his dirty feet in dirty socks resting on the pillows, watching a tennis match at top volume. They were *never* allowed to go into the master bedroom or sit on the bed, even if they kept their feet on the floor, nor were they allowed to watch television without an express invitation. Cal didn't lift his eyes from the screen or give the smallest recognition of their arrival as they passed.

Holly was behind them, close enough to bump when they stopped walking. "I was thinking that all four of us could dance in white nightgowns. Would that be okay? We could start practicing this afternoon. I've got some ideas about the choreography if you want to see."

As for there being four girls in the dance recital, only three were in evidence. Jeanette was MIA. No one had noticed she was gone, but Franny's cat Buttercup was missing as well. Buttercup had not come to the door to greet Franny as surely she would have after two weeks away. Buttercup, the lifeline to normalcy, was gone. Beverly, drowning in the sea of child-life, had no clear memory of the last time she'd seen the cat, but Franny's sudden, paralyzing sobs prompted her to do a thorough search of the house. Beverly found Jeanette beneath a comforter on the floor in the back of the linen closet (how long had Jeanette been missing?). She was petting the sleeping cat.

"She can't have my cat!" Franny cried, and Beverly leaned down and took the cat from Jeanette, who hung on for only half a second and then let go. The entire time Albie followed Beverly around the house doing what the children referred to as "the stripper soundtrack":

*Boom* chicka-boom, *boom-boom* chicka-boom.

When their mother stopped walking the soundtrack stopped. If she took a single step it was accompanied by Albie saying only "boom" in a voice that was weirdly sexual for a six-year-old. She meant to ignore him but after a while he proved too much for her. When finally she snapped, screaming "Stop that!" he only looked at her. He had the most enormous brown eyes, and loose, loopy brown curls that made him look like a cartoon animal.

"I'm serious," she said, making an effort to steady her breathing. "You have to stop that." She tried to find within her own voice a sound that was reasonable, parental, but when she turned to walk away she heard the small, quiet chug, "*Boom* chicka-boom."

Beverly thought about killing him. She thought about killing a child. Her hands were shaking. She went to her room, wanting to close the door and lock it and go to sleep, but from the hallway she heard the thwack of a tennis ball, the roar of a crowd. She stuck her head around the doorframe. "Cal?" she said, trying not to cry. "I need my room now."

Cal didn't move, not a twitch. He kept his eyes on the screen. "It's not over," he said, as if she had never seen a tennis match before and didn't understand that when the ball was in motion it meant the game was still going on.

Bert didn't believe in television for children. At its most harmless he saw it as a waste of time, a bunch of noise. At its most harmful he wondered if it didn't stunt brain development. He thought Teresa had made a huge mistake letting the children watch so much TV. He had told her not to do it but she never listened to him when it came to parenting, when it came to anything. That's why he and Beverly had only one television in this house, and why it was in their bedroom, which wasn't open to children, or wasn't open to her children during the regular course of the year. Now Beverly wanted to unplug the television and cart it off to what the realtor had called "the family room," though no member of the family ever seemed to light there. She went down the hallway, Albie following at a safe distance, churning his music. Did his mother teach him that? Someone taught him. Six-year-olds didn't hang out in strip clubs, not even this one. Beverly went into the girls' room but Holly was there reading *Rebecca*.

"Beverly, have you ever read *Rebecca*?" Holly asked as soon as Beverly stepped into the room, her little face bright, bright, bright. "Mrs. Danvers is scaring me to death but I'm going to keep reading it. I don't care if I had the chance to live in Manderley. I wouldn't stay there if someone was being that creepy to me."

Beverly nodded slightly and backed out of the room. She thought about trying to lie down in the boys' room, the room that had once been Franny's, but it had a vaguely nutty smell reminiscent of socks and underwear and unwashed hair.

She went downstairs again and found Caroline banging around the kitchen in a rage, saying she was going to make brownies for her father and mail them to him so he'd have something to eat.

"Your father doesn't like nuts in his brownies," Beverly said. She didn't know why she said it. She was trying to be helpful.

"He does too!" Caroline said, turning on her mother so fast she spilled half a bag of flour on the counter. "Maybe he didn't when you knew him but you don't know him anymore. Now he likes nuts in everything."

Albie was in the dining room. She could hear him singing through the kitchen door. His single-pointed focus was astounding. Franny was in the living room, pulling the cat's front legs through the armholes of a doll's dress and crying so quietly that her mother was sure that every single thing she had ever done in her life up until that moment was a mistake.

There was no place to go, no place to get away from them, not even the linen closet because Jeanette hadn't come out of the linen closet since surrendering the cat. Beverly took the car keys and went outside. The minute she closed the door behind her she was underwater, the summer air hot and solid in her lungs. She thought about the back patio of the house in Downey, how she would sit outside in the afternoons, Caroline on her tricycle, Franny happy in her lap, the smell of the orange blossoms nearly overwhelming. Fix had had to sell the house in order to pay her half of what little equity they had and make the child support. Why had she made him sell the house? No one could sit outside in Virginia. She got five new mosquito bites just walking to the driveway and each one puffed up to the size of a quarter. Beverly was allergic to mosquito bites.

It was easily 105 degrees inside the car. She started the engine, turned on the air conditioner, turned off the radio. She lay across the scorching green vinyl of the bench seat so that no one looking out the front window of the house could see her. She thought about the fact that if she were in the garage rather than the carport she'd be killing herself now.

Because California public schools ran slightly longer than Virginia Catholic schools, Beverly and Bert had had five days alone in the house between her children's departure and his children's arrival. One night after dinner they made love on the dining room carpet. It wasn't comfortable. Beverly's weight had steadily dropped since their move to Virginia, and the bony protrusions of her vertebrae and clavicles were so clearly displayed she could have found work in an anatomy class. Every thrust pushed her back a quarter inch, dragging her skin against the wool blend. But even with the rug burns it made them feel daring and passionate. It hadn't been a mistake, Bert kept telling her as they lay on their backs afterwards, staring up at the ceiling. Beverly counted five places where the glass crystals on the chandelier were missing. She hadn't noticed it before.

"Everything that's happened in our lives up until now, everything we've done, it had to happen exactly the way it did so that we could be together." Bert took her hand and squeezed it.

"You really believe that?" Beverly asked.

"We're magic," Bert said.

Later that night he rubbed Neosporin down the length of her spine. She slept on her stomach. That was their summer vacation.

Here was the most remarkable thing about the Keating children and the Cousins children: they did not hate one another, nor did they possess one shred of tribal loyalty. The Cousinses did not prefer the company of Cousinses and the two Keatings could have done without each other entirely. The four girls were angry about being crowded together into a single room but they didn't blame each other. The boys, who were always angry about everything, didn't seem to care that they were in the company of so many girls. The six children held in common one overarching principle that cast their potential dislike for one another down to the bottom of the minor leagues: they disliked the parents. They hated them.

The only one who was troubled by this fact was Franny, because Franny had always loved her mother. During the regular part of the year they sometimes took naps together in the afternoons after school, spooning so close they fell asleep and dreamed the same dreams. Franny would sit on the closed toilet lid in the morning and watch her mother put on makeup, and she would sit on the toilet lid again at night and talk to her mother while her mother soaked in the bath. Franny was secure in the knowledge that she was not only her mother's favorite daughter, she was her mother's favorite person. Except in the summer, when her mother looked at her as if she were nothing more than the fourth of six children. When her mother was sick of Albie, she announced that all children had to go outside, and "all children" included Franny. Ice cream had to be eaten outside. Watermelon—outside. Since when had she not been trusted to eat watermelon at the kitchen table? It was insulting, and not just to her. Maybe Albie couldn't eat a dish of ice cream without dropping it on the floor but the rest of them were perfectly capable. They went outside all right. They went outside and slammed the door and took off down the street, loping across the hot pavement like a pack of feral dogs.

The four Cousins children didn't blame Beverly for their miserable summers. They blamed their father, and would have said so to his face had he ever been around. Cal and Holly gave no indication that they thought Beverly's behavior was inexcusable (and Jeanette never said anything anyway, and Albie, well, who knew about Albie), but Caroline and Franny were horrified. Their mother made everyone line up in the kitchen according to age and come to the stove with their plate instead of putting the food on the table in dishes as she did every other night of the year. In the summers they wandered out of the civilized world and into the early orphanage scenes of *Oliver Twist*.

2017

*Lincoln in the Bardo*

## XCII.

I am Willie    I am Willie    I am even yet
Am not
Willie
Not willie but somehow
Less
More
All is    Allowed now    All is allowed me now    All is
allowed lightlightlight me now
    Getting up out of bed and going down to the party, allowed
    Candy bees, allowed
    Chunks of cake, allowed!
    Punch (even rum punch), allowed!
    Let that band play louder!
    Swinging from the chandelier, allowed; floating up to ceil-
ing, allowed; going to window to have a look out, allowed
allowed allowed!
    Flying out window, allowed, allowed (the entire laugh-
ing party of guests happily joining behind me, urging me to
please, yes, fly away) (saying oh, he feels much better now, he
does not seem sick at all!)!
    Whatever that former fellow (willie) had, must now be
given back (is given back gladly) as it never was mine (never
his) and therefore is not being taken away, not at all!

As I (who was of willie but is no longer (merely) of willie) return
   To such beauty.
                          willie lincoln


# XCIII.

There in his seat, Mr. Lincoln startled.
                          roger bevins iii

Like a schoolboy jolting suddenly awake in class.
                          hans vollman

Looked around.
                          roger bevins iii

Momentarily unsure, it seemed, of where he was.
                          hans vollman

Then got to his feet and made for the door.
                          roger bevins iii

The lad's departure having set him free.
                          hans vollman

So quickly did he move that he passed through us before we could step aside.
                          roger bevins iii

And again, briefly, we knew him.
                          hans vollman

## XCIV.

His boy was gone; his boy was no more.
hans vollman

His boy was nowhere; his boy was everywhere.
roger bevins iii

There was nothing here for him now.
hans vollman

His boy was no more *here* than *anyplace else*, that is. There was nothing special, anymore, about *this* place.
roger bevins iii

His continued presence here was wrong; was wallowing.
hans vollman

His having come here at all a detour and a weakness.
roger bevins iii

His mind was freshly inclined toward *sorrow*; toward the fact that the world was full of sorrow; that everyone labored under some burden of sorrow; that all were suffering; that whatever way one took in this world, one must try to remember that all were suffering (none content; all wronged, neglected, over-looked, misunderstood), and therefore one must do what one could to lighten the load of those with whom one came into contact; that his current state of sorrow was not uniquely his, not at all, but, rather, its like had been felt, would yet be felt, by scores of others, in all times, in every time, and must not be prolonged or exaggerated, because, in this state, he could be of no help to anyone and, given that his position in the world situated him to be either of great help or great harm, it would not do to stay low, if he could help it.
hans vollman

All were in sorrow, or had been, or soon would be.
>> roger bevins iii

It was the nature of things.
>> hans vollman

Though on the surface it seemed every person was differ-ent, this was not true.
>> roger bevins iii

At the core of each lay suffering; our eventual end, the many losses we must experience on the way to that end.
>> hans vollman

We must try to see one another in this way.
>> roger bevins iii

As suffering, limited beings—
>> hans vollman

Perennially outmatched by circumstance, inadequately endowed with compensatory graces.
>> roger bevins iii

His sympathy extended to all in this instant, blundering, in its strict logic, across all divides.
>> hans vollman

He was leaving here broken, awed, humbled, diminished.
>> roger bevins iii

Ready to believe anything of this world.
>> hans vollman

Made less rigidly himself through this loss.
>> roger bevins iii

Therefore quite powerful.

> hans vollman

Reduced, ruined, remade.

> roger bevins iii

Merciful, patient, dazzled.

> hans vollman

And yet.

> roger bevins iii

And yet.

He was in a fight. Although those he fought were also suffering, limited beings, he must—

> hans vollman

Obliterate them.

> roger bevins iii

Kill them and deny them their livelihood and force them back into the fold.

> hans vollman

He must (*we* must, we felt) do all *we* could, in light of the many soldiers lying dead and wounded, in open fields, all across the land, weeds violating their torsos, eyeballs pecked out or dissolving, lips hideously retracted, rain-soaked/blood-soaked/snow-crusted letters scattered about them, to ensure that we did not, as we trod that difficult path we were now well upon, blunder, blunder further (we had blundered so badly already) and, in so blundering, ruin more, more of these boys, each of whom was once dear to someone.

*Ruinmore, ruinmore*, we felt, *must endeavor not to ruinmore.*

Our grief must be defeated; it must not become our master, and make us ineffective, and put us even deeper into the ditch.

roger bevins iii

We must, to do the maximum good, bring the thing to its swiftest halt and—

hans vollman

Kill.

roger bevins iii

Kill more efficiently.

hans vollman

Hold nothing back.

roger bevins iii

Make the blood flow.

hans vollman

Bleed and bleed the enemy until his good sense be reborn.

roger bevins iii

The swiftest halt to the thing (therefore the greatest mercy) might be the bloodiest.

hans vollman

Must end suffering by causing more suffering.

roger bevins iii

We were low, lost, an object of ridicule, had almost nothing left, were failing, must take some action to halt our fall, and restore ourselves to ourselves.

hans vollman

Must win. Must win the thing.
                        roger bevins iii

His heart dropped at the thought of the killing.
                        hans vollman


Did the thing merit it. Merit the killing. On the surface it was a technicality (mere Union) but seen deeper, it was something more. How should men live? How could men live? Now he recalled the boy he had been (hiding from Father to read Bunyan; raising rabbits to gain a few coins; standing in town as the gaunt daily parade drawled out the hard talk hunger made; having to reel back when one of those more fortunate passed merrily by in a carriage), feeling strange and odd (smart too, superior), long-legged, always knocking things over, called names (Ape Lincoln, Spider, Ape-a-ham, Monstrous-Tall), but also thinking, quietly, there inside himself, that he might someday get something for himself. And then, going out to get it, he had found the way clear—his wit was quick, people liked him for his bumbling and his ferocity of purpose, and the peach orchards and haystacks and young girls and ancient wild meadows drove him nearly mad with their beauty, and strange animals moved in lazy mobs along muddy rivers, rivers crossable only with the aid of some old rowing hermit who spoke a language barely English, and all of it, all of that bounty, was *for everyone,* for everyone to use, seemingly put here to teach a man to be free, to teach that a man *could* be free, that any man, any free white man, could come from as low a place as he had (a rutting sound coming from the Cane cabin, he had looked in through the open door and seen two pairs of still-socked feet and a baby toddling past, steadying herself by grasping one of the rutters' feet), and even a young fellow who had seen *that,* and lived among *those,* might rise, here, as high as he was inclined to go.

And that, against this: the king-types who would snatch the apple from your hand and claim to have grown it, even though what they had, had come to them intact, or been gained unfairly (the nature of that unfairness perhaps being just that they had been born stronger, more clever, more energetic than others), and who, having seized the apple, would eat it so proudly, they seemed to think that not only had they grown it, but had invented the very idea of fruit, too, and the cost of this lie fell on the hearts of the low (Mr. Bellway rushing his children off their Sangamon porch as he and Father slumped past with that heavy bag of grain drooping between them).

Across the sea fat kings watched and were gleeful, that something begun so well had now gone off the rails (as down South similar kings watched), and if it went off the rails, so went the whole kit, forever, and if someone ever thought to start it up again, well, it would be said (and said truly): The rabble cannot manage itself.

Well, the rabble could. The rabble would.
He would lead the rabble in managing.
The thing would be won.

roger bevins iii

*Our* Willie would not wish us hobbled in that attempt by a vain and useless grief.

hans vollman

In *our* mind the lad stood atop a hill, merrily waving to us, urging us to be brave and resolve the thing.

roger bevins iii

But (*we* stopped ourselves short) was this not just wishful thinking? Weren't we, in order to enable ourselves to go on, positing from our boy a blessing we could not possibly verify?
Yes.
Yes we were.

hans vollman

315

But we must do so, and believe it, or else we were ruined.
roger bevins iii

And we must not be ruined.
hans vollman

But must go on.
roger bevins iii

We saw all of this in the instant it took Mr. Lincoln to pass through us.
hans vollman

And then he was out the door, and into the night.
roger bevins iii

## XCV.

We black folks had not gone into the church with the others.

Our experience having been that white people are not especially fond of having us in their churches. Unless it is to hold a baby, or prop up or hand-fan some old one.

Then here came that tall white man out the door, right at me.

I held my ground as he passed through and got something along the lines of *I will go on, I will. With God's help. Though it seems killing must go hard against the will of God. Where might God stand on this. He has shown us. He could stop it. But has not. We must see God not as a Him (some linear rewarding fellow) but an IT, a great beast beyond our understanding, who wants something from us, and we must give it, and all we may control is the spirit in which we give it and the ultimate end which the giving serves. What end does IT wish served? I do not know. What IT wants, it seems, for now, is blood, more blood, and to alter things from what they <u>are</u>,* *to what IT wills they <u>should</u> be. But what that new state is, I do not know, and patiently wait to learn, even as those three thousand fallen stare foul-eyed at me, working dead hands anxiously, asking, What end might this thing yet attain, that will make our terrible sacrifice worthwh—*

Then he was through me and I was glad.

Near the front gate stood Mr. Havens, square in that white man's path, as I had been, but doing, then, something I had not the nerve (nor desire) to do.

mrs. francis hodge

# Nicole Krauss

## 2017

## *Forest Dark*

I was too weak to drag anything but the bed back inside. I left it in the middle of the room, and discovered that from there I could see out through all three windows. The only book I had in English was *Parables and Paradoxes*, and after rereading the section on Paradise a few times, I looked out the windows and was struck by the thought that I'd misunderstood something about Kafka, having failed to acknowledge the original threshold at the source of every other in his work, the one between Paradise and this world. Kafka once said that he understood the Fall of Man better than anyone. His sense came from the belief that most people misunderstood the expulsion from the Garden of Eden to be punishment for eating from the Tree of Knowledge. But as Kafka saw it, exile from Paradise came as a result of *not* eating from the Tree of Life. Had we eaten from that other tree that also stood in the center of the garden, we would have woken to the presence of the eternal within us, to what Kafka called "the indestructible." Now people are all basically alike in their ability to recognize good and evil, he wrote; the difference comes after that knowledge, when people have to make an effort to act in accordance with it. But because we lack the capacity to act in accordance with our moral knowledge, all our efforts come to ruin, and in the end we can only destroy ourselves trying. We would like nothing more than to annul the knowledge that came to us when we ate in the Garden of Eden, but as we are unable to do so, we create rationalizations, of which the world is now full. "It's possible that the whole visible world," Kafka mused, "might be nothing more than the rationalization of a man wanting to find rest for a moment." Rest how? By pretending that knowledge can be an end in itself. Meanwhile, we go on overlooking the eternal, indestructible thing inside ourselves, just as Adam and Eve fatally overlooked the Tree of Life. Go on overlooking it, even while we can't live without the faith that it is there, always within us, its branches reaching upward and its leaves unfurling in the light. In this sense, the threshold between Paradise and this world may be illusory, and we may never have really left Paradise, Kafka suggested. In this sense, we might be there without knowing it even now.

It became clear that no one was coming back for me. Maybe they'd forgotten. Or maybe whoever was in possession of the whole story had been called away or killed in the war. Kaddish for the whole story. I hadn't even tried to do my part: the suitcase sat untouched where Schectman left it. But, no, that isn't entirely true. Before I fell ill, and at times in my fever, too, I'd thought a lot about Kafka's afterlife. I imagined his gardens most of all. Maybe it was the barrenness of the desert all around that gave me a thirst for lushness, for the heavy, almost sickeningly overripe smell of crowded leaves, but I found myself repeatedly conjuring their fragrant paths, busy with insect life, their arbors, fruit trees, and vines. And always Kafka among them, at work or at rest, mixing peat or lime, fingering hard buds, untangling root balls, watching the work of the bees while still dressed in the dark suit of an undertaker. I never pictured him in clothes appropriate to outdoor work or the heat. Even after my vision of his gardens fell into keeping with what I knew could grow there, after I filled them with honeysuckle and pomegranate trees, I still couldn't see him in anything but that stiff suit. The suit, and sometimes that odd bowler hat that always looked too small for his head, as if the merest wind might knock it off. If I couldn't fully accept the idea of him shedding his old clothes, however inappropriate in his new life, I suppose it was because I couldn't fully accept that he would prefer to plant a tree, to water and fertilize and prune, than to organize the light through its leaves, to put it through the paces of three hundred years in a sentence or two, and to kill it at last in a hurricane that brought too much salt to its roots and left it as fodder for the ax. Could not, finally, accept that he would want to toil under nature's harsh and limiting conditions when his powers extended to being able to surpass them for something that, in his prose, had always been soldered to the eternal.

There was a Hebrew dictionary on the shelf, and I turned its pages, trying to imagine that after his death in Prague Kafka really had crossed over into Hebrew, and gone on writing in those ancient letters. That the results of the union between Kafka and Hebrew was what had really lain hidden all this time in the fortress of Eva Hoffe's Spinoza Street apartment, protected by a double cage and her paranoia. Was there such a thing as late Kafka? Was it possible that the unspoken subtext of the ongoing court case between the National Library of Israel and Eva Hoffe, acting as Brod's agent, was really that: the struggle to preserve the myth, versus the struggle to claim Kafka by the state that regards itself as the representative and culmination of Jewish culture, and which depends on an overcoming of the Diaspora, on the Messianic notion that only in Israel can a Jew be authentically a Jew? The knowing smile that played on Friedman's lips that day he'd dropped me at my sister's apartment came back to me again: *You think your writing belongs to you?* Only now that he was gone was I ready to argue with him, to tell him that literature could never be employed by Zionism, since Zionism is predicated on an end—of the Diaspora, of the past, of the Jewish problem—whereas literature resides in the sphere of the endless, and those who write have no hope of an end. A journalist interviewing Eva Hoffe once asked her what she thought Kafka would have made of it all had he been alive. "Kafka wouldn't have lasted two minutes in this country," she'd shot back.

The dog watched me from her place in the corner as I got up to return the Hebrew dictionary to the shelf. She had sat there all through my fever, whining only when she had to go outside

to relieve herself. Otherwise she didn't leave my side. I won't
soon forget the look in her dark, wet eyes: as if she understood
what I myself didn't. But now she seemed to know that the
fever had broken, and began to stretch and move about, and
even thump her tail against the floor, as if she also sensed that
time was returning to us. When I went to the kitchen to get
her some water, she leaped up and trotted after me with a new
spring in her step, as if in the course of my fever she had shed
many years. There was nothing left to eat, the kitchen was bare.
I had no interest in discovering what it felt like to starve, or to
watch the dog starve. All night I'd heard her stomach bubbling
with hunger.

The suitcase was still waiting by the door. The moment I laid
my fingers on the handle, the dog began to pant with excitement. I pulled it across the empty room while she watched. It
was far lighter than I'd expected. So light that for a moment
I wondered whether the army had left the wrong suitcase, or
whether Friedman had really taken anything from Spinoza
Street at all.

I filled some large jars with water and put them in the musty
canvas backpack I'd found in the closet. I was still wearing the
coat that might have been Kafka's coat, but instead of returning
it to the hanger, I buttoned it up to my chin. Then I took one last
look around the room, which seemed to hold no more memory
of his time here than it did of mine. I drew the thin curtains,
which did little to keep out the light. Kaddish for Kafka. May his
soul be bundled in the bundle of life. He might have lived there,
but I never could. I had children who needed me, and whom
I needed, and the time when I might have been able to live
confined to what was unquestionably within myself had passed
when they were born.

I opened the door, and the dog didn't hesitate. She ran out
thirty or forty paces ahead, then turned to wait for me. She
seemed to want to show me that she knew the way, and could
be trusted to lead. The furniture was still laid out under the sky.
The slippers stood waiting side by side on the dusty ground for

whoever would come. Soon the rain would arrive and come down on everything. I looked back on the house, which seemed even tinier from the outside.

The dog hurried ahead, alternately sniffing the ground and turning back to be sure I was following. The suitcase bumped along behind me over the rocky ground. What at first seemed light soon became heavy, as is always the way. If I lagged too far behind, the dog circled back and trotted at my heels, and when I stopped and sat down on the ground, she whined and licked my face.

We walked for hours. The sun began to fall toward the west, sending our shadows ahead of us. The skin of my palms became raw and blistered, my arms had lost their feeling, and by then my belief in the dog's preternatural ability to guide me had been worn thin by exhaustion and fear that I would die out there, and never see my children again because I'd been foolish. It was not without disgust with myself that I abandoned the job of wheeling a suitcase that I was afraid to find out was empty across the floor of a desert that once had been the bottom of a sea. The dog looked at it pitifully for a moment, then raised her nose to the sky and sniffed the air, as if to demonstrate that she was already on to other things.

It was late by the time we reached the road. I wanted to get down on my knees and cry into the tarmac that someone had taken the trouble to lay down there. I shared out the last of the water with the dog, and we curled against each other for heat. I slept intermittently. It must have been nearly six in the morning when we heard the rising hum of an engine approaching from the other side of the hill. I jumped to my feet. The taxi came tearing around the bend, and I waved frantically at the driver, who slammed on the brakes, glided slowly toward us, and lowered his window. We were lost, I explained, and not in good shape. He turned down the Mizrahi music coming from the stereo and smiled, revealing a gold tooth. He was on his way back to Tel Aviv, he said. I told him that's where we were headed, too. He looked skeptically at the dog, whose body had become tense and rigid. She seemed prepared to spring forward and sink her teeth into his jugular, if necessary. She looked nothing at all like a shepherd, neither German nor any other, but in the end Friedman was right, that's what she was. She was an extraordinary dog; to think that I almost gave her up to the soldier. After I got out of the hospital, I tried to find her. I'd half expected her to be waiting on her haunches exactly where I left her outside the entrance to the emergency room. But she must have been long gone by the time I was released. She'd done her part, and had gone off in search of her master. Later I looked for him, too. But there was no trace of Friedman. At the offices of Tel Aviv University, they told me that they had no record of any Eliezer Friedman—no one by that name had ever been employed by the department of literature, or any other department, for that matter. I'd lost the card he'd given me. I checked the telephone listings, too, but though there were hundreds of Friedmans in Tel Aviv, there was no Eliezer there, either.

# Madeline Miller

## 2018

## *Circe*

He asked me once, why pigs. We were seated before my hearth, in our usual chairs. He liked the one draped in cowhide, with silver inlaid in its carvings. Sometimes he would rub the scrolling absently beneath his thumb.

'Why not?' I said.

He gave me a bare smile. 'I mean it, I would like to know.'

I knew he meant it. He was not a pious man, but the seeking out of things hidden, this was his highest worship.

There were answers in me. I felt them, buried deep as last year's bulbs, growing fat. Their roots tangled with those moments I had spent against the wall, when my lions were gone and my spells shut up inside me, and my pigs screamed in the yard.

After I changed a crew, I would watch them scrabbling and crying in the sty, falling over each other, stupid with their horror. They hated it all, their newly voluptuous flesh, their delicate split trotters, their swollen bellies dragging in the earth's muck. It was a humiliation, a debasement. They were sick with longing for their hands, those appendages men use to mitigate the world.

Come, I would say to them, it's not that bad. You should appreciate a pig's advantages. Mud-slick and swift, they are hard to catch. Low to the ground, they cannot easily be knocked over. They are not like dogs, they do not need your love. They can thrive anywhere, on anything, scraps and trash. They look witless and dull, which lulls their enemies, but they are clever. They will remember your face.

They never listened. The truth is, men make terrible pigs.

In my chair by the hearth, I lifted my cup. 'Sometimes,' I told him, 'you must be content with ignorance.'

He did not like that answer, yet that was the perversity of him: in a way he liked it best of all. I had seen how he could shuck truths from men like oyster shells, how he could pry into a breast with a glance and a well-timed word. So little of the world did not yield to his sounding. In the end, I think the fact that I did not was his favourite thing about me.

But I am ahead of myself now.

A ship, the nymphs said. Very patched, with eyes upon the hull.

That caught my attention. Common pirates did not have the gold to waste on paint. But I did not go look. The anticipation was part of the pleasure. The moment when the knock came and I would rise from my herbs, swing wide the door. There were no pious men anymore, there had not been for a long time. The spell was polished in my mouth as a river-stone. I added a handful of roots to the draught I was making. There was moly in it, and the liquid gleamed.

The afternoon passed, and the sailors did not appear. My nymphs reported they were camped on the beach with fires burning. Another day went by, and at last on the third day came the knock.

That painted ship of theirs was the finest thing about them. Their faces had lines like grandfathers. Their eyes were blood-shot and dead. They flinched from my animals.

'Let me guess,' I said. 'You are lost? You are hungry and tired and sad?'

They ate well. They drank more. Their bodies were lumpish here and there with fat, though the muscles beneath were hard as trees. Their scars were long, ridged and slashing. They had had a good season, then met someone who did not like their thieving. They were plunderers, of that I had no doubt. Their eyes never stopped counting up my treasures, and they grinned at the tally they came to.

I did not wait any more for them to stand and come at me. I raised my staff, I spoke the word. They went crying to their pen like all the rest.

The nymphs were helping me set right the toppled benches and scrub away the wine stains when one of them glanced at the window. 'Mistress, another on the path.'

I had thought the crew too small to man a full ship. Some of them must have waited on the beach, and now one had been sent to scout after his fellows. The nymphs set out new wine and slipped away.

I opened the door at the man's knock. The late sun fell on him, picking out the red in his neat beard, the faint silver in his hair. He wore a bronze sword at his waist. He was not so tall as some, but strong, I saw, his joints well seasoned.

'Lady,' he said, 'my crew has taken shelter with you. I hope I may as well?'

I put all my father's brightness into my smile. 'You are as welcome as your friends.'

I watched him while I filled the cups. Another thief, I thought. But his eyes only grazed my rich trappings. They lingered instead on a stool still upended on the floor. He bent down and set it upright.

'Thank you,' I said. 'My cats. They are always tumbling something.'

'Of course,' he said.

I brought him food and wine, and led him to my hearth. He took the goblet and sat in the silver chair I indicated. I saw him wince a little as he bent, as if at the pull of recent wounds. A jagged scar ran up his muscled calf from heel to thigh, but it was old and faded. He gestured with his cup.

'I have never seen a loom like that,' he said. 'Is it an Eastern design?'

A thousand of his kind had passed through this room. They had catalogued every inch of gold and silver, but not one had ever noticed the loom.

I hesitated for the briefest moment.

'Egyptian.'

'Ah. They make the best things, don't they? Clever to use a second beam instead of loom weights. So much more efficient to draw the weft down. I would love to have a sketch.' His voice was resonant, warm, with a pull to it that reminded me of ocean tides. 'My wife would be thrilled. Those weights used to drive her mad. She kept saying someone ought to invent something better. Alas, I have not found time to apply myself to it. One of my many husbandly failings.'

*My wife.* The words jarred me. If any of the men in all those crews had had a wife, they never mentioned her. He smiled at me, his dark eyes on mine. His goblet was lifted loosely in his hand, as if any moment he would drink.

'Though the truth is, her favourite thing about weaving is that while she works, everyone around her thinks she can't hear what they're saying. She gathers all the best news that way. She can tell you who's getting married, who's pregnant, and who's about to start a feud.'

'Your wife sounds like a clever woman.'

'She is. I cannot account for the fact that she married me, but since it is to my benefit, I try not to bring it to her attention.'

It surprised me to a huff of laughter. What man spoke so? None that I had ever met. Yet at the same time there was something in him that felt nearly familiar.

'Where is your wife now? On your ship?'

'At home, thank the gods. I would not make her sail with such a ragged bunch. She runs the house better than any regent.'

My attention was sharp on him now. Common sailors did not talk of regents, nor look so at home next to silver inlay. He was leaning on the carved arm of the chair as if it were his bed.

'You call your crew ragged?' I said. 'They seem no different from other men to me.'

'You are kind to say so, but half the time I'm afraid they behave like beasts.' He sighed. 'It's my fault. As their captain, I should keep them in better line. But we have been at war, and you know how that can tarnish even the best men. And these, though I love them well, will never be called best.'

327

He spoke confidingly, as if I understood. But all I knew of war came from my father's stories of the Titans. I sipped my wine.

'War has always seemed to me a foolish choice for men. Whatever they win from it, they will have only a handful of years to enjoy before they die. More likely they will perish trying.'

'Well, there is the matter of glory. But I wish you could've spoken to our general. You might have saved us all a lot of trouble.'

'What was the fight over?'

'Let me see if I can remember the list.' He ticked his fingers. 'Vengeance. Lust. Hubris. Greed. Power. What have I forgotten? Ah yes, vanity, and pique.'

'Sounds like a usual day among the gods,' I said.

He laughed and held up his hand. 'It is your divine privilege to say so, my lady. I will only give thanks that many of those gods fought on our side.'

*Divine privilege.* He knew I was a goddess then. But he showed no awe. I might be his neighbour, whose fence he leaned over to discuss the fig harvest.

'Gods fought among mortals? Who?'

'Hera, Poseidon, Aphrodite. Athena, of course.'

I frowned. I had heard nothing of this. But then, I had no way to hear anymore. Hermes was long gone, my nymphs did not care for worldly news, and the men who sat at my tables thought only of their appetites. My days had narrowed to the ambit of my eyes and my fingers' ends.

'Fear not,' he said, 'I will not tax your ear with the whole long tale, but that is why my men are so scraggled. We were ten years fighting on Troy's shores, and now they are desperate to get back to home and hearth.'

'Ten years? Troy must be a fortress.'

'Oh, she was stout enough, but it was our weakness that drew the war out, not her strength.'

This too surprised me. Not that it was true, but that he would admit it. It was disarming, that wry deprecation.

'It is a long time to be away from home.'

'And now it is longer still. We sailed from Troy two years ago. Our journey back has been somewhat more difficult than I would have wished.'

'So there is no need to worry about the loom,' I said. 'By now your wife will have given up on you and invented a better one herself.'

His expression remained pleasant, but I saw something shift in it. 'Most likely you are right. She will have doubled our lands too, I would not be surprised.'

'And where are these lands of yours?'

'Near Argos. Cows and barley, you know.'

'My father keeps cows himself,' I said. 'He favours a pure-white hide.'

'They are hard to breed true. He must husband them well.'

'Oh, he does,' I said. 'He cares for nothing else.'

I was watching him. His hands were wide and calloused. He gestured with his cup now here, now there, sloshing his wine a little, but never spilling it. And never once touching it to his lips.

'I am sorry,' I said, 'that my vintage is not to your liking.'

He looked down as if surprised to see the cup still in his hand. 'My apologies. I've been so much enjoying the hospitality, I forgot.' He rapped his knuckles on his temple. 'My men say I would forget my head if it weren't on my neck. Where did you say they've gone again?'

I wanted to laugh. I felt giddy, but I kept my voice as even as his. 'They're in the back garden. There's an excellent bit of shade to rest in.'

'I confess I'm in awe,' he said, 'they're never so quiet for me. You must have had quite an effect on them.'

I heard a humming, like before a spell is cast. His gaze was a honed blade. All this had been prologue. As if we were in a play, we stood.

'You have not drunk,' I said. 'That is clever. But I am still a witch, and you are in my house.'

'I hope we may settle this with reason.' He had put the goblet down. He did not draw his sword, but his hand rested on the hilt.

'Weapons do not frighten me, nor the sight of my own blood.'

'You are braver than most gods then. I once saw Aphrodite leave her son to die on the field over a scratch.'

'Witches are not so delicate,' I said.

His sword hilt was hacked from ten years of battles, his scarred body braced and ready. His legs were short but stiff with muscles. My skin prickled. He was handsome, I realised.

'Tell me,' I said, 'what is in that bag you keep so close at your waist?'

'A herb I found.'

'Black roots,' I said. 'White flowers.'

'Just so.'

'Mortals cannot pick moly.'

'No,' he said simply. 'They cannot.'

'Who was it? No, never mind, I know.' I thought of all the times Hermes had watched me harvest, pressed me about my spells. 'If you had the moly, why did you not drink? He must have told you that no spell I cast could touch you.'

'He did tell me,' he said. 'But I have a quirk of prudence in me that's hard to break. The Trickster Lord, for all I am grateful to him, is not known for his reliability. Helping you turn me into a swine would be just his sort of jest.'

'Are you always so suspicious?'

'What can I say?' He held out his palms. 'The world is an ugly place. We must live in it.'

'I think you are Odysseus,' I said. 'Born from that same Trickster's blood.'

He did not start at the uncanny knowledge. He was a man used to gods. 'And you are the goddess Circe, daughter of the sun.'

My name in his mouth. It sparked a feeling in me, sharp and eager. He was like ocean tides indeed, I thought. You could look up, and the shore would be gone.

'Most men do not know me for what I am.'

'Most men, in my experience, are fools,' he said. 'I confess you nearly made me give the game away. Your father, the cowherd?'

He was smiling, inviting me to laugh, as if we were two mischievous children.

'Are you a king? A lord?'

'A prince.'

'Then, Prince Odysseus, we are at an impasse. For you have the moly, and I have your men. I cannot harm you, but if you strike at me, they will never be themselves again.'

'I feared as much,' he said. 'And, of course, your father Helios is zealous in his vengeances. I imagine I would not like to see his anger.'

Helios would never defend me, but I would not tell Odysseus that. 'You should understand your men would have robbed me blind.'

'I am sorry for that. They are fools, and young, and I have been too lenient with them.'

It was not the first time he had made that apology. I let my eyes rest on him, take him in. He reminded me a little of Daedalus, his evenness and wit. But beneath his ease I could feel a roil that Daedalus never had. I wanted to see it revealed.

'Perhaps we might find a different way.'

His hand was still on his hilt, but he spoke as if we were only deciding dinner. 'What do you propose?'

'Do you know,' I said, 'Hermes told me a prophecy about you once.'

'Oh? And what was it?'

'That you were fated to come to my halls.'

'And?'

'That was all.'

He lifted an eyebrow. 'I'm afraid that is the dullest prophecy I've ever heard.'

I laughed. I felt poised as a hawk on a crag. My talons still held the rock, but my mind was in the air.

'I propose a truce,' I said. 'A test of sorts.'

'What sort of test?' He leaned forward a little. It was a gesture I would come to know. Even he could not hide everything. Any challenge, he would run to meet it. His skin smelled of labour and the sea. He knew ten years of stories. I felt keen and hungry as a bear in spring.

'I have heard,' I said, 'that many find their trust in love.'

It surprised him, and oh, I liked the flash of that, before he covered it over.

'My lady, only a fool would say no to such an honour. But in truth, I think also only a fool would say yes. I am a mortal. The moment I set down the moly to join you in your bed, you may cast your spell.' He paused. 'Unless, of course, you were to swear an oath you will not hurt me, upon the river of the dead.'

An oath by the River Styx would hold even Zeus himself. 'You are careful,' I said.

'It seems we share that.'

No, I thought. I was not careful. I was reckless, headlong. He was another knife, I could feel it. A different sort, but a knife still. I did not care. I thought: give me the blade. Some things are worth spilling blood for.

'I will swear that oath,' I said.

# Tim Pears

## 2019

## *The Redeemed*

Twice a week, dances were held on the upper deck of *Benbow*. The band played for an hour, from 6 p.m. The men danced in pairs, one taking the woman's part. They did the valeta, the two-step, lancers. Many men did not dance but stood and watched. On occasion Leo was one such. He listened silently as the other spectators made ribald observations, to cover their confusion.

★

As a rest and a change from the fleet routine, ships were sent in turn to anchor for a few days off the north shore of the Flow. Normal duties were performed in the morning, but at noon a make and mend was granted. Then men could sail or fish or visit the shops in Kirkwall or otherwise do as they pleased.

Boats ferried them to the shore. Leo did not join his fellows but walked off alone. He headed inland along lanes that wound round bleak farms in the open, rolling landscape. There were few trees except for odd specimens around some of the settlements. Coarse-haired little sheep and squat cattle and small, round-bellied ponies inhabited the wind-ridden pastures. There was little cereal grown that he could see.

When he spotted, in a field to his right-hand side, a boy on a white pony coming towards him, it seemed for a moment like some uncanny vision, that Leo was seeing himself as he once was, cantering across the grass out of the past. The sun shone but the breeze was cool, yet the boy wore no shirt. He rode

333

bareback, jouncing off the horse's spine. As he neared the wall between the field and the lane, the boy turned the young horse and rode along in a wide curve around the field, jumping the horse over fences each made from two long rough poles crossed over, like a flattened letter X.

The horse was a white filly. She had long legs, unlike the other, sturdy ponies Leo had noticed on the island. She did not look strong enough to pull a cart. The slight boy was about as much weight as she looked able to carry. Maybe a saddle as well would have been too much. She was spindly, but fast. The boy hung on as he disappeared over the rising ground.

When they reappeared, Leo had climbed the wall and jumped down into the field and was waiting for them. He waved the boy over. The rider slowed the filly and walked her warily over to the tall young sailor.

'What are ye doin in our field?' he asked.

'That there's a fine animal,' Leo said.

The boy halted the pony a yard or two away. 'Aye,' he said, in a voice as yet unbroken. He had red hair and pale skin. He turned the horse. Should this stranger make an untoward move, he could gallop away.

'You ride her well,' Leo said. He judged the boy to be eleven or twelve years old. He did not speak or otherwise respond to the compliment but sat upon the white filly, waiting to be released.

'The race is on next week,' the boy said, 'and I plan to win.'

Leo asked what race this was. The boy could not believe the seaman had not heard of it and told him it was the highlight of the annual county show. Leo asked if only lads rode. The red-headed boy said men of any age could but the smaller they were, the faster, so riders were mostly young. There was one dwarfish old man who raced every year. He'd won two or three times long ago, but he must be in his thirties now and in the boy's opinion would never win again. 'It's my turn now,' he said.

Leo could not tell how deep the boy's bravado went. Was it sincere or merely superficial?

'Do you wish to ride faster?' he asked.

The boy gazed blankly back at him. Perhaps the question was too difficult. Then he nodded.

Leo stepped forward slowly. He spoke to the horse, and stroked her neck. Then he looked up at the Orcadian boy and said, 'You're holdin her back. You wants to sit higher up, on her withers. She'll fly as swift as a winged beast, if you can bear it. Do you reckon you can?'

The boy had been gazing at Leo with his blank expression. Now he smiled. 'Aye.'

'My name's Leo Sercombe,' he said, raising his hand to shake the boy's, who said that he was called Jamie Watt.

And so Leo had the boy sprint the filly, and each time encouraged him to ride a little forward, as he himself had once done. He showed him how to use his knees, and to loosen the reins. He explained that these were not principles of equitation but skills he himself had discovered by chance.

The Orcadian boy galloped the horse across the field and came back beaming. 'It's brilliant,' Jamie said. 'She's so speedy, I can hardly hold on to her.'

When it came to the jumps, however, Jamie Watt leaned right back, his spine almost touching that of the horse. The boy hung on to the filly's mouth.

'All your weight's over the pony's loins,' Leo told him. 'You're interferin with her liftin and with her spread, and makin it more difficult for her to get her quarters over. And then when she lands she wants to use the muscles of her loins to push off again. You needs to lean forward.'

Once Jamie put this novel instruction into practice, Leo could see that the horse was appreciative and the boy could feel it too. He began to lean forward before he made his mount accelerate for the last strides of their approach to a fence. Leo told him that he should aim to time his own movements in exact conformity to those of the horse, but until this stage of perfection was reached it would be better to be a little in advance of the horse than to be left behind. After a couple of hours the filly began to tire and Leo brought the lesson to an end, despite the boy's protests.

'She won't learn if her's weary,' Leo told him. 'She'll revert to old habits.'

'I thought it was me who was doing things different,' Jamie said.

Leo smiled and said the horse was as much a pupil as the boy was, if a little smarter. Jamie asked the seaman to hold the reins while he pulled on a single upper garment over his bare torso, a thick blue woollen pullover.

Leo said that to understand a horse you had to appreciate how its senses differed from those of man. The boy said surely a horse had five senses just like us.

Leo nodded. 'They do. Your filly sees but she is colour blind.' He turned and with a sweep of his arm indicated the wide vista before them. 'She does not see this landscape as we do. Green fields, blue sky, grey water. All is grey to her, a patchwork, a mosaic of grey. Some parts darker, others lighter. If I stood in the field and my clothes were of the same shade as the grass, she would not see me unless I moved.'

The boy listened intently. 'Can they all see the same, then?' he asked. Were horses not like men, unique?

Leo said that naturally each horse was different. Yet it was useful to know the strong and weak points common to all or most members of a species. Many horses suffered from astigmatism to a greater or lesser extent, for neither the corneas nor the lenses of their eyes were shaped with a true curvature. 'She can hear much better than we can, though. Like a dog, there are many sounds she can hear that we cannot. The officer on my last ship told me that his hunters would sometimes get all excited in their stables for no reason anyone could see. They neighed, broke out in a lather of sweat, and refused to settle until night fell. Why? Because they'd heard the sound of a horn and the calls of the hounds, from miles away.'

The boy nodded, to show he was listening but also to encourage Leo to speak more.

'And, of course, a horse can detect vibrations in the ground in a way we no longer can, if us ever could.' He gestured in the direction of the road down which he had come. 'Another horse walks along that road. Your filly is standing still on her four feet. Her front limb bones, the radius and ulna, the knee bones, canons and pasterns, are locked. So vibrations rise through them, are carried to the skull, and register in the ear.'

'Will you come again?' Jamie Watt asked.

Leo said that he would like to but could not. He had to rejoin his ship and would not get another shore leave for some time. He wished the boy good fortune in the forthcoming race. Leo turned and walked away towards the road, but the boy called after him, 'Sir.'

Leo turned back and Jamie Watt said, 'What's a horseman doing in the Royal Navy?'

'That's a good question,' Leo said. 'A very good question.' He turned away again and waved goodbye to the boy behind him.

# Colum McCann

## 2020

### Apeirogon

65

זה לא ייגמר עד שנדבר

It will not be over until we talk.

66

He clicks back to third to accommodate the rising road.

Further up the hill is the bird-ringing station at Talitha Kumi, the steep streets, the stone walls, the centre of town, the Christian churches, the careful iconography, the tin roofs, the high lime-stone houses looking out over the lush valley, the hospital, the monastery, the small countries of light and dark rushing across the vineyard, all the atoms of the approaching day stretching out in front of him.

Today, like most days, just another day: a meeting with an international group – seven or eight of them, he has heard – in the Cremisan monastery.

He turns the corner at the top of Manger Street.

67

In the distance, over Jerusalem, the blimp rises.

68

He followed the blimp one Sunday, a year ago, for a couple of hours, surveilling it, surveilling him, wondering if he could find a pattern to its movement.

He went corner to corner, street sign to street sign, out into the countryside, then parked his bike at the overlook at Mount Scopus, sat on the low stone wall, shaded his eyes and stared upwards, watching the blimp drift in the blue. He had heard from a friend that it was a weather machine, gauging moisture levels and checking air quality. There was always a backup for the truth. And, in truth, how many sensors? How many cameras? How many eyes in the sky looking down?

Rami often felt that there were nine or ten Israelis inside him, fighting. The conflicted one. The shamed one. The enamoured one. The bereaved one. The one who marvelled at the blimp's invention. The one who knew the blimp was watching. The one watching back. The one who wanted to be watched. The anarchist. The protester. The one sick and tired of all the seeing.

It made him dizzy to carry such complications, to be so many people all at once. What to say to his boys when they went off to military service? What to say to Nurit when she showed him the textbooks? What to say to Bassam when he got stopped at the checkpoints? What to feel every time he opened a newspaper? What to think when the sirens sounded on Memorial Day? What to wonder when he passed a man in a kaffiyeh? What to feel when his sons had to board a bus? What to think when a taxi driver had an accent? What to worry about when the news clicked on? What fresh atrocity lay on the horizon? What sort of retribution was coming down the line? What to say to Smadari? What is it like being dead, Princess? Can you tell me? Would I like it?

Below him, on the slope, young boys lazed on the hillside on the backs of thin Arabian horses. The boys wore immaculate white jeans. Their horses muscled beneath them. Rami wished he could somehow reach out to them, approach them, say a word. But they knew already who he was from his license plate, *what* he was, just from the way he carried himself. They would know from his accent too, even if he spoke to them in Arabic. An older man on a motorbike. His pale white skin. His open face. The hidden fear. I should go and tell them. I should stride across and look them directly in the eye. Her name was Smadar.

Grape of the vine. A swimmer. A dancer too. She was this tall.
She had just cut her hair. Her teeth were slightly crooked. It was
the start of the school year. She was out shopping for books. I
was driving to the airport when I got the news. She was missing.
We knew. My wife and I. We knew. We went from hospital to
police station, back again. You cannot imagine what that is like.
One door after another. Then the morgue. The smell of antisep-
tic. It was unspeakable. They slid her out on a metal tray. A cold
metal tray. She lay there. Your age. No more. No less. Let's be
honest here, guys. You would have been delighted by the news.
You would have celebrated. Cheered. And I would once have
cheered for yours too. And your father's. And your father's father.
Listen to me. I admit it. No denial. Once, long ago. What do you
think of that? What sort of world are we living in? Look up. It's
watching us, all of us. Look. Look. Up there.

After a while the blimp began to press down further upon
him, like a light hand upon his chest, the pressure growing
firmer, until all Rami wanted to do was find a place where he
could not be seen. It was so often like this. The desire to vanish.
To have all of it gone in a single smooth motion. To wipe it all
clean. Tabula rasa. Not my war. Not my Israel.

Show me, then. Convince me. Roll back the rock. Return
Smadar. All of her. Gift her back to me, all sewn up and pretty and
dark-eyed again. That's all I ask. Is that too much? No more whining from me, no more weeping, no more complaints. A heavenly
stitch, that's all I ask. And bring back Abir too, for Bassam, for me,
for Salwa, for Areen, for Hiba, for Nurit, for all of us. And while
you're at it bring back Sivan and Ahuva and Dalia and Yamina and
Lilly and Yael and Shulamit and Khalila and Sabah and Zahava
and Rivka and Yasmine and Sarah and Inaam and Ayala and
Sharon and Talia and Rashida and Rachel and Nina and Mariam
and Tamara and Zuhal and Riva and every other one under this
hot murdering sun. Is that too much to ask for? Is it?

He felt the bike galloping underneath him as he drove back
to his house and sat in his office, closed the curtains, rearranged
the photographs on his desk.

69

Smadar. From the Song of Solomon. The grapevine. The opening of the flower.

70

Abir. From the ancient Arabic. The perfume. The fragrance of the flower.

71

He has only ever been stopped once on his motorbike. He had heard that the back road from the West Bank was closed, but it was the easiest and quickest way home. The rain hammered down in slanting sheets. He took the chance. What was the worst that could happen: to be stopped, to be questioned, to be turned away?

He had, he knew – even at his age – an impish grin, a chubby face, a soft pale gaze. He sat low and throttled the engine. The bike sprayed up droplets behind him.

A sudden spotlight funnelled a shot of fear down his spine. He throttled back, sat up on the bike. His visor was blurry with raindrops. The spotlight enveloped him. He braked in the pool of brightness. The back wheel skidded slightly in the oily rain.

A shout insinuated itself into the night. The guard was trembling as he ran through the downpour. The light was scattershot with silver spears of rain. The guard pointed his gun at Rami's helmet. Rami raised his hands slowly, opened the visor, greeted him in Hebrew, *Shalom aleichem, shalom,* in his thickest accent, showed him his Israeli identity card, said he lived in Jerusalem, he had to get home.

—The road's closed, sir.

—What do you want me to do, go back *there*?

A raindrop fell from the barrel of the soldier's rifle: Go back, yes, sir, go back, right now, this road is off-limits.

A tiredness had crawled into Rami's bones. He wanted to be home with Nurit, in his comfortable chair, a blanket over his knees, the simple life, the ordinary mundanities, the private pain, not this forsaken rain, this roadblock, this cold, this shaking gun.

He lifted the visor further: I was lost, I got lost, and you want me to go back there, are you mad? Look at my ID I'm Jewish. I got lost. Lost, man. Why in the world would you want me to go back?

The boy's gun swung back and forth wildly.

—Go back, sir.

—Are you fucking crazy? You think I have a death wish? I got lost, I took the wrong road, that's all.

—Sir. I'm telling you it's closed.

—Tell me this –

—What?

—What Jew in their right mind would go to the West Bank in the first place?

The boy's face puzzled. Rami tightened the throttle, gave the engine some throat.

—Go ahead, habibi, shoot me if you have to, but I'm going home.

He watched a fault line develop further on the boy's brow, a little earthquake of confusion as Rami closed the visor, turned on his hazards and drove on, his whole body conspired into the bike, all the time thinking of the gun aimed at him, a bullet slamming into the small of his back.

## 72

When, the next day, in the office of the Parents Circle, he began to tell Bassam the checkpoint story, he stopped short and remembered the shiny blue shoe sailing through the air and the bullet ripping into the back of Abir's skull. He had no desire to tell last night's story any more.

## 73

The shopkeeper was named Niesha the Ancient, even though she was just thirty-four years old. She heard the pops. One, two, three, four. A screech of tyres. For a moment there was silence. Her hands remained on the long wooden counter. Then the shouting began: the high pitch of schoolchildren, girls mostly, an unusual sign: the girls were usually quiet. Niesha reached for her keys from the cash register.

Outside, a commotion. A child on the pavement. A blue skirt. A white cotton collar blouse. A discarded shoe. Niesha dropped to her knees. She knew the child's name. She leaned down to check the pulse.

—Wake up, Abir, wake up.

Screams rang out. A crowd huddled over the child. She was unconscious. Men and women keyed their phones for a signal. Word went around that traffic had been blocked by the soldiers at the far end of the road. Nothing was being allowed through: no ambulances, no police, no paramedics.

—Wake up, wake up.

Minutes passed. A young teacher crossed the roundabout, wailing. A battered taxi pulled up. The young driver waved his arms. Kids streamed from the school gates.

Niesha helped pick Abir from the ground and bundle her into the back seat of the taxi. She wedged herself into the well between the front and back seats to keep the child from rolling off. The driver glanced over his shoulder and the taxi lurched. Someone had thrown the lost shoe into the back of the car. Niesha slipped it on Abir's foot. She felt the warmth of the toes. She knew instantly that she would never forget the surprising warmth of the flesh.

The taxi raced through the heart of the marketplace. Word had already jumped around Anata and Shu'fat. Calls went out from the mosques, the balconies, the side streets. Kids ran from the alleyways, streamed down towards the school. The driver braked only for the speed bumps. He hit traffic on the far side of the market. He laid his hand on the car horn. The cars around them joined in the hellish symphony.

Niesha lay on the floor beneath Abir, reaching up, keeping the child's head still. Abir's eyes fluttered. She made no sounds. Her pulse was slow and irregular. Niesha touched the child's toes once more. They had grown colder.

The windows of the taxi were down. Loudspeakers outside. Flags unfurling. The prospect of riot. The car jolted forward. The driver invoked the name of Allah. The tumult rang in Niesha's ears.

The hospital building was low-slung and dingy. A team waited on the steps. Niesha took her hand from Abir's head and opened the rear door before the taxi had even stopped. Shouts went up for a trolley. The front steps of the hospital were mayhem.

Niesha watched the trolley disappear in a swamp of white coats. These were the days of small shrouds: she had seen so many of them carried along the streets.

She suddenly recalled that she had forgotten to lock the door of her shop. She put her forearm to her eyes and wept.

74

The cameras in the blimp remotely swivelled and the lenses flared. Already helicopters were circling over Anata.

75

Down below, the shebab threw stones. They landed on rooftops, bounced against light poles, clattered against water tanks.

76

On the day Smadar was killed, the television cameras were there even before the ZAKA paramedics.

Rami saw part of the footage years later in a documentary: the outdoor restaurant, the afternoon light, the milling bodies, the overturned chairs, the table legs, the shattered chandeliers, the splattered tablecloths, the severed torso of one of the bombers like a Greek statue-piece in the middle of the street.

Even listening with his eyes closed was unbearable: the rush of footsteps, the sirens.

After the screening, he realised that he had clasped his hands so tightly together that his fingernails had drawn blood.

What he wanted the film-makers to do was to somehow crawl inside time and rewind it, to upend chronology, reverse it and channel it in an entirely different direction – like a Borges story – so that the light was brighter, and the chairs were righted, and the street was ordered, the café was intact, and Smadar was suddenly walking along again, her hair short, her nose pierced, arm in arm with her schoolgirl friends, sauntering past the café, sharing her Walkman, the smell of coffee sharp in her nostrils, caught in the banality of not caring what happens next.

## 77

The sky was a radiant blue. The cobblestone street was crowded with September shoppers. Music was being piped from a raffia-fronted loudspeaker. The blasts ruptured the sound system. The silence afterwards was uncanny, a stunned interval, until the street erupted in screams.

## 78

In Aramaic, *Talitha Kumi* means: Rise up, little girl, rise up.

## 79

The bombers were dressed as women, their explosive belts strapped around their stomachs. They had shaved closely and wore headscarves to hide their faces.

They had all come originally from the village of Assira al-Shamaliya in the West Bank. It was, for two of them, the first time they had ever been in Jerusalem.

## 80

Jorge Luis Borges, when walking with guides through Jerusalem in the early 1970s, said he had never seen a city of such clean searing light. He tapped his wooden cane on the cobbles and the sides of the buildings to figure out how old the stones might be.

The stones, he said, were pink as flesh.

He liked walking in the Palestinian neighbourhoods, around the souks where as a blind storyteller he was treated with particular reverence. There had always been a tradition of the blind among Arabs. The imam in the marketplace. Abdullah ibn Umm Maktum. Al-Ma'arri. Those who were *basir*, sighted in the heart and mind. Their ways of seeing, their ways of telling.

Crowds of young men followed Borges, hands clasped behind their backs, waiting for a chance to talk to the famous Argentinian writer, the *rawi*. He wore a grey suit jacket, shirt and tie, even in the warm weather. He had been given a red fez as a welcome present. He wore the hat unabashedly.

When he stopped, the crowd stopped with him. He enjoyed the sound of the alleyways, the flitter of laundry, the swoop of pigeons, the remnants of ghosts. In particular he liked the trinket shops in the Old City where he could pick small charms from the trays, attempt histories from the feel of them alone.

Borges sat drinking coffee in the small shops, amid the smoke and the bubbling water pipes, listening to ancient stories of larks and elephants, of streets that turned endlessly, of pillars that contained every sound in the universe, of flying steeds, of mythical marketplaces where the only things for sale were hand-written poems that scrolled out infinitely.

81

*Being with you, and not being with you, is the only way I have to measure time.*

BORGES

# Jhumpa Lahiri

## 2021

## *Whereabouts*

### At His Place

Ever since that trip together with his children I've been feeling off-kilter. I've wondered what it would be like to take things further, and I think, too often, about the way he laughs, the way his voice reverts to the high pitch of a little boy's, and the hairs on his wrists and scattered on the backs of his hands, and the humorous messages he still sends me now and then. I wait but he doesn't get in touch, it's been a while since I've seen him in the neighborhood, but then one day the phone rings, and his name on the screen already smacks of impudence. My friend is usually at work at this hour, their children are at school. What will he suggest this time? A bite to eat at the bar on the corner?

Instead when I hear his voice I realize something's happened. He explains it all quickly: my friend's father has had a stroke and the outlook is grim. They got the call early in the morning and they left the dog and the house without tending to either. The barista on the corner has the keys.

I head over right away, the dog needs to go out. It's the first time I've been at their place alone. Until now all I've known is the table set for a dinner, the bathroom used by guests, the kitchen crowded with pots and pans. This morning it's all under control in spite of the call before dawn, the hasty departure. The plates in the dishwasher are clean, and the coffeepot on the stove is the only thing to wash. Someone spilled a bit of sugar on the countertop.

347

I look into the bedrooms. The bright one, uncluttered, with white linen curtains, that he shares with my friend, and the one right next to it, less spacious, crowded with toys and a bunk bed. But even there, it's all relatively tidy. The hallway is lined with photos of the two of them and of the children, photos of the four of them, moments of parenting they treasure, with their children at the seaside, or abroad, or in their laps. I pull down a few window shades and turn off the lever for the gas. I spread a blanket over the bed. I tie the garbage bag. This is the private morphology of a family, of two people who fall in love and have children: an enterprise as mundane as it is utterly specific. And all at once I see how they form an ingenious organism, an impenetrable collective.

I find the leash that hangs by the door and take the dog out. I walk him to the villa behind my house, carrying a few plastic bags in my pocket. We walk past the dirty fountains, beneath the sclerotic palms, past the pockmarked statues flecked with lichen and moss.

He's a good dog, it doesn't take long for him to trust me. He doesn't bark, he leads me along the grounds of the villa, and I like the tinkling of the tags around his collar. He stops to drink water from a fountain, in front of a she-lion who crushes a skull with her paw, and another, recumbent, eating an apple.

Three times a day, for the next three days, until they've buried my friend's father, until they come back, the dog and I make the same rounds. I grow fond of the animal, of his ears, always alert, and of his careful gait, his determined muzzle. Our walks together thrust me forward, and though he pulls me, I'm the one holding the leash. Every step puts distance between me and my infatuation until it's no longer dangerous, until our romance, which never took hold to begin with, loses its hold over me.

## At the Bar

"What's new?" my barista asks one day.
"I'm thinking of leaving for a while."

"What do you mean?"

"I've received a fellowship to go to a place I've never been before."

"What would you do there?"

"I'd work on my own in the mornings. Then twice a day I'd sit at a long table to eat lunch and dinner with other scholars. I'd get to know them, have discussions, that sort of thing."

"Sounds nice. And how long would this last?"

"A year."

"You're torn about it?"

"I've never left this city."

"This city is a big fat drag."

I finish my coffee and leaf distractedly through the newspaper someone else has left behind, and at one point, toward the bottom of the page, I recognize a face: the curly mass of hair, the large limpid eyes, the fine features. It's the philosopher who was next door to me in that dreadful hotel. He's probably accepted lots of invitations like the one I'm considering. Maybe it's a sign.

I'm pleased to come across him again, to recall our riding up and down the elevator together, our unspoken accord. I still mean to read one of his books.

I remember how he used to speak excitedly in a foreign language, one I never managed to identify. In the picture he's got that same smile, polite but ironic, ever so slightly malicious, that had somehow withstood the tedium of the conference. I haven't forgotten his generous gaze, at once absent and piercing.

Below the picture there's a block of text, just one column. I assume it's an article about him, maybe a review of his latest book. After a long illness, it says. I'd had no idea.


## Upon Waking


Today when I wake up I stay put. I don't go to the bathroom to weigh myself or to the kitchen to drink a glass of tepid water before preparing the coffeepot. The city doesn't beckon or lend me a shoulder today. Maybe it knows I'm about to leave. The sun's dull disk defeats me; the dense sky is the same one that will carry me away. That vast and vaporous territory, lacking precise pathways, is all that binds us together now. But it never preserves our tracks. The sky, unlike the sea, never holds on to the people that pass through it. The sky contains nothing of our spirit, it doesn't care. Always shifting, altering its aspect from one moment to the next, it can't be defined.

This morning I'm scared. I'm afraid to leave this house, this neighborhood, this urban cocoon. But I've already got one foot out the door. The suitcases, purchased at my former stationery store, are already packed. I just need to lock them now. I've given the key to my subletter and I've told her how often she needs to water the plants, and how the handle of the door to the balcony sometimes sticks. I've emptied out one closet and locked another, inside of which I've amassed everything I consider important. It's not much in the end: notebooks, letters, some photos and papers, my diligent agendas. As for the rest, I don't really care, though it does occur to me that for the first time someone else will be using my cups, dishes, forks, and napkins on a daily basis.

Last night at dinner, at a friend's house, everyone wished me well, telling me to have a wonderful time. They hugged me and said, Good luck!

He wasn't there, he had other plans. I had a nice time anyway, we lingered at the table, still talking after midnight.

I tell myself: A new sky awaits me, even though it's the same as this one. In some ways it will be quite grand. For an entire year, for example, I won't have to shop for food, or cook, or do the dishes. I'll never have to eat dinner by myself.

I might have said no, I might have just stayed put. But something's telling me to push past the barrier of my life, just like the dog that pulled me along the paths of the villa. And so I heed my call, having come to know the guts and soul of this place a little too well. It's just that today, feeling slothful, I'm prey to those embedded fears that don't dissipate.

# Valzhyna Mort

## 2022

## *Music for the Dead and Resurrected*

### Washday

Amelia does her washing by the wall
so bare you'd think she shaved it.

The window's open, anyone can see.
Soap hisses. An air-raid warning rings
like a telephone from the future.
Her dress is nailed to the laundry line.

From this grey garment, that is either guarding
or attacking the house, three yards of darkness
fall across the floorboards. She stands inside,
as at the bottom of a river, her heart an octopus.

Her hands so big, next to them
her head is a small o
          (the neighbours squint),

stuffed hungrily with stubborn hair.

# Paul Baggaley

## The Future

Editor-in-Chief, 2021–ongoing

The launch of Bloomsbury in 1986 was an exciting time for publishing and bookselling. I was a fledgling bookseller at the newly founded Waterstone's, and the timing of these two new ventures reflected a changing world for our industry – and these companies were at the forefront of that change.

Most of what I remember from Bloomsbury at the time came from Freddie Baveystock, a friend who had been appointed the company's first London rep. He wasn't the hard-bitten salesman, with bags stuffed full of catalogues and stocklists. He'd finished an English degree at Oxford, looked like he'd stepped straight out of *Brideshead Revisited*, and he charmed London booksellers into excitedly over-ordering vast quantities of Bloomsbury's first books. This seemed to reflect Bloomsbury at the time. Ambitious, classy – but with decided eccentricities.

What else do I remember of those glamorous early years? There was the end of a long night (was it at the Ritz?) where I observed the Bloomsbury publicist writing a cheque for many thousand pounds for the champagne at the launch party for Jay

McInerney's *Brightness Falls*. I've just found my signed copy, from 1992. That was the same year that Michael Ondaatje's *The English Patient* was joint winner of the Booker Prize, a book I sold to almost every customer who crossed the threshold of the Waterstone's in Charing Cross Road I managed. Within five years, Bloomsbury had already published many of the best writers.

I was now a close neighbour to Bloomsbury's Soho Square offices and there always seemed to be good reasons for visiting editors, being introduced to authors and soaking up the atmosphere of a unique publisher – one of the last independent literary houses.

By 2002, I'd moved over to the other side, and when the publisher I was working for became another victim of a take-over by a conglomerate, I was suddenly on the lookout for a job. I nervously went up the stairs to be interviewed by Alexandra Pringle for a vacancy for which I had little qualification. Never has anyone so tactfully turned someone down for a job, and made the rejected applicant feel that this was absolutely the right decision.

But when I got word in late summer 2019 that Nigel Newton was interested in meeting me to talk about the role of editor-in-chief, I was of course flattered and intrigued. It came at a time when it felt like Bloomsbury was on the up again. As the publisher of Picador, I started noticing how we'd started losing books at auctions to a new hungry group of editors. It seemed that there was an opportunity to build on this remarkable heritage, and I couldn't say no. Plus it brought me together with Alexandra Pringle at last, many years after her classy response to my job application, and she has been a valuable guide to the gems on Bloomsbury's list, and its rising stars.

Two weeks into my new role, as the first lockdown was announced, I left the office before I'd settled in. But we already had plans to develop our lists, to build on the first thirty-five years of publishing exceptional fiction and non-fiction. Our first step was to announce a poetry list. Devised by Alexis

Kirschbaum and with the distinguished poet and writer Kayo Chingonyi as its founding editor, this would be a poetry list unlike any other, and the first books will be published this year. The list will showcase the most innovative and original poets today, often coming to poetry from other forms such as perform-ance and music, and representing the full breadth and diversity of Anglophone poetry and work in translation.

Over the next year, we will be announcing many new publish-ing ventures which will build on the values of the first thirty-five years: the qualities of independence and internationalism; writing that entertains and enlightens; and a commitment to bringing to readers voices which are often unheard. We will build on the values and heritage from Liz Calder's and Alexandra Pringle's stewardship of Bloomsbury – and run up the odd champagne bill on the way.

# A Note on Nigel Newton, Liz Calder and Alexandra Pringle

**Nigel Newton** was born and spent his childhood in San Francisco. In 1973 he moved to England to read English at Selwyn College, Cambridge.

His publishing career began in London as a graduate trainee at Macmillan. At the age of twenty-nine whilst working at Sidgwick & Jackson Publishers he decided to start a new publishing company from his kitchen in Putney. He approached first David Reynolds who worked with him on the business plan and then Alan Wherry and Liz Calder to join him in starting the company.

His mission as founder and chief executive of Bloomsbury from the start in 1986 to this day was for Bloomsbury to be a publisher of works of excellence and originality.

He is President of the Publishers Association and of Book Aid International. In 2021, he was awarded a CBE in the New Year Honours List for services to the publishing industry.

**Liz Calder** was born in London in 1938 and educated in New Zealand, where her family emigrated in 1949.

Her publishing life began in 1970 at Victor Gollancz, where, after a stint in the publicity department, she was made an editor and published Salman Rushdie's first novel, *Grimus*. It wasn't a success. However her acquisition of John Irving's *The World According to Garp* inspired MD Tom Maschler to offer her a job at Jonathan Cape, and she moved there as Editorial Director in 1978. At Cape she published Rushdie's novel *Midnight's Children*, which won the Booker Prize in 1981.

In 1987 she joined Nigel Newton, David Reynolds and Alan Wherry to set up Bloomsbury Publishing. On retiring in 2009, Liz moved to Suffolk, where she became one of the founding directors of Full Circle Editions, publishing books with an East of England theme.

Liz has honorary doctorates from the University of Suffolk and the University of Canterbury in New Zealand. She was awarded an honour in Brasília from the then President Lula for helping to start Brazil's first literary festival, FLIP, and in 2018 was awarded a CBE for services to literature.

**Alexandra Pringle** was born and grew up in Chelsea, London. She began her career in publishing on the art magazine *Art Monthly* and joined Virago Press as the office skivvy in 1978. She went on to edit the Virago Modern Classics series and become Editorial Director. The first debut novel she ever published was Lucy Ellmann's *Sweet Desserts* which she commissioned on no material and which won the *Guardian* Fiction Prize.

In 1990 she moved to Hamish Hamilton as Editorial Director, where the first debut novels she published were Elspeth Barker's *O Caledonia* (which she commissioned on three pages of writing) and Esther Freud's *Hideous Kinky*. Four years later she left publishing and corporate life to become a literary agent, where she acted for Amanda Foreman, Geoff Dyer, Maggie O'Farrell and Ali Smith amongst others.

Alexandra joined Bloomsbury in 1999. She has been awarded honorary degrees of Doctor of Letters from Anglia Ruskin University and Warwick University. She is a patron of Index on Censorship, a director of the charity Reprieve and an Honorary Fellow of the Royal Society of Literature.

# Thank you to our Authors

*The Passion* by **Jeanette Winterson** is reprinted with kind permission of the author. Copyright © Jeanette Winterson, 1987.

*A Case of Knives* by **Candia McWilliam** is reproduced with kind permission of the author. Copyright © Candia McWilliam, 1988.

*A Prayer for Owen Meany* by **John Irving** is reproduced with kind permission of the author. Copyright © John Irving, 1989.

*A Village Affair* by **Joanna Trollope** is reproduced from A VILLAGE AFFAIR by Joanna Trollope (Copyright © Joanna Trollope, 1989) by permission of United Agents LLP on behalf of Joanna Trollope.

*An Immaculate Mistake* by **Paul Bailey** is copyright © Paul Bailey 1990. Reproduced by permission of the author c/o Rogers, Coleridge & White Ltd., 20 Powis Mews, London W11 1JN.

*The Quantity Theory of Insanity* by **Will Self** is reproduced with kind permission of the author. Copyright © Will Self, 1991.

*The English Patient* by **Michael Ondaatje** is reproduced with kind permission of the author. Copyright © Michael Ondaatje, 1992.

# A Note on the Type

The text of this book is set in Bembo, which was first used in 1495 by the Venetian printer Aldus Manutius for Cardinal Bembo's *De Aetna*. The original types were cut for Manutius by Francesco Griffo. Bembo was one of the types used by Claude Garamond (1480–1561) as a model for his Romain de l'Université, and so it was a forerunner of what became the standard European type for the following two centuries. Its modern form follows the original types and was designed for Monotype in 1929.